Connecting Social Problems
and Popular Culture

Connecting
Social Problems and
Popular Culture

WHY MEDIA IS NOT THE ANSWER

Karen Sternheimer

A Member of the Perseus Books Group

Published by Westview Press,
A Member of the Perseus Books Group

Find us on the World Wide Web at www.westviewpress.com.

Westview Press books are available at special discounts for bulk purchases in the
United States by corporations, institutions, and other organizations. For more
information, please contact the Special Markets Department at the Perseus
Books Group, 2300 Chestnut Street, Suite 200, Philadelphia, PA 19103, or
call (800) 810-4145, ext. 5000, or e-mail special.markets@perseusbooks.com.

Designed by Brent Wilcox

Library of Congress Cataloging-in-Publication Data
Sternheimer, Karen.
   Connecting social problems and popular culture : why media is not the answer /
Karen Sternheimer.
      p.   cm.
   Includes bibliographical references and index.
   ISBN 978-0-8133-4417-1 (alk. paper)
   1. Mass media—Moral and ethical aspects—United States.   2. Popular
culture—Moral and ethical aspects—United States.   3. Mass media and
culture—United States.   4. Social problems—United States.   I. Title.
   HN90.M3.S75 2010
   302.23—dc22
                                                          2009014007

10 9 8 7 6 5 4 3 2

For Frieda Fettner,
whose wisdom and encouragement
will be with me always

Contents

Acknowledgments

Just as John Donne said "no man is an island," no author ever really writes a book without the help and support of many others. I had many people who have contributed significantly to the finished product. First, many thanks to my editor, Alex Masulis, for encouraging me to write this book. Along with Alex, the staff at Westview Press, Cathleen Tetro, and others who have since moved on, including Jill Rothenberg and Greg Houle, have been supportive for many years. Their encouragement and enthusiasm has made a world of difference to me. Many thanks to Erica Lawrence, Meredith Smith, and Anais Scott for your contributions as well.

I am also very thankful for my student researchers who helped find articles for this book. William Rice, Jessica Sackman, and Mishirika Scott spent hours online finding many of the news stories that populate this book. They and many other undergraduate students at the University of Southern California have been a pleasure to work with; their input in my classes helps keep me grounded in youth culture as time takes me further away from being anywhere near pop culture's cutting edge. Anonymous reviewers also provided useful comments and suggestions, and I thank them for helping make this book stronger.

The department of sociology at the University of Southern California has been my professional home for many years, and I could not have written this book without years of academic nurturing. In particular, Mike Messner, Barry Glassner, Elaine Bell Kaplan, Jon Miller, Tim Biblarz, and former faculty members Darnell Hunt, Cheryl Maxson, Malcolm Klein, and Barrie Thorne have been incredibly supportive through the years. A special thanks to the department's staff, Melissa Hernandez, Stachelle Overland, Lisa Rayburn-Parks, and Amber Thomas for your help. Other colleagues and friends provided invaluable support as sounding boards, especially Sally Raskoff, Elisabeth Burgess, and Molly Ranney. Thanks to Jean Summer and Portia Cohen for our walk-and-talk get-togethers and your grounded advice.

Most centrally, I couldn't have published one word without the continued support and encouragement of my family. Special thanks to Barbara Cohen, Linda Cohen, Saul Fettner, Nancy and Larry Friedman. My parents, Toby Sternheimer and Lee Sternheimer, have always encouraged even my most dubious endeavors; thanks to Laura, Linda, and Jacob for their support throughout the years. And Eli, thanks for your own brand of encouragement, even though you can't read just yet.

Media Phobia: Why Blaming Popular Culture for Causing Social Problems Is a Problem

"They're here!" Carol Anne exclaims in the 1982 film *Poltergeist*. "Who's here?" her mother asks. "The TV people!" answers the wide-eyed blonde girl, mesmerized by the "snow" on the family's television set. What follows is a family's sci-fi nightmare: Carol Anne is taken away by the angry spirits terrorizing their home. Her only means of communication to her family is through the television set.

This film's plot serves as a powerful example of American anxieties about media culture. The angelic child is helpless against its pull and is ultimately stolen, absorbed into its vast netherworld. She is the family's most vulnerable victim, and as such is drawn into evil without realizing its danger. Carol Anne's fate highlights the fear of what television in particular and popular culture more generally may "do to" children: take them someplace dangerous and beyond their parents' reach. Ultimately Carol Anne is saved with the help of a medium, but the imagery in the film reflects the terror that children are somehow prey to outsiders who come into unsuspecting homes via the TV set.

More than twenty-five years after this film was released media culture has expanded well beyond television; unlike in Carol Anne's day,

1

kids today use iPods, the Internet, cell phones, video games, DVDs, and other technology that their parents may not even know how to use. Cable television was in its infancy in 1982: MTV was one year old, CNN was two. Today there are hundreds of channels, with thousands more programs available on demand at any time. Unlike in 1982, television stations no longer sign off at night. Our media culture does not rest. What does this mean for young people today?

For many people, this explosion of media over the past decades brings worry. Are kids so distracted by new technology that they don't study as much? Does our entertainment culture mean kids expect constant entertainment? Do kids know too much about sex thanks to the Internet? Does violent content in video games, movies, and television make kids violent? Promiscuous? Materialistic? Overweight? Anorexic? More likely to smoke, drink, or take drugs? Become racist, sexist, or homophobic from listening to rap music?

This book seeks to address these questions, first by examining the research that attempts to connect these issues to popular culture. Despite the common-sense view that media must be at least partly to blame for these social problems, the evidence suggests that there are many more important factors that create serious social problems in the United States today. Popular culture gets a lot of attention, but is rarely a central causal factor. Throughout the book we will also take a step back and think about exactly *why* it is that so many people fear the effects of popular culture. You might have noticed that all of the questions posed above focus on young people's relationship with media and leaves most adults out of the equation. As we will see, a great deal of our concern about media and media's potential effects on kids has more to do with uncertainty about the future and the changing experiences of childhood and adolescence. In addition to considering why we are concerned about the impact of popular culture, this book also explores why many researchers and politicians encourage us to remain afraid of media culture, and of kids themselves.

The Big Picture

Blaming media for changes in childhood and social problems has shifted our public conversation away from addressing the biggest problems that impact children's lives. The most pressing crisis facing American children today is not media culture but poverty. The National Center for Children in Poverty reported in 2007 that nearly 13 million children (approximately 17 percent of Americans under eighteen) live in poverty, a rate two to three times higher than that in other industrialized nations.[1] Reduced funding for families in poverty has only exacerbated this problem, as we are now starting to see the effects of 1996 welfare reform legislation that threatens to take away the safety net from children. Additionally, our two-tiered health care system often prevents poor children from receiving basic health care, as 12 percent of American children had no health insurance in 2006.[2] These are often children with parents who work at jobs that offer no benefits.

These same children are admonished to stay in school to break the cycle of poverty, yet many of them attend schools without enough books or basic school supplies. Schools in high-poverty areas are more likely to have uncertified teachers; for instance, 70 percent of seventh through twelfth graders in such schools are taught science by teachers without science backgrounds.[3] We worry about kids being in danger at school but forget that the most perilous place, statistically speaking, is in their own homes. In 2006, for instance, over 1,100 children were killed by their parents, compared with fourteen killed at school during the 2005–2006 school year.[4] By continually hyping the fear of media-made child killers, we forget that the biggest threat to childhood is adults and the policies adults create.

As we will see throughout this book, many of the problems that we tend to lay at the feet of popular culture have more mundane causes. The roots of the most serious problems American children face, problems like lack of a quality education, violent victimization, early pregnancies, single parenthood, and obesity, poverty plays a starring role; popular culture is a bit player at best. And other problems that this book addresses, such as materialism, substance use, racism, sexism, and homophobia might be highly visible in popular culture, but it is the adults around young people, as well as the way in which American society is structured, that contributes the most to these issues. Yes, once again these issues are made most visible in popular culture, but their causes are more complex. We will examine these causes in the chapters that follow.

The media have come to symbolize society and provide glimpses of both social changes and social problems. Changes in media culture and media technologies are easier to see than the complex host of economic, political, and social changes Americans have experienced in the past few decades. Graphic video games are easier to see than changes in public policies, which we hear little about even though they better explain why violence happens and where it happens. We criticize single mothers on television because it is difficult to explore the real and complex situations that impact people's choices and behavior. The point of this book is to expose that what lies behind our fear of media culture is anxiety about an uncertain future. This fear has been deflected onto children, symbolic of the future, and onto media, symbolic of contemporary society.

The terrorist attacks of September 11, 2001, and the ongoing conflicts in Afghanistan and Iraq are dramatic reminders that we are living in a time of flux and fear. The Cold War logic that shaped American foreign policy for nearly forty years is now obsolete, and previous conceptions of allies and enemies are now all but meaningless. Twentieth-century icons of American power and prosperity—the Pentagon, the World Trade Center, and aviation—were proven vulnerable in ways unimaginable before that day. Our sense of security was violated, as two oceans can no longer be enough for us to feel safe. In many ways the future has never seemed so unknowable. These issues have turned up the volume and the vitriol about what has gone wrong in the United States. Culture seems like a plausible answer for some.

In addition to political changes, we have experienced economic shifts over the past few decades, such as the increased necessity for two incomes to sustain middle-class status, which has reshaped family life. Increased opportunities for women have created greater independence, making marriage less of a necessity for economic survival. Deindustrialization and the rise of an information-based economy have left the poorest and least skilled workers behind and eroded job security for many members of the middle class. Ultimately these economic changes have made supervision of children more of a challenge for adults, who are now working longer hours.

Since the Industrial Revolution, our economy has become more complex and adults and children have increasingly spent their days separated from one another. From a time when adults and children worked together on family farms to the development of institutions specifically for children, like age-segregated schools, day care, and organized after-school activities, daily interaction in American society has become more separated by age. Popular culture is another experience that kids may enjoy beyond adult supervision. An increase of youth autonomy has created fear within adults, who worry that violence, promiscuity, and other forms of "adult" behavior will emerge from these shifts and that parents will have a declining level of influence on their children. Kids spend more time with friends than with their parents as they get older, and more time with popular culture too. These changes explain in large part why children's experiences are different now than in the past, but are not just the result of changes in popular culture.

A Brief History of Media Fears

Fear that popular culture has a negative impact on youth is nothing new: It is a recurring theme in history. Whereas in the past, fears about youth were largely confined to children of the working class, immigrants, or racial minorities, fear of young people now appears to be a more generalized fear of the future, which explains why we have brought middle-class and affluent youth into the spectrum of worry. Like our predecessors we are afraid of change, of popular culture we don't like or understand, and of a shifting world that at times feels out of control.

Fears about media and children date back at least to Plato, who was concerned about the effects the classic Greek tragedies had on children.[5] Historian John Springhall describes how penny theaters and cheap novels in early nineteenth-century England were thought to create moral decay among working-class boys.[6] Attending the theater or reading a book would hardly raise an eyebrow today, but Springhall explains that the concern emerged following an increase in working-class youths' leisure time. As in contemporary times, commentators blamed youth for a rise in crime and considered any gathering place of working-class youth threatening. Young people could only afford admission to penny theaters, which featured entertainment geared towards a working-class audience, rather than the "respectable" theaters catering to middle- or upper-class patrons. Complaints about the performances were very similar to those today: Youngsters would learn the wrong values and possibly become criminals. Penny and later dime novels garnered similar reaction, accused of being tawdry in content and filled with slang that kids might imitate. Springhall concludes that the concern had less to do with actual content and more to do with the growing literacy of the working class, shifting the balance of power from elites to the masses and threatening the status quo.

Examining the social context enables us to understand what creates underlying anxieties about media. Fear of comic books in the 1940s and 1950s, for instance, took place in the McCarthy era, when the control over culture was high on the national agenda. Like the dime novels before, comic books were cheap, based on adventurous tales, and appealed to the masses. Colorful and graphic depictions of violence riled critics, who lobbied Congress unsuccessfully to place restrictions on comics' sale and production.[7] Psychiatrist and author Frederic Wertham wrote in 1953 that "chronic stimulation . . . by comic books are contributing factors to many children's maladjustment."[8] He and others believed that comics were a major cause of violent behavior, ignoring the possibility that violence in postwar America could be caused by anything but the reading material of choice for many young boys. Others considered pinball machines a bad influence; the city of New York even banned pinball from 1942 to 1976 as a game of chance that allegedly encouraged youth gambling.

During the middle of the twentieth century, music routinely appeared on the public enemy list. Historian Grace Palladino recounts concerns about swing music in the early 1940s.[9] Adults feared that kids wasted so much time listening to it they could never become decent soldiers in World War II (sixty years later Tom Brokaw dubbed these same would-be delinquents "the greatest generation").[10] Palladino contends that adult anxieties stemmed from the growing separation between "teenagers," a term coined in 1941, and the older generation in both leisure time and cultural tastes. Just a few years later similar concerns arose when Elvis Presley brought traditionally African American music to white Middle America. His hips weren't really the problem; it was the threat of bringing traditionally black music to white middle-class teens during a time of enforced and de facto segregation.

Later, concerns about subliminal messages—ever try to play an LP backwards to find a satanic message? (If you're not sure what an LP is, ask your parents)—and panic over Prince's "1999" lyrics about masturbation in the 1980s led to the formation of Tipper Gore's Parents Music Resource Center (PMRC), Senate hearings, and parental warning labels. Both stem from parents' discomfort with their children's cultural preferences and the desire to increase their ability to control what their children know. Today, fears of media culture stem from the decreased ability to control content and consumption. While attending the theater or reading newspapers or novels elicits little public concern today, fears have shifted to newer forms of cultural expression like television, video games, and the Internet. Throughout the twentieth century, popular culture became something increasingly consumed privately. Before the invention of radio and television, popular culture was more public, and controlling the information young people were exposed to was somewhat easier. Fears surrounding newer media have largely been based on the reduced ability of adults to control children's access. MP3 players, DVDs, smart phones, and laptops make it nearly impossible for adults to seal off the walls of childhood from the rest of society.

These recurring concerns about popular culture are examples of what sociologist Stanley Cohen refers to as "moral panics," fears that are very real but also out of proportion to their actual threat.[11] Underneath the fear lies the belief that our way of life is at stake, threatened by evildoers—often cast as popular culture or its young consumers—who must be controlled. The rhetoric typically takes on a shrill and angry tone, joined by people nominated as experts to attest to the danger of what might happen unless we rein in the troublemakers. Cohen calls those blamed for the crisis "folk devils," the people or things that seem to embody everything that is wrong with society today. Typically moral panics attempt to redefine the public's understanding of deviance, recasting the folk devils as threats in need of restraint.

Moral panics typically have a triggering event that gathers significant media attention, much like the Columbine High School shootings in Littleton, Colorado, did in 1999. The tragic murder of twelve students and a teacher shocked the nation, who could view nonstop live coverage of the event on a variety of news networks. Drawing on previous concerns about youth violence and popular culture, a panic began surrounding video games, music, and the use of the Internet to post threats and gather information about carrying out similar attacks. In the aftermath, commentators linked the perpetrators' pop culture preferences to their actions, suggesting that it was highly predictable that violent music and video games would lead to actual violence. This panic cast both teens and violent media as folk devils, claiming that both were a threat to public safety.

Is there any wonder that many young people feel disconnected from adult authority figures? We call teens stupid and immoral, condemn them for the video games, music, and movies they like, and try to take what freedoms they have away. We wonder why, after hearing politicians blame them for many of our nation's problems, they haven't typically rushed to the polls to vote when they turn eighteen. In addition to blaming media for social problems, we all too often blame young people themselves.

Rather than promote an atmosphere in which we discuss the realities of children's and adolescents' lives and reconsider the pressure adults and adult-run institutions place on them, by, for instance, cutting education budgets, the conversation following this panic turned towards attempting to further restrict young people. Curfews and harsher sentences for juvenile offenders have grown in popularity despite the dearth of empirical evidence in support of these punitive policies. Calls for further media restrictions are also heard, including a group in the Senate who in spring 2001 introduced the Media Marketing Accountability Act, which would fine producers who advertise adult-oriented entertainment to teenagers.

Young people are routinely the folk devils in moral panics about popular culture, both threatened and threatening. Commentators often see them as oversexed, dangerous, self-centered fools, creating a rather convenient class of scapegoats for difficult social problems. Articles like the *Washington Post*'s "Why Johnny Can't Feel" reveal a sense that a new problem has emerged among the young.[12] According to a story called "It's Hard to See the Line Where Alienation Turns to Violence," being a teenage outcast today is somehow worse than ever before.[13] "It never seemed to matter as much as it does now," the authors stated, and asserted that kids today are "more sensitive than ever," which could potentially lead to violence.[14] Allegedly "the difference between alienated youths and violent youths may be little more than an inadvertent bump or whispered taunt."[15] Stories like these would have us believe that kids are ticking time bombs, waiting to blow. The reality is that young people are becoming less violent, yet they are continually maligned in public discourse. The "epidemic" of school shootings is used to support the contention that more and more young people are becoming cold-blooded killers, in spite of the fact that homicides in schools decreased in the past decade.[16] The facts only get in the way of creating a sensational story about the tragic downfall of the next generation.

Panics about popular culture ebb and flow throughout history. They are often masked attempts to condemn the tastes and cultural preferences of less powerful social groups. Popular culture has always been viewed as less valuable than "high culture," the stuff that is supposed to make you more refined, like going to the ballet, the opera, or the symphony. Throughout history people have been ready to believe the worst about the "low culture" of the common folk, just as bowling, wrestling, and monster truck rallies often bear the brunt of put-downs today. It's more socially acceptable to make fun of something working-class people might enjoy than to appear snobby and insensitive by criticizing people for their economic status. The same is true of criticizing rap music rather than African American youth directly. In other words, popular culture is frequently used as a proxy for hostility, and so we condemn a group's cultural preferences rather than openly express enmity towards the group.

Popular culture often creates power struggles. Every new medium creates new freedom for some, more desire to control for others. For instance, although the printing press was regarded as one of the greatest inventions of the second millennium, it also destabilized the power of the church when literacy became more widespread and people could read the Bible themselves. Later, the availability of cheap newspapers and novels reduced the ability of the upper class to control popular culture created specifically for the working class. Fears of media today reflect a similar power struggle, although now the elites are adults who fear losing control of what their children know, what their children like, and who their children are.

Constructing Media Phobia

Ironically, we are encouraged to fear media by the news media itself, because doomsday warnings sell papers, attract viewers, and keep us so scared we stay glued to the news for updates. "TV is leading children down a moral sewer!" the late entertainer Steve Allen claimed in several full-page ads in the *Los Angeles Times*. Other headlines seem to concur—"Cartoon violence is no laughing matter," said the *Kansas City Star*.[17] "Health Groups Link Hollywood Fare to Youth Violence," announced the front page of the *Los Angeles Times*.[18] "Number of Youths Awaiting Trial in D.C. Jails Triples," the *Washington Post* reported.[19] These and hundreds of other stories nationwide imply that the media are a threat to children, and more ominously, that children are subsequently a threat to the rest of us. Media are a central facet of American culture, but media culture is not the root cause of American social problems, as our ongoing public discussion would suggest. Instead, our anxieties about a changing world, uncertain future, and seemingly unsolvable social ills are deflected onto popular culture, which serves as a visible target when the real causes are harder to pin down. The news media are central within American public thought, maybe not telling us what to think, but, to borrow a popular phrase, focusing our attention on what to think about.[20] The abundance of news stories similar to the ones listed above directs us to think about entertainment as public enemy number one for kids.

Problems do not emerge fully formed; they need to be created in order to claim the status as important and worthy of our attention and concern. In their 1977 book, *Constructing Social Problems*, sociologists John Kitsuse and Malcolm Spector argue that social problems are the result of the work of claims makers, people who actively work to raise awareness and define an issue as a significant problem. This is not to suggest that problems don't really exist, only that to rise to the level of a *social* problem, issues need to have people who lobby for greater attention to any given topic. The constructionist approach to social problems requires us to look closely not just at the issue at hand, but at how we have come to think of it as a problem and who wants us to view it as such. The popular culture problem is one example, created by a variety of people, including academics who do research testing for negative effects and provide commentary attesting to its alleged harm; activist groups that seek to raise public awareness about pop culture's supposed threat; and, as noted earlier, the news organizations that report on these claims. Politicians also campaign against popular culture, hold hearings, and propose legislation to appear to be doing something about the pop culture problem.

Author Cynthia Cooper analyzed nearly thirty congressional hearings held on this issue, finding them to be little more than an exercise in public relations for the elected officials, yet hearings add to the appearance of a weighty problem in need of federal intervention.[21] A fall 2000 report by the Federal Trade Commission (FTC) concluded that movies with violence were marketed to teenagers. Action movies like the *Rambo*, *Die Hard*, and *Lethal Weapon* franchises have been a staple for male teenage audiences for decades, but nonetheless this report was treated like a smoking gun. The attorney general from South Carolina once threatened to file a class action suit against major Hollywood studios similar to those filed against the tobacco industry.[22] Corporations also sometimes jump on the bandwagon, furthering the appearance that there is a real problem and that they are part of the solution. Following the FTC report, Wal-Mart announced that they were considering a ban on sales of videos containing violence.

This is ironic, considering a January 2001 *60 Minutes* report revealed that the chain had covered up incidents of violence within its stores, including children shot by guns on their shelves. The California attorney general's office found that the chain had committed almost 500 violations of the state's gun laws, including skirting the ten-day waiting period and selling weapons to felons.[23] Yet Wal-Mart did not announce a ban on sales of actual guns.[24]

These claims makers do not simply raise awareness in response to a problem, their actions help create our sense that problems exist in the first place. Claims makers also shape the way we think about an issue, and frequently "distort the nature of a problem," as sociologist Joel Best details in his analysis of crime news.[25] He acknowledges that claims makers might not do this on purpose, and often have good intentions. After all, if people see what they believe to be a serious problem, raising awareness makes sense. For example, consider the surgeon general's report on youth violence, released in January 2001. This report indicated that poverty and family violence are the best predictors of youth violence. Nonetheless, the report concludes: "Exposure to violent media plays an important causal role," based on research that is highly criticized by many media studies scholars.[26] Two Los Angeles area newspapers capitalized on this single statement, running stories with the headlines "Surgeon General Links TV, Real Violence," and "Media Dodges Violence Bullet."[27] Even when studies point to other central causal factors, media violence often dominates the story.

You might be wondering what the harm could be in conducting research, holding hearings, and reporting on this issue. After all, media culture is very pervasive, and if it *could* be even a minor issue, shouldn't we pay attention to it? There is danger, however, in taking our attention away from potentially serious issues. The pop culture answer diverts us from delving into the other questions. Focusing on the media only in a cause-and-effect manner fails to help us understand the connection between media culture and politics and power, as well as the ways in which the media are central to American culture, not merely an influence on individuals' behavior. An emphasis on media as the cause of kids' bad behavior prevents us from asking deeper questions about the use of violence to solve problems on a national and global level, for instance, or why boys grow up learning to save face at any cost, to be tough and never vulnerable.

But most ominously, the effects question crowds out other vital issues affecting the well-being and future of young people. These issues play out more quietly on a daily basis and lie hidden underneath the more dramatic fear-factor type headlines. Sociologist Barry Glassner, author of *The Culture of Fear*, refers to this as social sleight of hand, a magician's trick that keeps us focused on one hand while the other actually does the work, encouraging us to think of a trick as real magic. He warns that these diversions encourage us to fear the wrong things, while the real roots of problems go unexamined, and often don't rise in public awareness.

But there are those who benefit from the continued focus on popular culture. Not only is this an issue that politicians can use to connect with middle-class voters, but researchers can get funding from a host of sources to continue to seek negative media effects. David L. Altheide, sociologist and author of *Creating Fear: News and the Construction of Crisis*, suggests that fear-based news helps support the status quo, justifies further social control, and encourages us to look for punitive solutions to perceived problems. In the case of popular culture and young people, heightened fear translates into justification for further restriction and infantilization. Meanwhile, more significant causes of American social problems fall by the wayside.

To consider how social problems are constructed does not mean that there are no real problems, but instead that some receive attention and public indignation, while others loom beneath the surface. Likewise, media phobia is not just a figment of our imaginations, but reflects a unique social context that encourages us to think about individuals and popular culture rather than structured patterns of inequality. Americans in particular have a hard time doing this; within our culture of individualism it is often hard to see these patterns and why they matter.

Deconstructing Media Phobia

This book uses the constructionist approach to understand how claims makers blame popular culture for causing social problems. But there is a danger in taking this approach to mean that all problems are just invented crises. In fact, we can observe many issues that impact a large number of people. Within each chapter, we will examine the unglamorous causes that tend not to attract massive attention or news coverage. Issues such as the persistence of poverty, unequal access to quality education, reduced information about birth control, overall disparities in opportunity, and the continued presence of racial and gender inequality explain many of the problems we hear blamed on popular culture.

In addition to examining how media phobia is constructed and why it is not the central cause of social problems, we will examine actual trends within each topic to best understand that many of the problems attributed to popular culture are actually blown out of proportion. Yet sometimes the problems are very serious (such as violence and educational disparities) and an emphasis on media serves to trivialize them. Studies purporting to find evidence of media culpability are often profoundly flawed or overstate their findings. Since research methodology can be complex and dry, the public almost never hears of how researchers actually conducted the studies discussed in the news. We will do that here, and in the process you will see that some of the research we hear so much about has serious shortcomings. When many people begin with the belief that popular culture is a damaging force, it doesn't take much evidence to provide "solid proof" that media is a major problem. In the following chapters, we will consider claims that popular culture promotes educational failure, violence, promiscuity, single parenthood, materialism, obesity and eating disorders, drinking, drug use, and smoking, as well as racism, sexism, and homophobia. These are important and often misunderstood issues that merit further exploration.

Media culture may not be the root cause of American social problems, but it is more than simply benign entertainment. The purpose of this book is not to simply exonerate media culture as inconsequential: In the book's final chapter I contend that media culture is a prime starting point for social criticism, but our look at social problems should never end with the media. Pointing out the real issues we should be concerned about does not absolve the entertainment industry of its excesses and mediocrity, particularly the news media, which often heightens our fears while providing little context or analysis. Fear is a powerful force, especially when children seem to be potential victims, so it is understandable that the public would be concerned about our ubiquitous media culture. However compelling news reports are, with attention-grabbing visuals and the constant competition for our interest, the fear that media are a central threat to children and the future of America is a tempting explanation, but at best misguided. Dangerously misguided when we consider all of the important (though not as sensational) issues that get pushed out of the headlines in favor of media fears. Poverty, family violence, child abuse and neglect, and the lack of quality education and health care are problems that merit public attention way before media culture. But these policy issues can seem dry and aren't what build big ratings, so they get pushed aside for stories that are more emotion-driven, where the "breaking news" or "live" banner can wave across the screen to excite us.

This fear of media was not invented out of thin air, nor is it only fanned by news stories suggesting media culture is dangerous. There is a parallel groundswell of public concern about the larger role of media culture in contemporary American society. Let's face it, a lot of media culture is highly sexualized, filled with violence, and seems to appeal to our basest interests. Many politicians and social scientists have made challenging popular culture central in their careers. Everyday citizens' letters to the editors of newspapers around the country reveal the widespread nature of the fear that media are ruining the next generation. The fear is everywhere.

Media act as a refracted social mirror, providing us with insights about major social issues such as race, gender, class, and the power and patterns of inequality. The media are an intricate element of our culture, woven into the fabric of social life. We can learn a lot about American society from media culture if we stop insisting on using only cause-effect logic.

Media Matters

I want to be clear that by arguing that popular culture isn't the central cause of our biggest problems I am *not* saying media has no impact on American society. Far from it. Our various forms of media shape our communication with each other and how we spend our time, and we use many forms in constructing our identities. Popular culture shapes what we talk about, how we think of each other, and how we think about ourselves. Media matters, but our relationship to its many forms is more complex and multifaceted than simple cause-effect arguments suggest.

I also understand why people are concerned about the content of popular culture. Many of us find it to be distasteful at times and wonder what its impact may be. Others don't like hearing foul language blasting from the stereo of the car next to ours and cringe when young girls seem to emulate sexy pop stars. Media culture has become very pervasive in the last few decades, and at times it feels like it bombards us—twenty-four-hour news streams, constant Internet chatter, texting, and other forms of media culture have reshaped our daily lives and interactions.

While media culture may not be the biggest threat to childhood, it certainly merits criticism in other arenas. For one, the news media are often guilty of peddling fascination rather than information. This book serves as a critique of the press coverage of social problems and why "the media made them do it" theme continually resurfaces. Aside from the news, media content is important too. Stereotypical images of women as sexual objects persist, as do narrow portrayals of racial, ethnic, and religious minority group members. Limited or absent representations of the elderly, the plus-sized, disabled, and people of color reflect the tendency of mass entertainment to focus on a narrow portrait of American life.

The quest to get the biggest box office opening or Nielsen ratings leads to lowest common denominator storytelling, which explains the overuse of sex and violence as plot devices. Profit, not critical acclaim, equals success in Hollywood (and on Wall Street). Sex and violence create fascination and are sold in popular culture like commodities to attract our attention, if only for a little while. I think concerns about sex and violence in entertainment stem from fears that real sex and violence may become just as meaningless as the multitude of empty images we often see.

So I understand critics who argue that graphic media depictions of sex and violence debase our culture. Hollywood's dependence on these tools often represents the failure to tell complex stories and the lack of courage to take artistic (and financial) risks. Rather than just ask for Hollywood for self-censorship, we should have more choices, more opportunities for our media culture to engage the complexities of life that the summer blockbusters seldom do. But business as usual often makes this impossible, when a handful of big conglomerates produce the lion's share of entertainment media and smaller producers have a difficult time getting attention. The 1996 Telecommunications Act, which eased media ownership restrictions, made it even harder for smaller media outlets to compete with the big conglomerates like Disney, Time-Warner, and Viacom.

That said, I know that sometimes at the end of a long day I prefer to be distracted and amused rather than informed or inspired. With the threat of terrorism, wars in the Middle East, and a faltering economy, maybe superficial entertainment serves a purpose. But deflected anxiety doesn't go away, it just resurfaces elsewhere. And in uncertain times such as our own, it is understandable that our concerns would eventually focus on children and the media culture that both reminds us of our insecurities and distracts us from them. But understanding the most important issues and their causes can help alleviate anxieties about both popular culture and young people. This book aims to do just that.

Notes

1. National Center for Children in Poverty, *Who Are America's Poor Children: The Official Story* (New York: NCCP, 2007), http://www.nccp.org/publications/pub_787.html.

2. Ibid.

3. The Children's Defense Fund, *The State of America's Children Yearbook, 2002* (Washington, DC: CDF, 2002).

4. U.S. Department of Health and Human Services, Administration on Children, Youth and Family, *Child Maltreatment 2006* (Washington, DC: Government Printing Office, 2007), http://www.acf.hhs.gov/programs/cb/pubs/cm06/chapter4.htm#status; U.S. Department of Education, *Indicators of School Crime and Safety* (Washington, DC: Government Printing Office, 2007), http://nces.ed.gov/programs/crimeindicators/crimeindicators2007/figures/fig_01_2.asp?referrer=report.

5. For further discussion of Plato's concerns, see David Buckingham, *After the Death of Childhood: Growing Up in the Age of Electronic Media* (Cambridge: Polity Press, 2000).

6. John Springhall, *Youth, Popular Culture and Moral Panics: Penny Gaffs to Gangsta-Rap, 1830–1996* (New York: St. Martin's Press, 1998).

7. For further discussion see ibid., chapter 5.

8. Frederic Wertham, "Such Trivia as Comic Books," in *The Children's Culture Reader*, ed. Henry Jenkins (New York: New York University Press, 1998).

9. Grace Palladino, *Teenagers: An American History* (New York: Basic Books, 1996).

10. Tom Brokaw, *The Greatest Generation* (New York: Random House, 1998).

11. Stanley Cohen, *Folk Devils and Moral Panics, 3rd ed.* (New York: Routledge, 2002).

12. Laura Sessions Stepp, "Why Johnny Can't Feel; Poor Relationships With Adults May Explain Youth Alienation," *Washington Post*, April 23, 1999, p. C1.

13. Matthew Ebnet and James Rainey, "It's Hard to See the Line Where Alienation Turns to Violence," *Los Angeles Times*, April 22, 1999, Orange County Edition.

14. Ibid.

15. Ibid.

16. U.S. Department of Education, *Indicators of School Crime and Safety*.

17. Leann Smith, "Cartoon Violence is No Laughing Matter," *Kansas City Star*, November 30, 2000, p. B6.

18. Marlene Cimons, "Health Groups Link Hollywood Fare to Youth Violence," *Los Angeles Times*, December 13, 2000, p. A34.

19. Robert E. Pierre, "Number of Youths Awaiting Trial in D.C. Jail Triples," *The Washington Post*, July 25, 2007, p. B1.

20. Maxwell E. McCombs and Donald L. Shaw, "The Agenda-Setting Function of the Mass Media," *Public Opinion Quarterly* 36, no. 2 (1972): 176–187.

21. Cynthia Cooper, *Violence on Television: Congressional Inquiry, Public Criticism and Industry Response—A Policy Analysis* (Lanham, MD: University Press of America, 1996).

22. James Bates and Faye Fiore, "Hollywood Braces for a Showdown on Capitol Hill," *Los Angeles Times*, September 24, 2000, p. A1.

23. Abigail Goldman and Joseph Menn, "Wal-Mart Halts Gun Sales After State Laws Broken," *Los Angeles Times*, April 5, 2003, p. A1.

24. In 2002 Wal-Mart did implement more stringent handgun purchasing policies, angering the National Rifle Association. The chain later agreed to temporarily stop selling guns in California, following the investigation conducted by the attorney general's office. See Eric Lichtblau, "Wal-Mart Gun Policy Praised, Scorned," *Los Angeles Times*, July 4, 2002, p. A12.

25. Joel Best, *Random Violence: How We Talk About New Crimes and New Victims*, (Berkeley: University of California Press, 1999), xiii.

26. U.S. Department of Health and Human Services, *Youth Violence: A Report of the Surgeon General* (Washington, DC: GPO, 2001). For more discussion of the research on which the statement was based, see Chapter 2.

27. Jeff Leeds, "Surgeon General Links TV, Real Violence," *Los Angeles Times*, January 17, 2001, p. A1; Jesse Hiestand, "Media Dodges Violence Bullet; Poverty, Peers More To Blame," New York *Daily News*, January 18, 2001, p. B1.

Popular Culture Is Dumbing Down America

Can you name all of Brad and Angelina's kids? President Kennedy's siblings? The sisters in Louisa May Alcott's *Little Women*? Jacob's sons from the Old Testament? My guess is the first question is easiest for most readers coming of age in the twenty-first century, whether we are actually interested in knowing the Jolie-Pitt children's names or not. After all, you don't have to try very hard to hear them mentioned in celebrity gossip or fan magazines that feature their pictures. Television, magazines, and the Internet help us much more with the first question than the others.

The other questions require us to draw on knowledge of history, literature, and the Bible, information that is not circulating as freely and rapidly as information about contemporary popular culture. I admit that my ability to name any of Jacob's sons is solely based on memories of the play *Joseph and the Amazing Technicolor Dream Coat*. Is popular culture turning us into a nation of shallow idiots?

Many critics of popular culture are certain that the answer is yes. By now you have probably heard some of the complaints: Kids know the names of the Three Stooges but not the three branches of the federal government, they know that Bart Simpson is from Springfield but not that Abraham Lincoln is from Springfield, Illinois, and

21

other comparisons that suggest our brain space is occupied with pop culture trivia to the exclusion of other knowledge.[1]

News reports, like one in the *Washington Times* called "The Pull of Pop Culture," imply that young people must choose between "the pull of the popular or the push of schooling," and that kids consistently choose the former, or 50 Cent over Shakespeare.[2] A *Chicago Sun-Times* story, "Successful Kids Reject Pop Culture's Message," notes that being able to graduate from high school is based on kids' "ability to reject the nonsense they are exposed to in our pop culture."[3] A 2008 book, *The Dumbest Generation: How the Digital Age Stupefies Young Americans and Jeopardizes our Future*, reflects this same concern.

Within these stories, popular culture is cast as antithetical to education and knowledge, something that prevents learning. Communications scholar Neil Postman's 1985 book, *Amusing Ourselves to Death*, explored this issue in depth. He argued that as the United States shifted from "the magic of writing to the magic of electronics" public discourse changed from "coherent, serious and rational" to "shriveled and absurd," thanks largely to television.[4] Drawing from Aldous Huxley's *Brave New World*, Postman decries what he sees as the rejection of books in favor of a show business mentality that has pervaded every aspect of public life, from politics and religion to education. He believed that these amusements undermine our capacity to think, encouraging us to move away from the written word—rationality, in his view—towards television and visual media.

Postman got it partly right. This new media world does act as a never-ending shiny object that grabs our attention. It distracts us from knowing too much about the way American society is structured, being too aware of social problems that might seem boring in the face of so much other interesting stuff out there to pay attention to. But instead of impeding knowledge and discourse across the board, new media like the Internet have *increased* public discourse, along with the number of amusements available to distract us. Television news programs now use interactive media to further engage citizens, through live blogs and using sites like YouTube in presidential debates, rather than just enabling people to be passively entertained. In fairness to Postman, who wrote before the Internet age, these developments are still unfolding. But rather than replacing traditional means of informing the public and furthering the flow of knowledge, new media and even popular culture are sometimes used to create new ways to educate.

This chapter considers the complaints that popular culture interferes with education and has created an intellectually lazy population. As we will see, changes in visual media and the increased ability to communicate electronically have altered how people interact and exchange information. Television, texting, and a culture awash in seemingly frivolous gossip may appear to be the causes of educational failure, but the reality is far less entertaining. Problems within education stem from factors beyond popular culture: lack of resources, inconsistent family and community support, and inequality. While some school districts have significant drop-out and failure problems, Americans are not as dumb as we are often told . . . at least no more so than we have been in the past. The vast divides of educational attainment and intellectual achievement cannot be explained by popular culture, but by the continuing reality of inequality in American society.

Television Zombies?

Does television put viewers into a hypnotic trance, injecting ideas into otherwise disengaged minds? During the 1970s, several books suggested that this was in fact the case. Marie Winn's 1977 book, *The Plug-in Drug,* described television as a dangerous addiction. Following Winn, in 1978 Jerry Mander's provocatively titled *Four Arguments for the Elimination of Television* concurred. According to Mander, television viewers are spaced out, "little more than . . . vessel[s] of reception" implanted with "images in the unconscious realms of the mind." Put simply, Mander argues that television viewing produces "no cognition."[5] Television viewing increases with age, and yet nearly all of the concerns about television dulling the intellect focused on children and teens. According to Nielsen Media Research, children and teens watch much less television than their elders: adults 65 and over watched an average of nearly 178 hours in May 2008, almost double that of children two to eleven, who averaged about 87 hours that same month.[6]

Both of these books rely upon anecdotal observations yet make important charges about the negative effects television supposedly has on thinking. Some of these claims seem like common sense: Television shortens one's attention span, reduces interest in reading, promotes hyperactivity, impedes language development, and reduces overall school performance. Yet research into these claims reveals that television is not exactly the idiot box its critics suggest.

It might surprise you to learn that one of the programs most heavily criticized in the 1970s was *Sesame Street*, the educational program many of us grew up watching. Cognitive psychologist Daniel R. Anderson studied claims that preschoolers get transfixed in zombielike fashion while viewing *Sesame Street*, as well as the contradictory complaint that it contributes to hyperactivity. Studies where researchers observed three- to five-year-olds watch television found that their attention is anything but fixed: They look away 40 to 60 percent of the time, draw letters with their fingers in the air along with characters, and pay more attention to segments compatible with their current cognitive aptitude level. There was no evidence of hyperactivity after watching, and *Sesame Street* viewers had larger vocabularies and showed greater readiness for school than other children.[7]

Anderson and several colleagues conducted a long-term study, following 570 children from preschool into adolescence to see if a relationship between preschool television viewing and academic performance exists. Their findings cast serious doubt on the speculation that television impedes learning later in life. In contrast to the claims that the nature of television itself dulls intellectual ability, their data repeatedly reveals that content matters: Children—especially boys—who watched what they call "informative" programming as preschoolers had higher grade point averages and were likely to read *more* as teens. These findings counter a well-worn idea that television primes children to expect to be entertained at all times, leading to intellectual laziness and the idea that learning is boring.[8]

Their study also challenges the idea that television has a "displacement" effect: People spend more time watching television, and thus less time engaged in more rigorous intellectual activities like reading. Anderson and colleagues found that this effect was small, complicated, and only observed in middle- and high-income kids. Children who watched fewer than ten hours a week actually had poorer academic achievement than those who averaged about ten hours of viewing per week, and those who watch a lot more than ten had slightly lower academic achievement than those in the middle. The authors conclude that there is no evidence that television viewing displaces educational activities; instead it is likely that television viewing replaces other leisure activities, like listening to music, playing video games, and so forth. The authors also found that more television viewing did not necessarily translate into doing less homework.[9]

The authors list other studies to support their claims, finding that television does not ruin reading skills, lower IQ, or otherwise interfere with education. This does not mean that parents should let kids watch as much television as they want and let them do their homework when they feel like it. We should not presume from this study that television is children's best teacher, but that it does not necessarily have the damaging effect critics have suggested. In fact, the best predictor of student achievement is parents' level of education. It is likely that this effect is so strong—for better and for worse in some cases—that television cannot compete with the academic environment created by parents. Parents who encourage reading, read themselves, and emphasize the importance of education are a far more powerful source than television. Not surprisingly, reading more is a good predictor of school success, but watching television does not interfere with literacy skills as many critics charged.[10]

The critiques of educational television have had political underpinnings in some cases. Anderson describes how much of the concern about *Sesame Street* was driven by those who sought to cut funding for the Children's Television Workshop, and public television more generally, during the early 1990s.[11] If opponents could find that educational programming had no impact, or even deleterious effects, they could justify eliminating public funding as yet another form of budgetary pork. But such was not the case.

Television has never really left the hot seat. More recently, TV has been blamed for causing Attention Deficit Hyperactivity Disorder (ADHD) and even autism. While it may seem like television's electronic images can wreak havoc on the young brain's wiring process, research does not support this conclusion. It is likely that people who have grown up with electronic media think *differently* from those who did not, but different is not always pathological.

Let's look more closely at some of the research on ADHD and television. It is mostly based on correlations, and therefore causality cannot be assessed. But if you Google "television and ADHD" you will be told otherwise. One online article concludes "It's Official: Television Linked to Attention Deficit."[12] But the authors of the study cited by this article would not go that far.

The study in question, published in a 2004 issue of the journal *Pediatrics,* assessed the "overstimulating" effect television may have on children who watch TV as toddlers.[13] To do so, they asked parents about their children's television viewing at age one and three, and asked them questions regarding their children's attentional behavior at age seven. Although they did find a relationship between lower attentional behavior and more television viewing, the authors themselves acknowledge that "we have not in fact studied or found an association between television viewing and clinically diagnosed ADHD," because none of the children in the study had been diagnosed.[14] They also conclude that it is equally likely that a more lax or stressful environment might make television viewing more prevalent in early childhood, and that television viewing is associated, but not the *cause* of children's inattention.

Likewise, a 2006 study published in the *Archives of Pediatrics and Adolescent Medicine* found significant differences between children diagnosed with ADHD and their peers. The authors found "no effect of subsequent story comprehension in either group," and that for the non-ADHD children, "children who have difficulty paying attention may favor television and other electronic media to a greater extent than the media environment of children without attention problems."[15] Most interestingly, their study found that any effect that television watching had on attention was with the *non*-ADHD kids only; those diagnosed with ADHD showed no declines in attention after watching television. This study challenges the conventional wisdom that television has particularly adverse effects for children with ADHD; instead the authors conclude that, "the cognitive processing deficits associated with ADHD are so strongly rooted in biological predisposition that, among children with this diagnosis, environmental characteristics such as television viewing have a negligible effect on these cognitive processing areas."[16]

The research on television and autism is even more suspect. Nevertheless, it garnered coverage in a 2006 issue of *Time* magazine and in the online magazine *Slate.*[17] A study by economists found a correlation between autism rates and cable television subscription rates in

California and Pennsylvania. They did not measure what children watched (or if children were watching at all). Studies like this, although profoundly flawed, help maintain the doomsday specter of television. Easy answers for complex neurological processes are digestible to the public and thus make for interesting speculation, but probably will yield little in the way of solving serious problems like autism.

The cumulative effect of questionable studies helps create an environment where television seems to be the answer for all educational failures. The American Academy of Pediatrics (AAP) insists that parents should not allow children under two to watch any television, for fear that it interferes with development, a claim that has yet to be scientifically supported. The AAP statement does not reference any research on infants, but instead focuses on research on older children and teens. Still, the AAP concludes that "babies and toddlers have a critical need for direct interactions with parents and other significant care givers (e.g., child care providers) for healthy brain growth and the development of appropriate social, emotional, and cognitive skills."[18] While television does not provide the direct one-on-one interaction babies need and can never replace human interaction, there is no evidence of direct *harm* from television. A 2003 Kaiser Family Foundation (KFF) report found that the majority of children under two—74 percent—have watched television (or at least their parents admit that they have), and 43 percent watch every day.[19]

I am not suggesting that propping infants up in front of the TV set is a good idea, especially if children are left unattended (in the KFF report 88 percent of parents said they were with their children all or most of the time). But there is no evidence that television has a *negative* impact on infants either, only that it does not necessarily contribute to their development. If parents decide they would like to keep their children away from television, they have the right to make that choice. But many parents are made to feel guilty for choosing to allow some television viewing when there is no concrete evidence of harm. The TV blackout is especially difficult for parents with older children who might watch, or those who enjoy watching TV themselves.

In contrast to the widespread belief that television interferes with intelligence, writer Steven Johnson suggests that the opposite might be true. In his book, *Everything Bad is Good for You: How Today's Popular Culture is Actually Making us Smarter,* Johnson argues that television has actually become more complex and cross-referential, and that the best dramas and comedies of today require significantly more of viewers than in the past. He cites programs like *24,* which expect that viewers think along with the show and draw from plot twists and information from previous shows, in contrast to older television, which provided more exposition, if any was needed at all. He says that these kinds of shows are "cognitive workouts," and that even reality shows sometimes encourage us to develop greater social intelligence.[20]

While I'm not sure that television makes most people smarter—I would hypothesize that those who are already intelligent can use television to improve upon an already strong intellect—we cannot lay educational failure at the base of the television set. It is a tempting but dangerous diversion, to put too much focus on the TV explanation.

Newer Media

While concerns about television will probably never completely fade away, tweens and teens spend more time online than they do watching television, according to a 2008 study by research firm Youth Trends.[21] Adults are even more likely to spend time online than children or teens: Adults aged thirty-five to forty-four spent an average of nearly thirty-nine hours online in May, compared with just over twelve hours for teens twelve to seventeen, according to Nielsen Media Research.[22] And video games also cut into television time, especially for boys.

A 2007 study, published in the *Archives of Pediatrics and Adolescent Medicine,* found that 36 percent of their respondents in a nationally representative sample played video games, averaging an hour a day (and an hour and a half on weekends). Gamers reported spending less time reading and doing homework than nongamers.[23] While this may indicate that video gamers' schoolwork will suffer, other studies—including two that I discussed above—have found no evidence that video games were associated with lower academic performance. In one of these studies, published in *Pediatrics* in 2006, the authors seem to contradict themselves. In their analysis they state that "video game use [was] not associated with school performance," yet conclude that "television, movies and video game use during middle school years is uniformly associated with a detrimental impact on school perform-ance." They also neglect to add that television use itself has no neg-ative impact, just heavy viewing *during* the school week, according to their own findings.[24]

Another researcher responded to this contradiction by writing to the journal that the "conclusions are not warranted," and yet the au-thors refused to accept their own study's findings, responding that "from this 'displacement' perspective, we have little reason to believe that four hours of video game time would be any different from four hours of television time."[25] The reality is that very few people actu-ally play video games for four hours a day, as the 2007 study found; in the *Pediatrics* study 95 percent of kids played fewer than four hours a day. Their unfounded conclusion that video game playing must neg-atively affect academic achievement reflects the persistent belief that video games are problematic.

For people who have played video games, the question about gam-ing and academic achievement might seem backwards. Wouldn't games that require you to learn often complex rules at increasingly difficult levels actually provide intellectual *benefits*? Steven Johnson, author of *Everything Bad is Good for You,* makes this argument, using

The Sims as an example, where users need to master a host of rules as they play the game about urban planning. Yes, common sense dictates that people (of all ages) should not neglect their other responsibilities in favor of playing, but the games themselves tend to offer a kind of mental workout, especially improving spatial skills. I admit that I am not much of a gamer, but have at times gotten into games like Tetris, Free Cell, and Snake, mostly on my computer or cell phone. As a child I was weakest in spatial intelligence, and remember taking timed tests with shapes that I struggled with. After playing Tetris and Snake just a little, I have noticed improvement in this area. And these are really simple games—for people who play others, it is clear that they are getting, as Johnson says, "a cognitive workout," one that critics and many researchers belittle by insisting that games make people less intelligent.[26]

I suspect the disdain for video games and other new media comes from a lack of familiarity. The games are so much more complex now than when they first came out in the 1970s that they compel users to play a lot more than Pong, Merlin, or Atari did when I was growing up. Back then the games were much like other children's toys that kids played occasionally and mostly grew tired of. By contrast, games today are likely to be serious endeavors that kids don't give up after a few weeks, but instead are likely to play into adulthood.

Video games bear little resemblance to their predecessors from decades ago, and thus seem like a strange new development for many older adults. But at least some people over forty have a frame of reference for video games, unlike texting, a relatively new development. Recently texting has come under fire for presumably ruining young peoples' ability to spell and write coherently. Many complaints come from people I can relate to: college professors who read students' papers and e-mails. A Howard University professor told the *Washington Times* that electronic communication has "destroyed literacy and how students communicate."[27] A University of Illinois professor wrote to the *New York Times* that she is concerned about the informality in written communication, with no regard for spelling and grammar.[28] A tutor wrote an op-ed in the *Los Angeles Times* of the "linguistic horrors" she frequently reads in students' essays. "The sentence is dead and buried," the author concludes, asking teens to "step away from MySpace" while doing homework.[29]

I can relate to these concerns, especially when I get rambling e-mails in all lowercase letters from students. But to tell the truth I have not seen a decline in students' ability to write since e-mail and texting became so widespread. And according to a Pew Internet and American Life study, teens don't confuse texting with actual writing. A surprising 93 percent of those surveyed indicated that they did some form of writing for pleasure (journaling, blogging, writing music lyrics, and so on). Most teens—82 percent—also thought that they would benefit from more writing instruction at school.[30]

Others are also optimistic. Michael Gerson of the *Washington Post* writes, "A command of texting seems to indicate a broader facility for language. And these students seem to switch easily between text messaging and standard English."[31] Texting reminds me of another form of language use that is all but obsolete: shorthand. This used to be considered a skill, taught in school often to prepare students for secretarial work. Court reporters also master a language within a language in their daily work. But because texting is associated with young people, critics presume it is a detriment rather than a new skill. And like television, video games, and the Internet, texting is not just a young person's activity. According to industry research, the average age of a texter is 38.[32]

Perhaps at the heart of these concerns are uncertainties about these new media. Will they distract people from being productive citizens? Enable too many shortcuts? Much has been written recently about teens and multitasking, mostly with an undercurrent of anxiety. "Some fear that the penchant for flitting from task to task could have serious consequences on young people's ability to focus and develop analytical skills," warns a 2007 *Washington Post* article.[33] *Time* magazine published an article in 2006 called "The Multitasking Generation," stating that "the mental habit of dividing one's attention into many small slices has significant implications for the way young people learn, reason, socialize, do creative work and understand the world. Although such habits may prepare kids for today's frenzied workplace, many cognitive scientists are positively alarmed by the trend." The article goes on to quote a neuroscientist who fears that multitaskers "aren't going to do well in the long run."[34]

It is interesting that rather than celebrate the possible positive outcomes of multitasking—which most mothers will tell you they have no choice but to learn—where young people are concerned the prognosis is grim. As *Time* rightly observes, multitasking is a valuable professional skill, as any brief observation of the frenzied Wall Street trader or busy executive reveals. The Kaiser Family Foundation (KFF) released a report on youth multitasking in 2006, and found that while doing homework the mostly likely other activity teens engage in is listen to music—something I do as I write too. Most of the multitasking comes while doing other leisure activities, like instant messaging and Web surfing at once. The KFF study seems to imply that using a computer to do homework invites distraction. "When doing homework on the computer is their primary activity, they're usually doing something else at the same time (65% of the time)," the report concludes.[35]

And yet computer use is a vital part of being educated in the twenty-first century. In creating access to a tremendous amount of information, the Internet also changes the nature of education. Items that had to be researched from a physical library can be recalled by computer or smart phone, basically eliminating the need for memorization of many facts. These shifts remind me of Albert Einstein's alleged ignorance of his own phone number, which he supposedly said he could look up if he needed to know. How many phone numbers do you know now that phones remember them for us?

Yes, the Internet and other technologies have created new ways to take intellectual shortcuts and to cheat. Education needs to evolve along with the technology, shifting the nature of learning away from memorization and onto teaching how to think. The Internet can and has been used to thwart cheating too, and rather than new media being the enemy, educators need to make peace with them and embrace them as much as possible. Just as the written word moved societies away from oral culture, visual media require a new intelligence that needs to be fully integrated into education today. Our continued reliance on standardized testing impedes this shift in many ways. But a new way of sharing information has arrived, and will likely continue to mutate in the coming years. Rather than fight it or bemoan the possibilities, we'd better start getting ready.

How Dumb Are We Really?

For those who glorify the past, the present or future can never compare. What's interesting is that complaining about how little the next generation knows never abates. As I discussed in my book *Kids These Days: Facts and Fictions About Today's Youth,* people have found young people's knowledge lacking for centuries, and commentators have grimly assessed Americans' intellectual abilities, whether it be math, reading skills, or geography, for over a century.[36] The complaint that we are superficial and only interested in amusements has been around for a long time. But are we really less knowledgeable than our predecessors?

One source of support critics look to is SAT (formerly known as the Scholastic Aptitude Test) scores. Between 1967 and 1980, average verbal scores fell 41 points, from 543 to 502, a fall of about 8 percent, and math scores fell 24 points, from 516 to 492. As you can see in the following figure, this appears to suggest that high school aptitude nose-

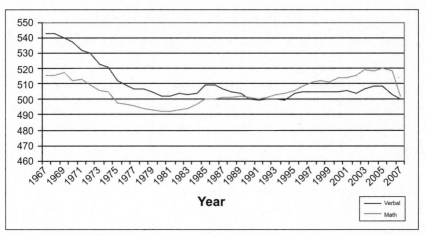

Average Verbal and Math SAT Scores, 1967–2007.
Source: College Board, 2008.

dived during the 1970s. Since that time, average math scores rose to an all-time high in 2005 before declining in the two years after. Verbal scores fluctuated but have yet to match levels of the late 1960s and early 1970s.

Critic Marie Winn, author of *The Plug-In Drug*, argues that television is the "primary cause" for this decline, claiming that as kids grew up watching more television in the late 1960s their ability to read declined.[37] But as the above-noted studies detail, television had little to do with high school grade point average, which are highly related to SAT scores.[38] Ironically, the decline in SAT scores from four decades ago reflects a *positive* trend: More high school students are taking the test and planning on attending college than in the past. According to the U.S. Department of Education, in 1972, 59 percent of high school seniors planned on attending college, compared with 79 percent in 2004.[39] Not only are more people attending college, many more African American and Latino students are attending college than in 1970, groups that have been historically underrepresented and tend to have slightly lower scores on average than whites or Asian Americans.[40] They are also more likely to attend underfunded and overcrowded urban schools with less qualified teachers, and in some cases English is their second language.[41] Blaming television takes the focus away from these significant disparities in public education, which I will discuss later in this chapter.

Donald P. Hayes, Loreen T. Wolfer, and Michael F. Wolfe of Cornell University suggest something else is to blame: the decline in the quality of textbooks. They examined eight hundred textbooks published between 1919 and 1991 and found that the newer texts are less comprehensive and, in their estimation, less likely to prepare students to master reading comprehension.[42]

Still others wonder if verbal abilities are really declining at all. Psychologists have studied scores on intelligence quotient (IQ) tests from the beginning of the twentieth century, when they were first administered, to 2001 and found that IQ scores are continually rising—so much so that they have had to be periodically recalibrated to reflect the population's average score. Called the "Flynn Effect" after psychologist James R. Flynn, total unadjusted IQ scores have risen about eighteen points between 1947 and 2002. This means the average IQ of someone in 2002—always scaled to 100—would have been about 118 in 1947 (the corollary means that a person of average intelligence in 1947 would have an IQ of 82 in 2002). Four of the points accounted for in the gain are from vocabulary.[43]

So are we smarter or dumber? Flynn says that "today's children are far better at solving problems on the spot without a previously learned method for doing so."[44] He also suggests that if we look at achievement tests of children's reading from 1971 to 2002, fourth and eighth grade students' reading skills improved, but by twelfth grade there were no differences over time.[45] Looking at the data to which he refers, what is most interesting is that nine-year-old boys in particular gained a great deal on reading scores—fifteen points between 1971 and 2004, compared with girls' more modest seven point gain.[46] In all age groups, significant racial/ethnic disparities persist, despite some reduction since 1971. This may partially explain why verbal SAT scores haven't risen (but not why they fell). In any case, these observations refute the notion that young children can't read because of television.

The case of IQ and SAT disparities remind us that these tests are only approximations of intelligence and aptitude, rife with problems of cultural bias and reflect the narrow ways that aptitude and intelligence are defined. The long-term changes in both measures tell us that people are better prepared for one test, but not for the other . . . and yet they purport to measure some of the same skills.

The National Center for Education Statistics (NCES) conducted assessments of adult literacy in 1992 and 2003, and found that overall results were virtually the same, but there were significant differences in terms of race, education, and age. Whites had higher scores than those in other racial categories, although their scores were virtually unchanged during the two time periods. Blacks and Asian Americans made gains in 2003, while Latino literacy scores declined. Not surprisingly, more education meant higher scores. Nineteen- to forty-nine-year-olds had the highest scores, with adults over sixty-five having the lowest.[47] Overall, people of all ages are reading less than a decade ago, according to a 2007 National Endowment for the Arts (NEA) report. As someone who writes books, this does not come as good news to me. But despite declines in leisure reading, the NEA study found that nearly 60 percent of adults twenty-five to forty-four still read for pleasure.[48] In contrast, a Harris Interactive Poll found that between 1995 and 2004, the percentage of adults who reported reading as their favorite leisure activity increased, from 28 to 35 percent (although in 2007 it fell to 29 percent); in every year reading was ranked the respondents' favorite leisure activity.[49]

Declines in reading have many causes and implications. We often think that this is a direct result of other media luring people away from books, but long-term studies have also found that in the last several decades Americans have less leisure time, period.[50] Since reading is a more intellectually taxing activity, it may be the first to go after a busy day. I am personally an avid reader, but after a long day at work my eyes and brain don't want to work that hard. I suspect that for other adults, who are working increasingly longer hours to make ends meet, this rings true. But we need to avoid viewing the past through rose-colored glasses, where entire families would have sat around reading books together. With high school graduation rates hovering below 25 percent until 1940, it is very likely that the number of people reading books was not as high as we might think.

While pleasure reading might not be increasing, educational attainment has risen dramatically since 1960. According to the U.S. Census, high school graduation rates more than doubled between 1960 and 2006, from just 41 percent of the population to about 86 percent. Less than 8 percent of Americans had a college degree in 1960, compared with 28 percent in 2006. Rates for African Americans and Latinos still lags behind whites, but these groups have made tremendous gains during this time as well. African American high school graduation quadrupled, and college graduation increased sixfold. Latino high school graduation rates have nearly doubled since 1970 (the first year data were collected), while college graduation has tripled in that time period.[51]

Overall, we are a more educated society, one that places a great deal of emphasis on higher learning as a vital skill in our information-based economy. But as continuing disparities in graduation, literacy, and SAT scores detail, race and socioeconomic status remain significant factors. This is *not* due to different innate abilities, as controversial theories suggest, or only to media use, but to different educational opportunities.

Unequal Education

More than a half-century has passed since the landmark Supreme Court ruling *Brown v. Board of Education*, which voided the "separate but equal" doctrine that had dominated American education. And yet children today still largely inhabit very separate public school systems: one that is largely effective in fulfilling its mission of providing students with a quality education, and one that fails miserably. The latter tends to be the only option for the nation's poorest children living in cities, helping to perpetuate the cycle of poverty. Focusing on television and other media as a primary source of educational failure enables us to overlook the pervasive nature of inequality, and the most important predictor of educational attainment.

This cycle predates television and has nothing to do with popular culture. Its roots are firmly planted in the days of slavery, where many states outlawed teaching slaves how to read. Education was viewed as a major threat to white supremacy, both during and after slavery. After slavery ended, schools for African American children lacked many of the basic resources, and most colleges and universities excluded them entirely.

While many children, like *Brown v. Board of Education*'s plaintiff Linda Brown, lived close to "white" schools, residential segregation ensured that many did not. Segregation actually increased after World War II, with the growth of suburbs that were off-limits for blacks and government policies that refused to underwrite loans for whites who lived in neighborhoods with African Americans. This practice, called "redlining," dictated the amount of risk involved in home loans, limiting who would get funding to live in a particular neighborhood or who could borrow money for home improvements. Until the passage of the Fair Housing Act in 1968, housing discrimination was rampant and legal, which helped to shuffle Americans into predominantly white or minority neighborhoods, as well as severely limit the property values in nonwhite neighborhoods. Since schools in the United States are typically funded by property tax revenues, those in areas with a lower tax base had less funding for local schools. Less funding means less money to pay teachers well, so those with more experience and training go to districts with a higher tax base. Those teaching low-income kids are more likely to have emergency credentials and lack training in the specific subject they teach. They are more likely to have older and fewer textbooks, which means that students cannot take their books home to study. The school itself is more likely to be overcrowded and in disrepair.[52]

As if these obstacles were not enough, as I discuss in later chapters, children living in low-income communities are more likely to experience family disruption and neighborhood violence, making it harder to focus on studying. One of the most important factors predicting educational success is having parents who actively support and are involved in their child's education. Low-income parents who might need to work several jobs, have little education themselves, or in some cases speak minimal English, might not be able to help their children as much as they might hope, despite their best intentions. Among the best predictors of high educational attainment is having a parent who has a high level of educational attainment—and thus the cycle unfortunately continues. Children who grow up with educated parents, who leverage their educations to obtain good paying jobs, can afford to live in neighborhoods with higher property values, a better tax base for its schools, and provide better preparation for college success. Public schools in affluent areas with insufficient public funding have the ability to raise private funds, so budget cuts and economic downturns affect them less.

These disparities reveal how socioeconomic status and race are deeply intertwined. While African Americans and Latinos have closed some of the achievement gaps in recent decades, they still persist. Think about the area where you live: Is it mostly segregated? Are there black or Latino neighborhoods that are mostly poor? If you are living near just about any American city, the answer would be yes. These communities developed and persist initially due to public policies that assured the continuation of racial inequality, even after the demise of slavery and Jim Crow laws, and the civil rights movement of the twentieth century.

In recent years, the federal government attempted to address these disparities through its No Child Left Behind (NCLB) policy. In theory, this program was supposed to assess how well schools worked, and provide options for those attending schools that were less effective, including tutoring, afterschool programs, or even transferring to another school.[53] Critics have argued that NCLB overemphasizes standardized testing and has not provided sufficient funding to help bolster failing schools. The policy also includes sanctions and penalties for schools that do not meet certain goals, which would further challenge schools in already difficult circumstances. Improving school achievement requires more than fixing failing schools—to significantly reduce the disparities in graduation rates and test scores we need to also begin to repair the communities which they serve to help break the cycle at all points.

As you can imagine, making changes like this takes time, investment, and commitment, things that we have been mostly unwilling to provide to America's poorest citizens. Throw in the contentious subject of race and inequality, and suddenly it seems much easier to talk about the problem of television, video games, and computers. We ought to be more concerned about the kids who *do not* have access to computers, who are not developing the same sort of computer skills as their peers. The digitally disempowered are most likely to be from low-income families and may live in communities with libraries that have no computers, no Internet access, or no public library at all.

According to a 2002 Annie E. Casey Foundation study, having access to a computer at home increases educational performance, even when factors like income are taken into account.[54] Not surprisingly, income is a major factor in determining who is likely to have a computer in their home. Census data from 2003 indicate a huge disparity between home computer access: Just 47 percent of children in families earning under $25,000 have a home computer, compared with 97 percent of those in families earning more than $100,000. Access is also a factor of race: while 85 percent of white and Asian American children have home computers, only 54 percent of black and Latino families have home computers.[55]

Clearly low-income families have more pressing needs, like food and rent, before buying a computer or subscribing to an Internet service provider. But can't these kids use computers at school? The Annie E. Casey Foundation report cited a 2001 study that found that only a quarter of kids without home computers had access at school.[56] Even when schools do have computers, they may not be up to date and the time students can individually spend using them is limited. Over time, this disparity in computer usage translates into less time to do homework assignments on a computer, less ease with computer software, fewer Internet research opportunities, and an overall educational disadvantage. Those without computer skills today already face serious employment setbacks, which are bound to multiply.

Common sense tells us that if someone is watching television, playing games, or otherwise avoiding their school (or work) responsibilities, that is not good. Planting one's self in front of the TV or computer screen for a long time does have consequences, and this chapter does not suggest otherwise. But those who argue that television and media are behind some of this country's serious educational problems are off the mark. For some, the only solution is to *never* watch television, or as Jerry Mander suggested in 1977, eliminate it altogether. Neither will happen any time soon. As our communications media shift, intellectual skills shift along with them. Rather than taking the glass half-empty approach, we might instead look to see what we gain from these changes, and how they can enhance education in the future. Beyond popular culture, we must also deal with the stubborn issue of inequality, which is the most important factor in understanding educational disparities—not simply whether someone watched *Sesame Street* as a toddler.

Notes

1. Bob Dart, "Teens Know About Pop Culture But Not Constitution," Cox News Service, September 2, 1998, http://constitutioncenter.org/Files/stooges.pdf.

2. Deborah Simmons, "The Pull of Pop Culture," *Washington Times,* January 18, 2008, p. A17.

3. Mary A. Mitchell, "Successful Kids Reject Pop Culture's Message," *Chicago Sun-Times,* June 7, 2001, p. 14.

4. Neil Postman, *Amusing Ourselves to Death: Public Discourse in the Age of Show Business* (New York: Penguin Books, 1985), pp. 13, 16.

5. Jerry Mander, *Four Arguments for the Elimination of Television* (New York: Morrow Quill Paperbacks, 1978), p. 204.

6. PR Newswire, "Under 35's Watch Video on Internet & Mobile Phones More Than Over 35's; Traditional TV Viewing Continues to Grow," Nielsen Reports TV, Internet and Mobile Usage Among Americans Press Release, PR Newswire, July 8, 2008, http://www.prnewswire.com/cgi-bin/stories.pl?ACCT=109&STORY=/www/story/07-08-2008/0004844888&EDATE=.

7. Daniel R. Anderson, "Educational Television is Not an Oxymoron," *Annals of the American Academy of Political and Social Science,* May 1998, 24–38.

8. Daniel R. Anderson, et al., "Early Childhood Television Viewing and Adolescent Behavior: The Recontact Study," *Monographs of the Society for Research in Child Development,* 66 (2001): 1–154.

9. Ibid, p. 41.

10. Gary D. Gaddy, "Television's Impact on High School Achievement," *The Public Opinion Quarterly* 50, no. 3 (1986): 340–359.

11. Daniel R. Anderson, "Educational Television is Not an Oxymoron," *Annals of the American Academy of Political and Social Science* 557 (May 1998): 24–38.

12. Jean Lotus, "It's Official: TV Linked to Attention Defecit," Post on White Dot, the International Campaign Against Television Blog, July 21, 2008, http://www.whitedot.org/issue/iss_story.asp?slug=ADHD%20Toddlers.

13. Dimitri A. Christakis, et al., "Early Television Exposure and Subsequent Attentional Problems in Children," *Pediatrics* 113 (2004): 708–713.

14. Ibid., p. 711.

15. Ignacio David Acevedo-Polakovich, et al., "Disentangling the Relation Between Television Viewing and Cognitive Processes in Children With Attention-Deficit/Hyperactivity Disorder and Comparison Children," *Archives of Pediatrics and Adolescent Medicine* 160 (2006): 358, 359.

16. Ibid., p. 359.

17. Claudia Wallis, "Does Watching TV Cause Autism?" *Time,* October 26, 2006, http://www.time.com/time/health/article/0,8599,1548682,00.html; Greg Easterbrook, "TV Really Might Cause Autism," *Slate,* October 16, 2006, http://www.slate.com/id/2151538.

18. American Academy of Pediatrics, "Policy Statement," *Pediatrics* 104 (1999): 341–343, http://aappolicy.aappublications.org/cgi/content/full/pediatrics;104/2/341.

19. Victoria J. Rideout, Elizabeth A. Vandewater, and Ellen A. Wartella, "Zero to Six: Electronic Media in the Lives of Infants, Toddlers and Preschoolers," The Henry J. Kaiser Family Foundation, 2003, http://www.kff.org/entmedia/entmedia 102803pkg.cfm.

20. Steven Johnson, *Everything Bad is Good for You: How Today's Popular Culture is Actually Making us Smarter* (New York: Riverhead Books, 2005), pp. 14, 96.

21. Katy Bachman, "Nielsen: Consumers Using TV, Web More Than Ever," *Mediaweek,* July 8, 2008; Katy Bachman, "Study: Teens Would Rather Hit Web, TV Than Read," *Mediaweek,* June 19, 2008, http://www.mediaweek.com/mw/content_display/news/media-agencies-research/e3i47ee828baa06c9e246f86eba4cd42c1a.

22. *Bachman,* "Study."

23. Hope M. Cummings and Elizabeth A. Vandewater, "Relation of Adolescent Video Game Play to Time Spent in Other Activities," *Archives of Pediatrics and Adolescent Medicine* 161 (2007): 684–689.

24. Iman Sharif and James D. Sargent, "Lack of Association Between Video Game Exposure and School Performance: In Reply," *Pediatrics (*2007): 1061, 1065.

25. Ibid., pp. 413–414.

26. Johnson, *Everything Bad is Good*, p. 14.

27. Shelley Widhalm, "OMG; How 2 Know Wen 2 Writ N Lingo?" *Washington Times,* January 24, 2008, p. B1.

28. Letter to the editor, "Email and the Decline of Writing," *New York Times,* December 11, 2004, p. A18.

29. Mary Kolesnikova, "Language That Makes You Say OMG; Teens are Letting Emoticons and Other Forms of Chat-Speak Slip into Their Essays and Homework," *Los Angeles Times,* May 13, 2008, http://www.latimes.com/news/opinion/la-oe-kolesnikova13-2008may13,0,4111689.story.

30. Amanda Lenhart, et al., "Writing, Technology, and Teens," Pew Internet and American Life Project, April 24, 2008, p. iv, http://www.pewinternet.org/pdfs/PIP_Writing_Report_FINAL3.pdf.

31. Michael Gerson, "Don't Let Texting Get U :-(," *Washington Post,* January 24, 2008, p. A19.

32. CellSigns, Industry text messaging statistics, March 2007, http://www.cellsigns.com/industry.shtml.

33. Lori Aratani, "Teens Can Multitask, But at What Costs?" *Washington Post,* February 26, 2007, p. A1, http://www.washingtonpost.com/wp-dyn/content/article/2007/02/25/AR2007022501600.html.

34. Claudia Wallis, "The Multitasking Generation," *Time,* March 19, 2006, http://www.time.com/time/magazine/article/0,9171,1174696,00.html.

35. "Media Multitasking Among American Youth: Prevalence, Predictors, and Pairings," Henry J. Kaiser Family Foundation, December 12, 2006, http://www.kff.org/entmedia/upload/7593.pdf.

36. Karen Sternheimer, *Kids These Days: Facts and Fictions About Today's Youth* (Lanham, MD: Rowman and Littlefield, 2006), pp. 8–9.

37. Marie Winn, *The Plug-In Drug: Television, Computers and Family Life* (New York: Penguin, 2002), p. 286.

38. See The College Board, "Mean SAT Scores by High School GPA: 1997 and 2007," http://www.collegeboard.com/prod_downloads/about/news_info/cbsenior/yr2007/tables/17.pdf.

39. U.S. Department of Education, National Center for Education Statistics, *National Longitudinal Study of the High School Class of 1972; High School and Beyond National Longitudinal Study of 1980 Seniors; National Longitudinal Study of 1988, Second Follow-Up; Student Survey, 1992; Education Longitudinal Study, 2002, First Follow-Up 2004,* http://www.icpsr.umich.edu/cocoon/ICPSR/SERIES/00107.xml.

40. U.S. Census Bureau, *Educational Attainment by Race and Hispanic Origin: 1960 to 2006,* U.S. Census of Population, 1960, 1970, and 1980, Vol. 1; and Current Population Reports P20-550 and earlier reports, http://www.census.gov/compendia/statab/tables/08s0217.pdf;

U.S. Department of Education, National Center for Education Statistics, *Digest of Education Statistics, 2006,* chapter 2, http://nces.ed.gov/programs/digest/d06/ch_2.asp; U.S. Department of Education, National Center for Education Statistics, *Status and Trends in the Education of Racial and Ethnic Minorities, 2006,* http://nces.ed.gov/pubs2007/minoritytrends/figures/figure_14.asp, and http://nces.ed.gov/fastfacts/display.asp?id=171.

41. Sternheimer, *Kids These Days,* pp. 69–71.

42. Donald P. Hayes, Loreen T. Wolfer, and Michael F. Wolfe, "Schoolbook Simplification and Its Relation to the Decline in SAT-Verbal Scores," *American Educational Research Journal* 33 (1996): 489–508.

43. James R. Flynn, *What is Intelligence?* (New York: Cambridge University Press, 2007), pp. 8–9.

44. Ibid., p. 19.

45. Ibid., p. 20.

46. U.S. Department of Education, National Center for Education Statistics, *Digest of Education Statistics, 2005* (NCES 2006–030), Table 108, http://nces.ed.gov/programs/digest/d05/tables/dt05_108.asp and http://nces.ed.gov/fastfacts/display.asp?id=147.

47. U.S. Department of Education, National Center for Education Statistics, *The Condition of Education 2007* (NCES 2007-064), Table 18-1, http://nces.ed.gov/programs/coe/2007/section2/table.asp?tableID=692 and http://nces.ed.gov/fastfacts/display.asp?id=69.

48. "To Read or Not to Read: A Question of National Consequence," National Endowment for the Arts, Research Report number 47, November 2007, p. 7, http://www.nea.gov/research/ToRead.pdf.

49. The Harris Poll, "Reading and TV Watching Still Favorite Activities, But Both Have Seen Drops," Telephone poll of 1,052 American adults aged eighteen and over, conducted October 16–23, 2007, http://www.harrisinteractive.com/harris_poll/index.asp?PID=835.

50. Anne H. Gauthier and Timothy Smeeding, "Historical Trends in the Patterns of Time Use of Older Adults," Paper presented at the Conference on Population Ageing in Industrialized Countries: Challenges and Issues, Tokyo, Japan March 19–21, 2001, http://www.oecd.org/dataoecd/21/5/2430978.pdf.

51. U.S. Census Bureau, *Educational Attainment by Race.*

52. Sternheimer, *Kids These Days,* pp. 70–71.

53. U.S. Department of Education, Office of the Secretary, Office of Public Affairs, *No Child Left Behind: A Parents Guide* (Washington, DC: Government Printing Office, 2003).

54. Tony Wilhelm, Delia Carmen, and Megan Reynolds, "Connecting Kids to Technology: Challenges and Opportunities," Annie E. Casey Foundation, June 2002, http://www.digitaldivide.net/articles/view.php?ArticleID=197.

55. Jennifer Cheeseman Day, Alex Janus, and Jessica Davis, "Computers and Internet Use in the United States: 2003 (P23-208)," Population Profile of the United States: Dynamic Version U.S. Census Bureau, http://www.census.gov/population/www/pop-profile/files/dynamic/Computers.pdf.

56. Wilhelm, Carmen, and Reynolds, "Connecting Kids."

MEDIA PHOBIA #2

Popular Culture Is Ruining Childhood

"Pop culture is destroying our daughters," a 2005 *Boston Globe* story declared, affirming what many parents and critics believe. The article, tellingly titled "Childhood Lost to Pop Culture," described young girls "walking around with too much of their bodies exposed," their posteriors visible while sitting in low-rise jeans. The concerns are not just in the U.S. either. A British newspaper warned readers of children's "junk culture," asking whether we have "poisoned childhood" with video games and other kinds of popular culture.[1] A Canadian newspaper asks, "Can the kids be deprogrammed?" noting that "concern is mounting that pop culture may be accountable for a wide range of social and physical problems that begin in childhood and carry through to adulthood."[2]

Stories like these reinforce what many people think is obvious: Childhood is under siege, and popular culture is the main culprit. From celebrities making questionable life choices to violent video games and explicit Web sites, there is certainly a deep well of pop culture to draw from in order to find examples of bad behavior.

But despite the plethora of potential bad influences, children and childhood are not in nearly as much danger from pop culture as many might fear.

Embedded within the fears about what popular culture might "do" to children lie many taken-for-granted assumptions that need to be examined. First among them is the meaning of childhood itself. If childhood looks different from what many people presume it should, we need to critically consider what it is supposed to be like and how we collectively create the meaning of childhood. Are children's lives really far from the ideal that pop culture is allegedly destroying?

Second is the presumption that the experience of childhood has changed for the worst. Some people are deeply concerned that children know things that they shouldn't—about sex, violence, and alcohol and drugs. But who decides what children should and shouldn't know (or when they should know it), and whether knowledge itself is dangerous? Before we convict popular culture, we need to consider whether children and childhood itself has really been damaged.

Finally, if children's experiences of childhood have changed, we often presume that popular culture is the main cause. But is it really?

In this chapter we will examine these three basic questions about children and popular culture. As we will see, childhood has not been ruined, nor is it ending earlier than in generations past. Yes, children's experiences are different now than they were when I was growing up and likely from when you were growing up too. When I was ten, cable television was just coming out (with only a few dozen channels), VHS and Betamax were starting their battle for household domination, and portable music mostly meant a transistor radio. But there were many other factors—more important factors—shaping the experiences of kids my age than our media consumption, just as there are for kids today.

Americans fear media in part because we are constantly told we should, but more importantly, because media are the most visible representation of the many changes that have altered the experiences of childhood. In this chapter I address why media are so often considered detrimental to childhood and the primary spoilers of innocence.

Instead of media being the true culprit, broader social, political, and economic changes over the past century have made adults uneasy about their ability to control children and the experience of childhood itself. Most centrally, fears about the demise of childhood make us nostalgic for our own lost childhoods. In a way we are longing for our lost selves when we think that childhood and children have been damaged by popular culture.

The Meaning(s) of Childhood

What is childhood? This may seem like an obvious question, but its definition is trickier than we might think. For one, Americans don't even agree on when a child's life begins—at conception? the second trimester of pregnancy? at birth? Once children are born the confusion doesn't end. Many might agree that people under ten can be classified as children, but we will probably not all agree on the sorts of experiences they should have. A religious education? Chores? Responsibility for younger siblings? A job? Underlying these decisions is a variety of basic ideas about what childhood should mean, and these decisions change over both time and place.

If we have trouble defining when childhood begins, we really have difficulty agreeing on when it ends. At eighteen? Twenty-one? Neither age is really the clear threshold to adulthood; after all, in some states children as young as ten can be tried as adults in criminal court.[3] On the other hand, some adults regard college students—many well over eighteen and even over twenty-one—as kids, not yet in the real world.

As a society we have mixed feelings about children and childhood. We all have different experiences of childhood ourselves. For some of us, this experience might have been fun and seem carefree (at least through the benefit of hindsight). For others, childhood might have been a painful experience, one best left behind. While people's experiences of childhood are quite varied, when I ask my students to define the term "child," they seem to have no trouble finding common adjectives. Words ranging from innocent, good, cute, pure, helpless, and vulnerable, to mischievous, impulsive, ignorant, and selfish come up year after year. A close analysis of these terms reveals that they certainly do not apply to all children, and they actually fit the behavior of some adults. Note that these words connote either sentimental or pejorative views of young people, a caricature of a vast and diverse group. Advertisers and politicians frequently use these symbols in order to sell products or their political platform.

But these words are not as benign as they might seem. Similar descriptors have historically been used to define women, people of color, and other minority groups to justify their inferior social status.[4] While most people now realize that one's race, ethnicity, gender, or religion cannot be used to identify personality traits, we still often view children as sharing a set of stable characteristics. Children are a group easily stereotyped, sentimentalized, and misrepresented.

At the same time there is a danger in viewing children as a singular group. Experiences of childhood are diverse and changing, yet often our standard for the ideal childhood in America (and adulthood for that matter) is based on white, middle-class, and usually suburban standards. If I'm not careful I can fall into this trap too, since this was my experience of childhood growing up in a Midwestern suburb not too far from where the mythical Cleavers of *Leave It to Beaver* supposedly lived. Childhood is rooted in social, economic, and political realities and is not a universal experience shared by all people of a certain age from the beginning of time. These realities, like the air we breathe, are often invisible and thus this experience of childhood might seem normal to those who once lived it.

Certainly each one of us can think of how children's experiences are different now than in the past. But they are also different based on the circumstances of the present. For instance, a girl growing up in my old neighborhood today will likely have a very different experience if her family's economic situation, ethnicity, and immigration status are different from mine. Across town, another girl of the same age who lost a parent and lives in public housing will have yet other experiences, as will the girl from another religious background who lives in a rural area miles away. Like snowflakes, no two experiences of childhood are exactly alike.

But we tend to define children as a unitary group and focus on how they are unlike adults. I know what you might be thinking—children aren't adults. This is true, but some of the differences are not as clear-cut as we might think. Some children have significant family responsibilities and can always be counted on to be there for the ones they love. Some adults cannot. Some children are very serious and stressed out, while some adults are not. And we all probably know some adults who are financially dependent on others and anything but emotionally mature. Just as some grown-ups don't meet the ideal definition of what it means to be an adult, many children don't necessarily fit the stereotype of the child.

This is why we must strive to understand the varied experiences of childhood, and to understand how they define their own reality, rather than simply how different they are from the dominant group. Just as the historical definition of women as less competent than men served to perpetuate male dominance, the social construction of childhood serves adult needs and reinforces adult power rather than best meeting the needs of young people. While young children are dependent upon adults in many ways, we tend to define them only by the qualities they lack rather than the competencies they possess.

We maintain these narrow beliefs about children because it is difficult to challenge a sentiment that seems natural. For many, rethinking childhood is a very threatening prospect. If childhood does not mean what we think it does, what is adulthood? When we realize that one of our society's central organizing principles is one that we ourselves actively construct and does not just emerge from nature, our reality must shift. What if we were to change the way we view children? Would parents have to stop telling their kids to eat their vegetables or when to go to bed? Changing the way we think about children and childhood is different from changing individual parent-child relationships, which can never be completely egalitarian. The solution is not to treat children as if they were adults, but to rethink what seems to be common-sense knowledge about who children as a social group really are.

The social construction of children as undeveloped adults needing more adult control feels appropriate because most of us have never considered an alternative, and on the surface this construction appears to be for children's own good. But the way that we think about children can be detrimental and even be dangerous. In her analysis of child sexual abuse, sociologist Jenny Kitzinger concludes that abuse may be facilitated by our conceptualization of "good" children as deferential to adult authority.[5] Child abuse stems largely from an abuse of power; perpetrators almost never use weapons. We so often forget that children are most likely to be victimized by someone within their own family, and that the adult power that supposedly protects children may contribute to their harm. David Buckingham, professor of education at the University of London, further explains the danger of thinking about children as fragile and only focusing on adult protection. Instead, he argues that we need to work towards *preparing* children to face the realities of the world around them.[6] Protection is an idea difficult to let go of—it sounds so noble and above reproach. To prepare rather than protect empowers children to make their own decisions, armed with the necessary information.

The definitions of childhood we create unwittingly contribute to children's disempowered status. Qualities like innocence, for example, are both idealized and demeaned: We fight to preserve what we believe to be children's innocence and yet consider them less competent, in part because of this "prized" trait. Of course children are dependent on adults for survival and support, but as they gradually become more independent we often still try to keep young people innocent (or ignorant) as long as we can.

Children who challenge the notion of innocence sometimes seem threatening. Knowledge is the antithesis of innocence, often seen as the antithesis of childhood itself. The "knowing" child, author Joe Kincheloe points out, is routinely seen as a threat within horror movies.[7] For example, he describes the 1960s British film *Village of the Damned*, where children can read adults' minds. Based on this perceived threat, the parents ultimately decide they must kill their own kids. Jenny Kitzinger notes in her study of abuse that a child who has knowledge about sex is often considered ruined and less a victim than a naïve counterpart.[8] Withholding knowledge is central to maintaining both the myth of innocence and power over children, which is at the heart of media fears. Media destabilize the myth of innocence and challenge adults' ability to withhold knowledge from children. This is the real threat popular culture poses; rather than threatening kids themselves, popular culture often challenges adult control.

Childhood is a construction we create rather than a fixed reality; it is of course a very real experience, but the meaning of childhood is shaped and defined by cultural expectations and beliefs. It is not just a biological phase that people pass through, but also an idea collectively constructed to serve adult needs. Childhood can remain a sacred shared fantasy, an illusion not unlike the Garden of Eden before eating from the tree of knowledge led to banishment. Ironically, adults mourn the expulsion from this fantasy land but also control the gates, seeking to keep people in even when they want to get out. Keeping kids "in" is seen as part of what adults should be doing as good parents. The media are accused of handing over the jailer's keys, allowing children to leave this mythical garden before adults deem them ready. Children's innocence/ignorance also serves to entertain adults, as in Art Linkletter's (and later Bill Cosby's) *Kids Say the Darndest Things.* Our conception of childhood reveals a major contradiction between the value of knowledge and the luxury of innocence. On the other hand, it is often through media that adults confront the reality that children do not necessarily embody innocence as much as adults might hope. We struggle to maintain the sense that childhood means carefree innocence and blame popular culture for getting in the way. The more closely we examine both media and the way we conceptualize childhood, the better we will understand the fear surrounding this relationship. We see how unclear the boundary between adulthood and childhood really is. Sometimes it is the media that help blur the line of demarcation; other times it is media that expose the ambiguity.

Reconsidering the meaning of childhood involves a redistribution of knowledge: At the core of the construction of childhood as a time of innocence lies the vain attempt to keep information from young people. We often perceive childhood innocence as a natural, presocial, and ahistorical state that all children pass through.[9] Idealizing childhood as a time of innocence causes us to panic when children know more than some think they should. We place a great deal of blame for this loss of innocence on media, as if innocence were something that would stick around longer without popular culture. As we will see in the next section, "innocence," before the age of electronic media, was likely to involve higher child mortality rates and an early introduction to hard work in factories, fields, and mills.

Childhood is constantly shifting and changing, and becomes defined based on the needs of society. The idea that childhood in the past was comprised of carefree days without worry is a conveniently reconstructed version of history. This fantasy allows adults to feel nostalgia for a lost idealized past that never was. Experiences of children have changed, but popular culture is at best a minor player in the story.

What Really Changed Childhood?

There should be no doubt that children's experiences of childhood change over time. In my own family history (and likely yours too), when we compare generations the differences become clear. I have a grandfather whose education ended in the eighth grade so he could work full time in the family business, something not unusual for his peers during the 1920s. Of course if my parents in the 1980s took me out of eighth grade to work, they would have been in big trouble. This isn't because people in the 1920s didn't care about children, but the needs in many families were different at that time and child labor wasn't as restricted. My grandfather was the seventh of eight children and lost his father in World War I, as did many children of his generation. Many like him were needed to contribute to their families to ensure basic survival.

By the time I came around much had changed, both in my family and within American society as a whole. The country had gone through a period of tremendous economic growth, making children's labor unnecessary. The passage of child labor laws and compulsory education laws made school attendance mandatory. And most importantly, the postindustrial, information-based economy created the need for a highly educated workforce. A lack of high school (and increasingly college) education would put economic survival in jeopardy for people of my generation. By contrast, my grandfather learned his family trade and eventually had his own business in the garment industry, something that would be more difficult today with the predominance of large retail chains.

These generational differences had much more to do with economics than culture. Yes, the array of media available was vastly different in my grandfather's day (and he took pleasure in buying me the stereo he never had), but popular culture did not alter the structural realities of either of our childhood experiences.

Not only have childhood experiences changed significantly over time, but the notion of the ideal childhood has too. In fact, even the idea that there is a distinct period of the life course called "childhood" is a relatively recent development, according to historian Phillipe Ariès, whose groundbreaking 1962 book *Centuries of Childhood: A Social History of Family Life*, claims that childhood did not exist as a separate social category in Western culture before the seventeenth century. Based on his analysis of paintings, Ariès observes that children were painted as miniature adults, mostly wearing the same type of clothing and drawn in adult proportions. Little seemed to separate the social roles between adults and children at that time. Although historians have challenged Ariès on several points, his work clearly demonstrates that childhood was conceptualized very differently in the past than it is today.

While Ariès's focus was on the children of French aristocrats, historian Karin Calvert describes how colonial American childhood was not regarded as an ideal time of life, as so often it is today.[10] She describes how high rates of infant mortality and childhood illness made childhood particularly risky, something to hurry up and survive rather than slow down and savor (or worry it is over too fast). Childhood itself became associated with illness. A colonist entering the New World often met with danger, and growing old was a form of conquest. Unlike today, when popular culture reveres all things youthful, maturity was highly regarded and looked forward to as a time of prestige. Think of the nation's founding fathers and their white powdered wigs and white stockings, which added years to their appearance. Calvert goes on to say that by the early nineteenth century American independence had changed the conception of childhood from a period of intense protection to one of greater freedom. She contends that coddling fell out of favor: Just as over-involvement of the mother country was seen as restrictive, parents were discouraged from being overprotective of their children. The belief was that children were made strong by a tough upbringing, while coddling only weakened them.

Calvert explains that during the Victorian era, when infant mortality rates began to fall, childhood evolved into a celebration of innocence and virtue. Families of wealth attempted to keep children pure by separating them from adult society, even from their own parents. Governesses and boarding schools attempted to prevent contamination from adults as long as possible. Childhood became an idealized time of life, reflected in advertisements, which used images of children to connote purity in products like food and soap.[11]

But the Victorian attempt to keep children away from the adult world was clearly only available to the affluent. For many children, carefree play and ignorant bliss do not mark past or present experiences of childhood. Death was much more likely to be part of childhood in previous centuries, with high rates of infant mortality, childhood illness, and shorter life expectancy. Historian Miriam Formanek-Brunnell notes that nineteenth-century children's doll play often involved mock funerals, reflecting anything but happy-go-lucky childhood experiences.[12] It is our recent conception that insists that childhood should mean freedom from knowledge of the darker side of life.

For other families, childhood meant work at far younger ages than we see now in the United States—although children in developing countries frequently work for wages today. In nineteenth-century America, children in rural areas were needed on family farms, and even if they attended school their labor was still a necessary part of the family economy. Learning a craft might have meant becoming an apprentice at age eight or nine. By twenty-first-century standards, children working for wages may seem inhumane, but for many families this was economically necessary. Households required full-time labor for tasks like cooking, cleaning, and sewing, particularly in the decades before World War I when poor and rural families were unlikely to have electricity. Since an adult was needed to do the work of maintaining the family, it was necessary for nearly 2 million children to work for wages in 1910.[13]

Working children often experienced a great deal of autonomy, especially those living in cities. As historian David Nasaw describes, city kids selling newspapers or shining shoes sold their goods and services late into the night, as newspapers published evening editions.[14] They kept a portion of their earnings for themselves, but gave most to their parents, who were often dependent on the extra money their kids brought. When reformers—mostly affluent white women who favored the idea that children should be protected from city life—attempted to get them into schools, many of these young peddlers resisted. Giving up their freedom and their incomes did not sit well with the kids, or with their parents who relied on their contributions.

Children's wages were vital sources of income around the turn of the century, particularly for immigrant families, and constructions of the ideal childhood reflected this need. The useful child was regarded as a moral child, mirroring the adage "Idle hands are the devil's workshop." Work and responsibility were considered fundamental values for children, which sociologist Viviana A. Zelizer notes date back to the Puritan ethic of hard work and moral righteousness in early colonial America. Work was viewed as good preparation for a productive adult life, while higher education remained the domain of elites. The industrial-based economy did not require a great deal of academic training from its labor force. Thus, receiving only an eighth-grade education, as my grandfather did, was not nearly as problematic in the first decades of the twentieth century as it is now.

Zelizer concludes that child labor "lost its good reputation" because children's labor became less necessary due to rising adult incomes and the growing need for a more educated labor force.[15] Compulsory education became more widespread in the early twentieth century, not just because it was more humane for children to be in school rather than factories, but because it became more economically necessary. The growth of automation reduced the need for children in the labor force, and the increasing enrollments in public schools stemmed from a desire to create a separate institution to keep children busy during the day in the interest of public safety, as the large number of immigrant children led to concerns about juvenile delinquency. Fearing that poor immigrants comprised a criminal class, compulsory education served as a way to legally enforce social control of this group.[16] Schools provided a way to Americanize children, keep them out of the labor force until needed, and remove them from the streets.

This is a defining moment in the history of American childhood: From this point on adults' and children's lives became increasingly divided. Children and adults went from sharing tasks on family farms or the shop floor before the 1930s to increasingly spending more time isolated from one another and creating distinct cultures.

The Creation of Childhood as We Know It

In a way, childhood as we think of it today is rooted in the fallout of the Great Depression years of the 1930s. Historian Grace Palladino contends that the separation between adults and children intensified during the depression, when adolescents were far more likely to attend high school than in years past due to the shrinking labor market. Children were all but expelled from the workforce.[17] Whereas only about 17 percent of all seventeen-year-olds graduated from high school in 1920, by 1935 the percentage had risen to 42 percent.[18] It is here that some of the early concerns about young people and popular culture began too. The shared space of high school led to the creation and growth of youth culture. Young people's tastes in music, for example, grew to bear more resemblance to their peers' than their parents'. Palladino cites swing music as a major cultural wedge between parents and youth in the late 1930s. Parents complained that young people wasted their time listening to the music and were not as industrious as prior generations, a reflection of children's exclusion from the labor force and increase in leisure time. This was particularly true following World War II, when economic prosperity coupled with mass marketing created even more distinction between what it meant to be a child, a teenager, and an adult.

The postwar economic boom fueled a consumption-based economy. Following strict rationing of goods during World War II, consumption and the widespread availability of goods expanded dramatically. The amount of consumer goods available to both adults and children exploded, and it became patriotic to spend instead of conserve. Families could also carry more debt with the introduction of credit cards, and home mortgages required much smaller down payments than in prewar days. Increases in wages and automation of household labor provided children with even more leisure time; this prosperity helped to create the new category called "teenager." Free from contributing to the family income, this young person had both more time and money than his or her parents had a generation earlier. Producers created movies, television, and music with this large demographic group in mind, particularly as baby boom children reached spending age in the late 1950s. But perhaps most centrally, market researchers recognized children as a distinct demographic group. Palladino details how market research firms that focused specifically on understanding youth culture emerged during the late 1940s to better sell products to this increasingly important consumer group. The perception of youth as a time for leisurely consumption of popular culture began.

Marketers sold the idea that postwar childhood and adolescence should be fun. Following the struggles of the depression and World War II, children born during the baby boom years were seen as symbols of a bright new future. Childhood illnesses like polio were gradually conquered, and basic survival was no longer most parents' major concern. Instead, happiness and psychological well-being, luxuries of prosperity, became central.

Rather than simply being a time of physical vulnerability, as in the colonial period, or moral vulnerability, as in the Victorian era, postwar childhood came to be defined as a psychologically vulnerable time. Following the popularity of Freud in the United States, parents were not only expected to produce healthy and productive children but were also charged with the responsibility of ensuring their psychological well-being. From a Freudian perspective, the adult personality is formed through childhood conflicts. If these conflicts go unresolved then neurosis or psychosis is likely to follow in adulthood, placing the burden of lifelong psychological health mainly on the mother, who, according to Freud, was central in these conflicts. This parenting approach reflected the political and economic realities of postwar America; the paranoid self-reflection of the McCarthy era is mirrored in psychoanalysis, in which one's own mother cannot be completely trusted.

This emphasis on children's psychological health also supported a rigid gender ideology. Middle-class mothers, herded out of the paid labor force following World War II, held the lion's share of responsibility to raise happy children, a relatively new mandate that would eventually suggest that parents—especially mothers—worry about their children's media use.

The growth of suburbs midcentury also influenced the meaning and experience of childhood. Shifts from an agrarian to an industrial-based economy led to the growth of cities in the late nineteenth and early twentieth centuries, and following World War II the expansion of American suburbs altered both the experiences and conceptions of childhood. With suburban life came the growing dependence on automobiles, often creating less mobility for young children dependent on parents for transportation, and more mobility for teens who had access to cars. The car culture symbolized American independence: Advertisements boasted of the adventures a car could offer on newly constructed superhighways. Teenagers could also congregate away from parental supervision, and in many ways the widespread availability of the automobile altered teen sexuality. Teens, now often free from the need to work to help their families, experienced less adult control, creating parental anxiety about their children's access to the world around them.

Cultural scholar Henry Jenkins notes that political discourse increasingly described families as individual "forts," or separate units striving to shield their children from the perceived harms of the larger community.[19] In this approach to understanding childhood, children are considered to be under siege, while individual family homes and white picket fences serve as bunkers of suburban safety. The perceived outside dangers include not only unknown neighbors, but also popular culture. This view of childhood as being in danger from the outside world and in need of parental protection continues more than fifty years later, in spite of important social changes that have altered the realities of parenting and family life since that time.

Recently, the postwar era has been held up as ideal, a benchmark against which childhood today is often compared. This has more to do with adults thinking back to their own midcentury childhood experiences and idyllic television shows than reality. While far fewer children lived in single parent families and divorce was less common than today, this era was itself the product of specific economic, political, and social realities of the time.[20] The prosperity after World War II, coupled with the strength of labor unions, meant that many more families could achieve and maintain middle class status with one wage earner's income. New homes in brand new suburbs could be purchased with little money down, thanks largely to the G.I. Bill, which also made it possible for many returning vets to attend college for the first time in their family's history. In many ways, the postwar years were golden.

But not for all.

Nostalgia for an allegedly carefree childhood of the past does not take into account the pervasive history of inequality in the United States. Economic prosperity was not shared by everyone: In 1955 African American families earned only 55 cents for every dollar white families earned.[21] Those who mourn the loss of childhood innocence in the twenty-first century tend to ignore the struggles faced by many children of color. In previous centuries children born into slavery, for instance, were regarded as individual units of labor and sometimes sold away from their families. We forget about inequality when we romanticize the happy days of the 1950s. Fifty-five percent of African American families, for instance, lived below the poverty line in 1959, and most suburbs were not just economically out of reach, but unfair housing practices kept suburbs white.[22] Our collective nostalgia for this mythical version of childhood calls upon memories of Cleaver-like families, when divorce and family discord were unheard of. In reality it was during the 1950s that divorce rates started to climb, and the families of old that we revere existed mostly on television.

As we will see in Chapter 5, the 1950s were not the age of sexual innocence we often believe today. Pregnancy precipitated many marriages in the 1950s, when the median age of marriage for women dipped to its lowest point in the twentieth century, down to twenty in 1950.[23] We often think that teenage pregnancy is a relatively new social problem, believed to be exacerbated by sexual content in media, but the reality is it has been steadily decreasing. In 1950 the pregnancy rate for fifteen- to nineteen-year-olds was 80.6 per thousand, whereas by 2005 the rate had dropped to an all-time low of 40.5 per thousand.[24] The difference is that pregnant teenagers now are less likely to be married or to be forced into secret adoptions or abortions. Teens also have more choices, including using birth control, having abortions, or keeping their babies without getting married. What has changed is our *perception* of teens and sex. Also changed is our idea of what it means to be a teenager: Before the mid–twentieth century, people in their teen years often held adult roles and responsibilities, including full-time jobs and parenting. We have redefined the teenage years as more akin to childhood than adulthood, making previously normative behavior unacceptable.

So childhood in the past was not necessarily as innocent as our collective memory incorrectly remembers. Nor was chewing gum or talking out of turn the biggest complaint adults had about children during that time, as a highly publicized, but made-up list claimed how benign children's problems used to be in the good old days.[25] People feared changes in youth at that time just as we do today: Juvenile delinquency and promiscuity were big concerns even during this hallowed time, something we conveniently forget today.

Perceptions of childhood now reflect adult anxieties about information technology, a shifting economy, a multiethnic population, and an unknown future. Not unlike the Victorian era, childhood innocence today is prized and we often attempt in vain to remove children from the adult world. Parents are viewed as the guardians of both their children and the meaning of childhood itself. Those who permit children to cross over into adulthood are demonized, particularly if they are poor or a member of a racial minority group. Many believe that childhood today ends too soon, with the media frequently cited as a cause of this "crisis." Innocence is seen as a birthright destroyed by popular culture or ineffective parents. Yet we often overlook the realities of children's experiences in both the past and the present that defy the assumption that childhood without electronic media was idyllic.

The Best Time to Be a Child?

Throughout the past three centuries, childhood has gradually expanded as our economy has enabled most young people to delay entry into the paid labor force.[26] We have also prolonged the time between sexual maturity and marriage, particularly as the onset of puberty happens sooner now for girls than in the past.[27] It is only within the past century that such a large group of physically mature people has had so few rights and responsibilities and been considered emotionally immature, a luxury of prosperity. So while we mourn the early demise of childhood, the reality is that for many Americans, childhood and adolescence have never lasted longer. At the beginning of the twentieth century, a large number of young people entered the labor force and took on many adult responsibilities at fourteen and earlier, compared with eighteen, twenty-one, or even later today. Childhood has been extended chronologically and emotionally, filled with meaning it cannot sustain. Contemporary childhood is charged with providing adults with hope for the future and remembrance of an idealized past. It is a complex and contested concept that adults struggle to maintain to offset anxiety about a changing world.

While the news provides a steady diet of doom-and-gloom reports about young people, on the whole the news is good. High school and college graduation rates are at an all-time high.[28] Youth violence has dropped considerably since the 1990s; the number of homicides involving a juvenile offender fell 65 percent between 1994 and 2002; juvenile crime in general fell nearly 57 percent between 1994 and 2003.[29] The teen birthrate fell 35 percent between 1991 and 2005.[30] According to the Centers for Disease Control and Prevention, fewer teens reported being sexually active in 2007 than in 1991, and those who are used condoms more often.[31] Fewer were involved in fistfights or reported carrying guns in 2007 compared with the early 1990s, and young people were much more likely to wear seat belts and avoid riding in a car driven by a drunk driver.[32] The percentage committing or contemplating suicide decreased steadily as well.[33]

As we will see in Chapter 8, the percentage of high school seniors who report drinking alcohol has been declining annually, as has drinking to intoxication.[34] Rates of both consumption and intoxication are substantially lower than the 1970s and 1980s, when their parents were likely teens. Likewise, illegal drug use has declined since the 1970s and 1980s.

So in spite of public perception and the fears that the new media technologies are breeding a violent, sex-obsessed, hedonistic, and self-indulgent young generation, young people are mostly more sober, chaste, and well-behaved than their parents were or than my generation was in the 1980s. Additionally, nearly 60 percent of teens volunteer, averaging three and a half hours of service each week.[35]

Certainly some changes in the experiences of childhood can be attributed to media and technological changes. For example, cell phones allow kids both greater freedom from and greater contact with parents. Kids can be physically tracked through Global Positioning System (GPS) software embedded in their phones. On the other hand, children can use their phones and the Internet to forge relationships with less parental intervention, but they can also be paged on the playground to return home. And young people do spend a lot of time using new technology.

Although many adults fear that playing video games or using the Internet will harm children, we forget that they also serve to prepare them to participate in a high-tech economy. Visual literacy has become more important in the last fifteen years, as video games and computers became staples in many homes that could afford them. The children we should be worried about are the ones that don't have access to these new technologies.

Changes in childhood may be most apparent when we see kids texting on smart phones while listening to iPods, but technology itself cannot single-handedly create change. The often hidden social conditions that alter experiences of childhood were also behind the creation of these new products; changes in the economy produce both the widespread use of new devices and also specific experiences of childhood. Media technologies are the icons of contemporary society; they represent and reflect what scares us most about the unknown future. We tend to see the most tangible differences and credit them with creating powerful social changes without scratching beneath the surface. To understand changes in childhood we must look further to see more than media.

Childhood has not disappeared. Instead it is constantly shifting and mutating with the fluctuations in society. The perceived crisis in childhood is derived from the gap between the fantasy of childhood and the reality. We have filled the idea of childhood with our hopes and expectations as well as our fears and anxieties. We want childhood to be everything adulthood is not, but in reality adults and children live in the same social setting and have more experiences in common than adults are often comfortable admitting. Our economic realities are theirs; they suffer when parents lose their jobs, and they feel the effects of political conflicts too. Although we would like to keep the realities of terrorism and violence away from them, unfortunately we cannot. For many young people, these are firsthand experiences, not mediated by television, movies, or popular culture at all.

If childhood has changed it is because the world has changed. Rapid change can be very frightening, even if the changes have many positive outcomes. Social life has been shifting so rapidly in the past few years that yesterday's technological breakthrough is tomorrow's dinosaur, obsolete and useless. Changes in family structure and economic realities render adult control of youth reduced. Automated households rarely require young people to perform lengthy chores to ensure the family's survival, so they are not needed at home as much as they were a few generations ago. And many young people have access to more information now than they did in the past. Yes, this is partially due to media, but it is also a reflection of changing attitudes about sexuality, for example, where open discussion of this topic is much more prevalent than in generations past.

This does not mean that adults should ignore the challenges of childhood—in fact, many of the problems children face are overshadowed by the fear of media. For instance, an up-close look at the roots of problems often blamed on media, like youth violence and teen pregnancy, reveals that poverty, not media, is the common denominator.[36] Poverty, not too much television, creates tangible far-reaching consequences for young people. When communications scholar Ellen Seiter studied adult perceptions of media effects on children, she found that the middle class and affluent were the most likely to blame media for harming children and causing social problems.[37] Lower income people have more experience with the reality of problems like violence to know that the media are not a big part of the equation in their struggles to keep their children safe in troubled communities. Yet our continued response is to attempt to focus on the supposed shortcomings of parents and to see popular culture as childhood enemy number one. Politicians often help us choose to focus on popular culture instead, making it seem like V-chips are more important for children than food stamps and health care.

Ultimately, it is easier to blame media than ourselves for policies that fail to adequately support children. School levies are routinely rejected because we don't want to pay more taxes or don't trust the adults who control school budgets. Affordable, quality child care is so difficult to find because as a society we do not monetarily value people who care for children: Those who do frequently earn less than minimum wage. It is not media that have changed childhood over the past century, it is our changing economy and the reluctance of the public to create programs that deal with the very real challenges children face.

Why We Blame Media Anyway

In spite of the fact that kids today are actually doing quite well by many measures, we worry anyway. Concerns about the next generation are anything but new; as I discussed in the previous chapter, fearing that the next generation is going downhill is a perennial concern. What is different is that now we have visual manifestations of these fears in the form of all kinds of new media.

In the worrier's defense, many people aren't aware that kids aren't in as much trouble as the news might often detail. And when looking for the source of the alleged problems, we need look no further than what's already in our face: popular culture. It's no wonder, then, that we focus on the most visible changes: In the last century one of the biggest transformations has been the growth of electronic media, which by their very nature command our attention. We have seen the development of movies, television, popular music, video games, and the Internet, each of which has received its share of public criticism. New technologies elicit fears of the unknown, particularly because they have enabled children's consumption of popular culture to move beyond adult control. Parents may now feel helpless to control what music their kids listen to, what movies they see, or what Web sites they visit. Over the past hundred years, media culture has moved from the public sphere (movies) to private (television) to individual (the Internet), each creating less opportunity for adult monitoring.

This is not to say that media content is unimportant, nor am I suggesting that parents ignore their children's media use. These are important family decisions, but on a societal level media culture is not the root cause of social problems. Media do matter, but not in the way many of us think they do. Communications scholar John Fiske describes media as providing "a visible and material presence to deep and persistent currents of meaning by which American society and American consciousness shape themselves."[38] Media are not the central cause of social change, but they are ever present and reflect these changes, and also bring many social issues to our attention.

Media have become an important American social institution intertwined with government, commerce, family, education, and religion.

Communications scholar John Hartley asserts that media culture has replaced the traditional town square or marketplace as the center of social life.[39] He and others argue that it is one of our few links in a large and increasingly segmented society, serving to connect us in times of celebration and crisis in a way nothing else quite can.[40] In a sense media have become representative of society itself. The media receive the brunt of the blame for social problems because they have become symbolic of contemporary American society.

Media culture also enables young people to develop separate interests and identities from their parents. The biggest complaints I have heard from parents is that their children like toys, music, movies, or television programs that they consider junk, and therefore must have harmful consequences. Listen to yourselves, parents—isn't this exactly what your parents told you about the music you liked? Adults attempt to exercise their power by condemning tastes that differ from their own sensibilities and displace their fears of the future onto popular culture.

Popular culture often reminds us that the myth of childhood innocence cannot be maintained, and that knowledge cannot be easily withheld from children. Media threaten to expose the illusion of childhood by revealing things some adults don't want kids to know about, and in some cases by offering content that challenges the wisdom and power of adults. Fears of media power represent displaced fears about social change and changes in childhood.

When we continually focus on media as the Big Bad Wolf devouring childhood, we overlook the historical conditions that shape both the experiences and preferred meaning of childhood. It becomes all too easy to sentimentalize children and childhood rather than understand the complexity of children's experiences. Instead, we often consider young people a potential threat that needs to be controlled, for our safety and theirs. If media can turn some children into cold-blooded killers, as some suspect, then restricting young people's behavior and access to popular culture seems reasonable. We are caught in a contradiction: Children are at once viewed as potential victims in need of protection, too weak and vulnerable to make their own decisions, yet as potential victimizers in need of control, too dangerous to ignore. Fear is a central part of our social construction of childhood.

When we relentlessly pursue the idea that media damage children, we are saying that children are damaged. Adults have always believed that kids were worse than the generation before, dating back to Socrates in ancient Greece, who complained about children's materialism, manners, and general disrespect for elders. Blaming the media is much like attempting to swim full force against a powerful riptide: You end up exhausted and frustrated and get nowhere. Understanding what is really happening will allow the swimmer to survive. Likewise, projecting our collective concern about both childhood and society onto media will not take us very far. It will force us to focus on only a small part of the equation and ultimately drive a wedge between generations.

Notes

1. Jenifer Johnston, "Have We Poisoned Childhood?" *The Sunday Herald* (United Kingdom), September 17, 2006.

2. Hal Niedzviecki, "Can We Save These Kids?" *Globe and Mail* (Canada), June 5, 2004.

3. Both Kansas and Vermont have statutes allowing children as young as ten to be transferred to adult criminal court.

4. For a comparison between children's and women's disempowerment see Barrie Thorne, "Re-Visioning Women and Social Change: Where are the Children?" *Gender and Society* 1 (1987): 85–109.

5. Jenny Kitzinger, "Who Are You Kidding? Children, Power, and the Struggle Against Sexual Abuse," in *Constructing and Reconstructing Childhood: Contemporary Issues in the Sociological Study of Childhood*, eds. Allison James and Alan Prout (London: Falmer Press, 1997).

6. David Buckingham, *After the Death of Childhood: Growing Up in the Age of Electronic Media* (London: Polity Press, 2000).

7. Joe Kincheloe, "The New Childhood: Home Alone as a Way of Life," in *Kinderculture: The Corporate Construction of Childhood*, eds. Shirley R. Steinberg and Joe L. Kincheloe (Boulder: Westview Press, 1998).

8. Kitzinger, "Who Are You Kidding," p. 168.

9. Henry Jenkins, "Introduction: Childhood Innocence and Other Myths," in *The Children's Culture Reader*, ed. Henry Jenkins (New York: New York University Press, 1998).

10. Karin Calvert, *Children in the House: Material Culture of Early Childhood, 1600–1900* (Boston: Northeastern University Press, 1992).

11. Stephen Kline, "The Making of Children's Culture," in *The Children's Culture Reader*, ed. Henry Jenkins (New York: New York University Press, 1998).

12. Miriam Formanek-Brunell, *Made to Play House: Dolls and the Commercialization of American Girlhood, 1830–1930* (New Haven: Yale University Press, 1993).

13. Viviana A. Zelizer, "From Useful to Useless: Moral Conflict over Child Labor," in *The Children's Culture Reader*, ed. Henry Jenkins (New York: New York University Press, 1998), p. 81.

14. David Nasaw, *Children of the City: At Work and at Play* (New York: Oxford University Press, 1986).

15. Zelizer, "From Useful to Useless," p. 84.

16. Anthony Platt, "The Child-Saving Movement and the Origins of the Juvenile Justice System," in *Juvenile Delinquency: Historical, Theoretical and Societal Reactions to Youth*, 2nd ed., eds. Paul M. Sharp and Barry W. Hancock (Upper Saddle River, NJ: Prentice Hall, 1998), pp. 3–17.

17. Grace Palladino, *Teenagers: An American History* (New York: Basic Books, 1996).

18. U.S. National Center for Education Statistics, 1900–1985, *120 Years of Education: A Statistical Portrait* (Washington, DC: Digest of Education Statistics, annual).

19. Jenkins, "Introduction," p. 4.

20. Judith Stacey, *Brave New Families: Stories of Domestic Upheaval in Late-Twentieth-Century America* (New York: Basic Books, 1990).

21. U.S. Census Bureau, Statistical Abstract of the United States, Tables P60-200 and P60-203, "Current Population Reports" (Washington, DC: Government Printing Office, 1999).

22. James Heintz, Nancy Folbre, and the Center for Popular Economics, *The Ultimate Field Guide to the U.S. Economy* (New York: The New Press, 2000).

23. U.S. Bureau of the Census, Statistical Abstract of the United States, "Current Population Reports Series P20-537" (Washington, DC: Government Printing Office, annual).

24. National Center for Health Statistics, *Natality*, Vital Statistics of the United States. (1937–), *Birth Statistics* (1905–1936) (Washington, DC: U.S. Bureau of the Census); Joyce A. Martin, et al., "Births: Final Data for 2005," *National Vital Statistics Reports* 56, no. 6 (Hyattsville, MD: National Center for Health Statistics, 2007), http://www.cdc.gov/nchs/fastats/teenbrth.htm and http://www.cdc.gov/nchs/data/nvsr/nvsr56/nvsr56_06.pdf.

25. A fake list of the top ten biggest problems in schools of the 1990s (robbery, drug abuse, pregnancy) compared with the supposed top ten problems in 1940 (gum chewing, running in the halls, improper clothing) was widely distributed and treated as real in spite of evidence otherwise. For a discussion see Mike Males, *Framing*

Youth: Ten Myths about the Next Generation (Monroe, ME: Common Courage Press, 1999).

26. James E. Côté and Anton L. Allahar, *Generation on Hold: Coming of Age in the Late Twentieth Century* (New York: New York University Press, 1994).

27. Marcia E. Herman-Giddens, et al., "Secondary Sexual Characteristics and Menses in Young Girls Seen in Office Practice: A Study from the Pediatric Research in Office Settings Network," *Pediatrics* 99 (4 April, 1997): 505–512.

28. Nicole Stoops, *Educational Attainment in the United States: 2003,* Current Population Reports (Washington, DC: U.S. Bureau of the Census), http://www.census.gov/prod/2004pubs/p20-550.pdf.

29. Howard N. Snyder and Melissa Sickmund, *Juvenile Offenders and Victims: 2006 National Report* (Washington, DC: U.S. Department of Justice, Office of Justice Programs, Office of Juvenile Justice and Delinquency Prevention, 2006), p. 64, http://ojjdp.ncjrs.org/ojstatbb/nr2006/downloads/chapter3.pdf (page 65) and http://ojjdp.ncjrs.org/ojstatbb/nr2006/downloads/chapter3.pdf.

30. Brady E. Hamilton, Joyce A. Martin, and Stephanie J. Ventura, "Births: Preliminary data for 2005," *National Vital Statistics Reports* 55, no. 11, (Hyattsville, MD: National Center for Health Statistics, 2007), http://www.cdc.gov/nchs/data/nvsr/nvsr55/nvsr55_11.pdf.

31. Department of Health and Human Services, "Trends in the Prevalence of Sexual Behaviors," *National Youth Risk Behavior Survey: 1991–2007* (Washington, DC: Centers for Disease Control and Prevention, 2008), http://www.cdc.gov/HealthyYouth/yrbs/pdf/yrbs07_us_sexual_behaviors_trend.pdf.

32. Department of Health and Human Services, "Trends in the Prevalence of Behaviors that Contribute to Violence," *National Youth Risk Behavior Survey: 1991–2007* (Washington, DC: Centers for Disease Control and Prevention, 2008), http://www.cdc.gov/HealthyYouth/yrbs/pdf/trends/2005_YRBS_Violence.pdf; Department of Health and Human Services, "Trends in the Prevalence of Behaviors that Contribute to Unintentional Injury," *National Youth Risk Behavior Survey: 1991–2007* (Washington, DC: Centers for Disease Control and Prevention, 2008), http://www.cdc.gov/HealthyYouth/yrbs/pdf/yrbs07_us_unintentional_injury_trend.pdf.

33. Department of Health and Human Services, "Trends in the Prevalence of Suicide Ideation and Attempts," *National Youth Risk Behavior Survey: 1991–2007* (Washington, DC: Centers for Disease Control and Prevention, 2008), http://www.cdc.gov/HealthyYouth/yrbs/pdf/yrbs07_us_suicide_related_behaviors_trend.pdf.

34. Monitoring the Future Study, "Long-Term Trends in Lifetime Prevalence of Use of Various Drugs for Twelfth Graders" (Survey Research Center, University of Michigan, Ann Arbor, 2008), http://www.monitoringthefuture.org/data/07data/pr07t14.pdf.

35. Marguerite Kelly, "Teens at 14 Are Still Living Self-Centered Life," *Milwaukee Journal Sentinel*, May 28, 1999, p. 1. Independent Sector Web site: www.independentsector.org/.

36. For discussion see Mike Males, *The Scapegoat Generation: America's War on Adolescents* (Monroe, ME: Common Courage Press, 1996).

37. Ellen Seiter, *Television and New Media Audiences* (Oxford: Oxford University Press, 1999), pp. 58–90.

38. John Fiske, *Media Matters: Everyday Culture and Political Change* (Minneapolis: University of Minnesota Press, 1994), p. xv.

39. John Hartley, *The Politics of Pictures: The Creation of the Public in the Age of Popular Media* (London: Routledge, 1992).

40. For further discussion see Daniel Dayan and Elihu Katz, *Media Events: The Live Broadcasting of History* (Cambridge: Harvard University Press, 1992).

Media Violence Causes Real Violence

Video games have supplanted movies as the form of popular culture that critics love to hate. Many—although certainly not all—feature high levels of mock violence. Could simulated violence in video games, movies, television, and music cause real violence?

For many the answer seems to be an obvious yes. Video games in particular appear to connect the dots between high-profile rampage shootings at schools during the 1990s. More recently, before a suspect was even identified after the 2007 shooting rampage at Virginia Tech, pundits were on the air blaming video games. While it turned out that the VT shooter rarely played video games, the 1999 Columbine High School shooters were allegedly aficionados of Doom, a game where the heavily armed protagonist stops demons from taking over the earth, and had used their classmates' images during their play target practice. John Leo of *U.S. News & World Report* described the murder scene as staged like a video game. According to Leo, their "cool and casual cruelty" pointed to "sensibilities created by the modern video kill games."[1] Leo concluded that "if we want to avoid more Littleton-style massacres, we will begin taking the social effects of the killing games more seriously."[2]

Video game graphics *are* much more realistic than they were in the days of Pac-Man and Frogger. And as the industry's multibillion-dollar revenues surpass movie profits, they have taken the mantle of most feared form of popular culture, especially as they have become the pastime of choice for many young men. In 2007, the American Psychiatric Association (APA) even convened to discuss the possibility of a new mental disorder: video game addiction. Although the APA has not yet elevated excessive video game playing to the level of mental illness, the mere consideration seemed to justify what many believe, that video games are training a new generation of obsessed and desensitized psychopaths.

Although video games have become the primary focus, concerns that movies, music, and other forms of popular culture contribute to violence still linger. After the shooting rampage at Columbine, critics also blamed music for inciting violence and for creating a sense of alienation in its listeners. Even though it is unclear whether the Columbine shooters were actually fans, the "shock rock" band Marilyn Manson garnered a lot of criticism. Dick Armey, then the House majority leader, alleged that the band's lyrics "tout suicide, torture, and murder."[3] Protesters followed the band to concert venues in the weeks following the shooting.[4]

Is simply discussing violence in music a form of promoting violence? Music that is admittedly angry and rage filled speaks to the experiences of some of its listeners. Contrary to the belief that it is music like Manson's that "brings our children into darkness," as a detractor told the *Milwaukee Journal Sentinel,* music like this finds many young people *already* in darkness.[5] "Sometimes music, movies and books are the only things that let us feel like someone else feels like we do," Marilyn Manson (born Brian Warner) wrote in *Rolling Stone.*[6] Instead of trying to understand why some people find solace in Marilyn Manson's music or consider the very real problem of bullying and alienation, we often choose to blame the music and to fear acts like Manson and their fans. Ultimately the fear of bands like Marilyn Manson promotes ostracizing and further alienating many young outcasts rather than reaching out to those rejected by their peers.

Media violence has a way of hitting a nerve like few other topics can—ironically, sometimes more than violence itself. Discussing the fear of media violence is like jumping into an argument where most people are no longer listening, just shouting louder and louder at each other. This is not just an intellectual issue for many people but one that is deeply personal. In fairness, the social science research isn't readily available (nor particularly interesting) for the public. So most people don't realize that the research is not nearly as conclusive as we are so often told, or that results suggest only a weak connection between violent programming and aggressive behavior.[7] It is fear that fuels the impassioned pleas to sanction Hollywood for "poisoning young minds" with media violence, as a woman wrote in a letter to the *San Francisco Chronicle*.[8] Everyday citizens fear "what this country is coming to" at the hands of "demented" writers and producers.[9] The fear and anger are very real, and unfortunately, often misplaced. A *Boston Globe* article conceded that a great deal of the evidence that popular culture causes problems is anecdotal, stating that "the real link between televised sex and violence and actual behavior has been difficult to prove," but only after seven paragraphs about the "growing concern of mental health specialists."[10] In spite of news reports about the "tremendous problem" of media violence allegedly demonstrated by "classic studies" and "sweeping new" research, as the *Boston Globe* and *Los Angeles Times* reported, this body of research contains leaps in logic, questionable methods, and exaggerated findings.[11]

There is a preponderance of evidence, not as a result of "thirty years of research and more than 1,000 studies," as the *St. Louis Post-Dispatch* described, but because Americans spend so much time, energy, and money researching this loaded question instead of researching violence itself.[12] If youth violence is really the issue of importance here, we should start by studying violence, before studying media. But media culture is on trial, not violence. These studies are smoke screens that enable us to continue along the media trail while disregarding actual violence patterns.

Interestingly, the media blamers seem to feel that they are against a great deal of media resistance to their cause. But there seems to be no shortage of newspaper editors willing and eager to play upon this fear in print. A *St. Louis Post-Dispatch* editorial called "Poisonous Pleasures" railed against "our caustic culture and pervasive appetite for violent and obscene entertainment."[13] The paper plainly stated that "media violence is hazardous to our health," but we are allegedly "a nation desperate to ignore it."

This chapter offers a critical view of the fear and assumptions contained within the contours of the panic surrounding media violence. The news media often guide us to think of media violence as the creator of real violence rather than the more complex causes, like poverty and the availability of guns. As Michael Moore's 2002 documentary *Bowling for Columbine* pointed out, we are a society that is ambivalent about gun control, so it becomes easier for the news media and the rest of us to focus on media culture and video game joysticks than to question our gun culture. While on the surface our fear seems to be about violence, we will see that actual violence has little to do with media violence. The fears surrounding media violence come from our individual-focused society; we have trouble understanding the collective social conditions that cause violence, and thus violent media seems like a very plausible explanation. Ultimately, focusing so much on media helps us ignore the very social conditions that create violence and serves to justify intensified control of children—typically *other* people's children.

I confess, I was once on the blame-the-media bandwagon for the very same reasons. When I began graduate work in psychology, the studies of effects of violent media on behavior seemed overwhelming.

The argument made sense to me at the time, especially since I hate violent movies. I had seen a movie called *Predator 2,* which I reluctantly agreed to watch with a very persistent boyfriend. I really can't tell you what the movie was about since I found it so offensive that I kept my eyes closed through most of it. I was really angry with him for taking me to see a movie in which people appeared to be skinned alive and vowed intellectual revenge by showing him that these movies were not just stupid and repulsive, but harmful too. Students of psychology are taught that the individual is the primary unit of analysis, and that something that may be bad for the individual can be multiplied many times over and thus become a social problem. This perspective is complementary to the American focus on individualism, where we often believe that our success or failure stems directly from our personal characteristics and actions rather than social forces.

But as I began to review the research, I saw that the results were not as compelling as I had hoped or had heard on the news. I eventually realized that my feelings about violent movies were driven more by my personal taste than social science. Other scholars, like psychologist Jonathan L. Freedman, challenge the conclusions of this research too. Freedman evaluated every study published in English that explored the media violence connection, and concluded that "the evidence . . . is weak and inconsistent, with more non-supportive results than supportive results."[14] Later, when I began graduate work in sociology, I saw that we need to consider sociological explanations in addition to focusing on individual behavior. Both media and violence are sociological as well as psychological phenomena.

Yet historically, psychologists have focused the bulk of the research about media and violence on individual effects that have been used to draw conclusions on a sociological level. Adding sociological analysis gives us information about the larger context. We will see that from a sociological perspective media violence is important, but not in the way we tend to think it is. It cannot help us explain real violence well, but it can help us understand American culture and why stories of conflict and violent resolution so often reoccur.

Media violence has become a scapegoat onto which we lay blame for a host of social problems. Sociologist Todd Gitlin describes how "the indiscriminate fear of television in particular displaces justifiable fears of actual dangers—dangers of which television . . . provides some disturbing glimpses."[15] Concerns about media and violence rest on several flawed, yet taken-for-granted assumptions about both media and violence. These beliefs appear to be obvious in emotional arguments about protecting children. So while these are not the only problems with blaming media, this chapter will address four central assumptions:

1. Children have become more violent as media culture has expanded.
2. Children imitate media violence with deadly results.
3. Real violence and media violence have the same meaning.
4. Research conclusively demonstrates that media violence causes real violence.

This chapter demonstrates where these assumptions come from, why they are misplaced, and what causal factors we ignore by focusing on popular culture.

Assumption #1: Children Have Become More Violent as Media Culture Has Expanded

Media culture has expanded exponentially over the last few decades. It's hard to keep up with the newest gadgets that make popular culture more portable: iPhones, BlackBerrys, and whatever new device is about to hit the market mean that we can be entertained virtually anywhere. Traditional media like television have expanded from a handful of channels to hundreds. Our involvement with media culture has grown to the degree that media use has become an integral part of everyday life. There is so much content out there that we cannot know about or control, so we can never be fully sure what children may come in contact with. This fear of the unknown underscores the anxiety about harmful effects. Is violent media imagery, a small portion of a vast media culture, poisoning the minds and affecting the behavior of countless children, as a *Kansas City Star* article warned in 2001?[16] "The lyrics kids listen to, the video games they play, often contain violent messages," a Boston area district attorney told the *Boston Globe* in 2006, contending that these factors are what is causing youth violence.[17] The fear seems real in part because it is repeated in news reports like these across the country.

An article in the *Pittsburgh Post-Gazette* is a case in point. Titled "Media, Single Parents Blamed for Spurt in Teen Violence," the article blames changes in family structure and the expansion of media culture with causing youth violence, claiming that kids are now more violent at earlier and earlier ages.[18] And while many people believe this is the case, the truth is that as media culture has expanded, young people have become *less* violent. During the ten year period between 1997 and 2006, arrests of juveniles for violent crimes (like murder, rape, and aggravated assault) declined 20 percent; for adults eighteen and older the violent arrest rate also declined, but by 10 percent.[19]

It's also important to keep in mind that adults are far more likely to commit violent crimes than juveniles are, although rates for both have fallen significantly in the last twenty years, as have rates of property crime. But most of our attention is placed on youth, especially when violent media is considered a motivating factor. We seldom hear public outcry about what motivates adults to commit crimes, although they are the most likely perpetrators.

Consider the fear that media violence is creating a new breed of young killers. True, we did see a rise in homicides committed by teens

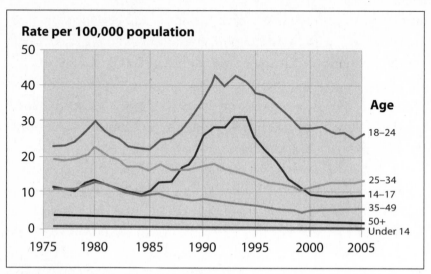

Rate per 100,000 population

Age

18–24

25–34
14–17
35–49
50+
Under 14

1975   1980   1985   1990   1995   2000   2005

Homicide Offending by Age, 1976–2005.
Source: Bureau of Justice Statistics.

in the late 1980s, but we also saw a rise in homicides committed by adults during that period.[20] Eighteen- to twenty-four-year-old adults have been and are now the age group most likely to commit homicide. After reaching their peak in 1993, homicide rates steadily declined in the late 1990s and leveled off in the 2000s. So there is no youth crime wave now; while there was in the late 1980s and early 1990s, it was matched by an *adult* crime wave. Those who blame media violence for an alleged wave of youth violence ignore these inconvenient facts.

Okay, so in the big picture juvenile violence rates have declined. But are kids becoming killers at earlier ages? The Federal Bureau of Investigation (FBI) began collecting data on homicide arrests for very young children in 1964, so we can test this quite easily, especially because very young perpetrators have a good chance of getting caught. Homicide arrest rates for children aged six to twelve are minuscule: In 2006 there were nine arrests out of a population of approximately 36 million children.[21] By contrast, 1,689 adults aged twenty-five to twenty-nine were arrested for homicide that year (and 93 people sixty-five or older).[22] Still, nine kids is nine too many, until we consider that this was the fewest number of arrests since the FBI began keeping separate numbers for young children in 1964. Overall, the period between 1968 and 1976 featured the highest arrest rates, with the numbers generally plummeting since. Young kids are actually *less* likely to be killers now than in the past.

So why do we seem to think that kids are now more violent than ever? A Berkeley Media Studies Group report found that half of news stories about youth were about violence and that more than two-thirds of violence stories focused on youth.[23] We think kids are committing the lion's share of violence because they comprise a large proportion of crime news. Chances are good that some, if not all, of those nine incidents made the news and stick in the viewers' memory. The reality is that adults commit most crime, but a much smaller percentage of these stories make news. Emotional stories draw our attention far more than statistics, which are often dry and left out completely in news stories that focus on young offenders.

But how do we explain the young people who *do* commit violence? Can violent media help us here? Broad patterns of violence do not match media use as much as they mirror poverty rates. While most people who are poor do not commit crimes and are not violent, there are large-scale patterns worth noting. Take the city of Los Angeles, where I live, as an example. Here, as in many other cities, violent crime rates are higher in lower-income areas relative to the population. The most dramatic example is demonstrated by homicide patterns. For example, the Seventy-Seventh Street division (near the flashpoint of the 1992 civil unrest) reported 12 percent of the city's homicides in 2007, yet comprised less than 5 percent of the city's total population. Conversely, the West Los Angeles area (which includes affluent neighborhoods such as Brentwood and Bel Air) reported less than 2 percent of the city's homicides but accounted for nearly 6 percent of the total population.[24] If media culture really was a major cause of violence, wouldn't the children of the wealthy, who have greater access to the Internet, video games, and other visual media be at greater risk for becoming violent? The numbers don't bear out because violence patterns do not match media use.

Violence can be linked with a variety of issues, the most important one being poverty. Criminologist E. Britt Patterson examined dozens of studies of crime and poverty and found that communities with extreme poverty, a sense of bleakness, and neighborhood disorganization and disintegration were most likely to have higher levels of violence.[25] Violence may be an act committed by an individual, but violence is also a sociological, not just an individual, phenomenon. To attribute actual violence to media violence we would have to believe that violence has its origins mostly in individual psychological functioning and thus that any kid could snap from playing too many video games. Ongoing sociological research has identified other risk factors that are based on environment: substance use, overly authoritarian or lax parenting, delinquent peers, neighborhood violence, and weak ties to one's family or community. If we are really interested in confronting youth violence, these are the issues that must be addressed first. Media violence is something worth looking at, but not the primary cause of actual violence.

What about the kids who aren't from poor neighborhoods and who come from supportive environments? When middle-class white youths commit acts of violence, we seem to be at a loss for explanations beyond media violence. These young people often live in safe communities, enjoy many material privileges, and attend well-funded schools. Opportunities are plentiful. What else could it be, if not media?

For starters, incidents in these communities are rare but extremely well publicized. These stories are dramatic and emotional and thus great ratings boosters. School shootings or mere threats of school shootings are often not just local stories but national news. Public concern about violence swells when suburban white kids are involved. Central-city violence doesn't raise nearly the same attention or public outcry to ban violent media. We seem to come up empty when looking for explanations of why affluent young white boys, for example, would plot to blow up their school. We rarely look beyond the media for our explanations, but the social contexts are important here too. Even well-funded suburban schools can become overgrown, impersonal institutions where young people easily fall through the cracks and feel alienated. Sociologists Wayne Wooden and Randy Blazak suggest that the banality and boredom of suburban life can create overarching feelings of meaninglessness within young people, that perhaps they find their parents' struggles to obtain material wealth empty and are not motivated by the desire for money enough to conform.[26] It is too risky to criticize the American Dream—the house in the suburbs, homogeneity, a Starbucks at every corner—because ultimately that requires many of us to look in the mirror. It is easier to look at the TV for the answer.

The truth is there is no epidemic of white suburban violence, but isolated and tragic examples have gained a lot of attention. White juvenile homicide arrest rates rose (along with black juvenile arrest rates) in the late 1980s and peaked in 1994. The number of African American juveniles arrested for homicide has tumbled even more sharply since its peak in the early 1990s and homicide arrest rates were at their lowest point in a generation.[27] Our media fears encourage us to overlook the good news about youth violence and blame young people for crimes they don't commit.

Assumption #2: Children Imitate Media Violence with Deadly Results

In 1999, retired Army Lieutenant Colonel David Grossman published a book, *Stop Teaching Our Kids to Kill,* claiming video games serve as military-like training that inspire young people to murder. Grossman's boot camp–instructor authority brought lots of attention and fed the video game fear. "There's a generation growing up that the media has cocked and primed for draconian action and a degree of bloodlust that we haven't seen since the Roman children sat in the Colosseum and cheered as the Christians were killed," he warned.[28] But as we saw in the previous section, crime data show us that kids are not displaying bloodlust, at least not the real unpixilated kind.

When young people *do* commit crimes or act violently, news reports often compare incidents to popular culture. Didn't the killer act like he was playing a video game? After the shootings at Columbine and other schools during the 1990s, video games bore the brunt of blame. Critics like Grossman argue that video games are even more influential than movies, television, or music because the player is actively participating in the game. This, of course, is what makes video games fun and exciting and sets them apart from other media where consumers take on more of a spectator role. Critics fear that players of violent games are rewarded for acts of virtual violence, which they believe may translate into learning that violence is acceptable. Straight out of B. F. Skinner, the fear stems from the idea that we learn from rewards, even vicarious rewards. The prevalence of violent video game playing among young boys troubles many for this reason.

Yet fears about violent media are not limited to video games. Couldn't a violent movie like *The Basketball Diaries*, which involves a school shooting, inspire imitation? Can a song lead a young, impressionable person to kill? Reporting on similarities between youth violence and popular culture does make for a dramatic story and good ratings, but too often the public never hears more about the context of the incident. By leaving out the nonmedia details, news reports make it easy for us to believe that the movies (or video games or music) made them do it.

In 1996, fourteen-year-old Barry Loukaitis shot three students and a teacher in Moses Lake, Washington, just east of Seattle, leaving all but one of the students dead.[29] The defense blamed alternative band Pearl Jam's song "Jeremy" (about a bullied boy who strikes back) for the shooting. His defense attorneys played the "Jeremy" video in court, insisting that the song triggered the shooting.[30] The song, released in 1991, describes a boy ignored by parents and taunted by classmates. The lyrics themselves are not nearly as apocalyptic as defense attorneys insisted. The song begins with Jeremy "at home drawing pictures" of himself on the top of a mountain, as "dead lay in pools of maroon below" in the drawing. The violence in school consists of "a surprise left," not a shooting spree.

Barry was clearly troubled; defense attorneys used his bipolar disorder as the basis for an insanity defense. His family life also appears to have been unstable. His father testified that the boy witnessed many arguments between his parents, who were separated at the time of the killings.[31] His mother testified that she told Barry about her suicidal fantasies of killing herself in front of her estranged husband and his girlfriend.

Barry was sentenced to life in prison for the murders. In this and other cases, courts have continually rejected the "media made me do it" defense.[32]

Nonetheless, parents will tell you that their kids often play fight in the same style as the characters in cartoons and other characters from popular culture. But as author Gerard Jones points out in *Killing Monsters: Why Children Need Fantasy, Super Heroes, and Make-Believe Violence,* imitative behavior in play is a way young people may work out pent-up hostility and aggression and feel powerful. Cops and robbers, cowboys and Indians are all modes of play where children, often boys, have acted out violent scenarios without widespread public condemnation. It is different from acting violently, where the intention is to inflict pain.

The idea that children will imitate media violence draws on Albert Bandura's classic 1963 "Bobo doll" experiment. Bandura and colleagues studied ninety-six children approximately three to six years old (the study doesn't mention details about the children's community or economic backgrounds). The children were divided into groups and watched various acts of aggression against a five-foot inflated Bobo doll. Surprise: When they had their chance, the kids who watched adults hit the doll pummeled it too, especially those who watched the cartoon version of the doll-beating. Although taken as proof that children will imitate aggressive models from film and television, this study is riddled with leaps in logic.

The main problem with the Bobo doll study is fairly obvious: Hitting an inanimate object is not necessarily an act of violence, nor is real life something that can be adequately recreated in a laboratory. In fairness, contemporary experiments have been a bit more complex than this one, using physiological measures like blinking and heart rate to measure effects. But the only way to assess a cause-effect relationship with certainty is to conduct an experiment, yet violence is too complex an issue to isolate into independent and dependent variables in a lab. Imagine designing a study where one group is randomly assigned to live in a neighborhood where dodging drug dealers and gang members is normal. Or where one group is randomly assigned to be verbally and physically abused by an alcoholic parent. What happens in a laboratory is by nature out of context, and real world application is highly questionable. We do learn about children's play from this study, but by focusing only on how they might become violent we lose a valuable part of the data.

So while this study is limited because it took place in a controlled laboratory and did not involve actual violence, let's consider a case that on the surface seems to be proof that some kids are copycat killers. In the summer of 1999, a twelve-year-old boy named Lionel Tate beat and killed six-year-old Tiffany Eunick, the daughter of a family friend in Pembroke Pines, Florida. Claiming he was imitating wrestling moves he had seen on television, Lionel's defense attorney attempted to prove that Lionel did not know that what he was doing would hurt Tiffany; he subpoenaed famous wrestlers like Hulk Hogan and Dwayne "The

Rock" Johnson in hopes that they would perform for the jury to show how their moves are choreographed. Ultimately, they did not testify, but his attorney argued that Lionel should not be held criminally responsible for what he called a tragic accident. The jury didn't buy this defense, finding that the severity of the girl's injuries was inconsistent with the wrestling claim. Nonetheless, the news media ran with the wrestling alibi. Headlines shouted "Wrestle Slay Boy Faces Life," "Boy, 14, Gets Life in TV Wrestling Death," and "Young Killer Wrestles Again in Broward Jail."[33] This case served to reawaken fears that media violence, particularly as seen in wrestling, is dangerous because kids allegedly don't understand that real violence can cause real injuries. Cases like this one are used to justify claims that kids may imitate media violence without recognizing the real consequences.

Lionel's defense attorney capitalized on this fear by stating that "Lionel had fallen into the trap so many youngsters fall into."[34] But many youngsters don't fall into this trap and neither did Lionel. Lionel Tate was not an average twelve-year-old boy; the warning signs were certainly present before that fateful summer evening. Most news reports focused on the alleged wrestling connection without exploring Lionel's troubled background. He was described by a former teacher as "almost out of control," prone to acting out, disruptive, and seeking attention.[35] A forensic psychologist who evaluated Lionel in 1999 described him as having "a high potential for violence" and "uncontrolled feelings of anger, resentment and poor impulse control."[36] Neighbors also described his neighborhood as dangerous, with a significant drug trade.

Evidence from the case also belies the claim that Lionel and Tiffany were just playing, particularly the more than thirty-five serious injuries that Tiffany sustained, including a fractured skull and massive internal damage. These injuries were not found to be consistent with play wrestling, as the defense claimed. The prosecutor pointed out that Lionel did not tell investigators he was imitating wrestling moves initially; instead he said they were playing tag but changed his story to wrestling weeks later. Although his defense attorney claimed Lionel didn't realize someone could really get hurt while wrestling, Lionel admitted that he knew television wrestling was fake.[37]

In spite of the fact that Lionel was deemed too naïve to know the difference between media violence and real violence, he was tried as an adult and received a sentence of life in prison without parole.

Ultimately, Lionel's new defense team arranged for his sentence to be overturned in 2003, this time saying that Lionel accidentally jumped on Tiffany when running down a staircase. He was released in January 2004 on the condition that he would remain under court supervision for eleven years. On appeal, a judge ruled that Lionel should have been granted a pretrial hearing to determine if he understood the severity of the charges against him. His case provides an example of the ultimate contradiction: If children really don't know any better than to imitate wrestling, why would we apply adult punishment? Completely lost in the discussion surrounding this case is our repeated failure as a society to treat children like Lionel *before* violent behavior escalates, to recognize the warning signs before it is too late.

Unfortunately this was not the end of Lionel Tate's troubles. Eleven months after his release, Lionel violated his probation when he was found out at 2:30 a.m. with a knife, and a judge extended his probation period to fifteen years.[38] In May 2005, Lionel was arrested for robbing a pizza delivery person at gunpoint, and in 2006 was sentenced to thirty years in prison for violating his probation.[39]

The imitation hypothesis suggests that violence in media puts kids like Lionel over the edge, the proverbial straw that breaks the camel's back, but this enables us to divert our attention from the seriousness of the other risk factors in Lionel's life. Chances are we would never have heard about Lionel or Tiffany if there was no wrestling angle to the story.

Another murder case demonstrates this point. In February 2001, an argument between two eleven-year-old boys at a Springfield, Massachusetts, movie theater resulted in the death of Nestor Herrera. In spite of the fact that the investigation concentrated on a dispute between the two boys, a *Boston Herald* story focused almost exclusively on the slasher movie, *Valentine,* which the accused stabber had just watched.[40] The article implied that the similarities between the stabbing and the movie could partly explain why Nestor was killed. Rather than explore why Nestor's killer was carrying a knife or investigate the family or community background, the *Herald* warned parents to limit their children's media use, or "the effects could be devastating."[41]

Two days after the initial report, the *Herald* ran another story, which revisited the gory details of the movie and noted almost as an aside that the suspect's home was plagued with violence. The suspect also had a history of discipline problems, which caused him to change schools.[42] The nature of the boys' argument (the *motive*) was apparently not as important as the movie in the *Herald*'s initial reports. As it turned out, the suspect was jealous; the victim was at the movie with a girl he liked. Although the district attorney prosecuting the case told the press that the movie clearly did not provoke the stabbing, a February 7 editorial in the *Herald* focused on media violence as the central problem, stating that "Hollywood's product is often as toxic as that of the tobacco industry."[43]

There is a problem here, but it's not the slasher film. The problem lies in how easy it is for news reports and subsequent public concern to overlook the central facts of a case like this: A troubled boy is shuffled around and does not receive appropriate intervention until he brings a knife to a movie and kills someone. The movie is not what we should be focusing on: Clearly family violence, a history of discipline problems, and the fact that the boy carried a weapon merit further examination.

The biggest problem with the imitation hypothesis is that it suggests that we focus on media instead of the other 99 percent of the pieces of the violence puzzle. When news accounts neglect to provide the full context, it appears as though media violence is the most compelling explanatory factor. It is certainly likely that young people who are prone to become violent are also drawn towards violent entertainment. For instance, the Columbine shooters probably used video games to practice acting out their rage onto others, but where the *will* to carry out such extreme levels of violence came from is much more complex. As Henry Jenkins, director of comparative media studies at MIT, explained, the boys "drew into their world the darkest, most alienated, most brutal images available to them and they turned those images into the vehicle of their personal demons."[44] Rather than implanting violent images, video games and other violent forms of popular culture enable people to indulge in dark virtual fantasies, to act out electronically in ways that the vast majority of them would never do in reality.

Here's what the media imitation explanation often leaves out: Children whose actions parallel media violence come with a host of other more important risk factors. We blame media violence to deflect blame away from adult failings—not simply the failure of parents but our society's failure to help troubled young people, who unfortunately we often overlook until it is too late.

Assumption #3: Real Violence and Media Violence Have the Same Meaning

While many young people who have committed violence have also consumed violent media, the majority of people who play video games, watch violent movies, or listen to music with violent lyrics never do. We might agree that some content is shocking and disturbing, as each new, more realistic looking, *Grand Theft Auto* video game release tends to be. But even though a scene from a film or lyric might be offensive to some, there is no way of knowing for certain how all viewers/listeners/players will actually make sense of the content. Yes, some acts of real violence have media parallels. But it is a problem to presume that popular culture simply implants violence in people's minds, even if the people are children. The fear of media violence is based on the belief that young people cannot discern fantasy from reality, and that this failure will condition kids to regard violence as a rewarding experience. It's important to note that the inability to distinguish fantasy from reality is a key indicator of psychosis in adults, but many seem to accept this as a natural condition of childhood and even adolescence.

It is a mistake to presume media representations of violence and real violence have the same meaning for audiences. Even if we have become emotionally immune to violence in popular culture, it by no means indicates that when violence *really* happens it has no effect. An anvil might fall on a cartoon character, the *CSI* sleuths investigate a new murder, but the meanings of each are quite different. A great deal of what counts as television violence today comes from the success of franchises such as *CSI, Law and Order,* and other police investigation shows that promote the power of law enforcement, not crime.

Ironically, studies that assess violence on television do not count real violence reported on the news. When we hear about violence on the news, we may feel a little more concerned but still experience minimal emotional reaction; after all, this is a daily feature of news broadcasts and it would be overwhelming to get upset every time we turn on the news. But when the event is close to home, the violence appears random, or we see the victims as people like us, the event becomes all the more meaningful. And of course *witnessing* violence in person has a different meaning than mediated violence. The fear that media violence may make kids violent is founded on the assumption that young people do not recognize a difference between media violence and real violence. Ironically, adults themselves seem to have problems distinguishing between the two. This is probably because many white middle-class adults have had little exposure to violence other than through media representations themselves.

I include myself in this category. Aside from the news and witnessing a fistfight or two at school, violence has mainly been a vicarious experience for me. While working as a researcher studying juvenile homicides, I discovered some of the differences between media violence and actual violence. This study required me and my research team to comb through police investigation files looking for details about the incidents. Just looking at the files could be difficult, so we tried to avoid crime scene and coroner's photographs to avoid becoming emotionally overwhelmed. One morning while I was looking through a case file, the book accidentally fell open to the page with the crime scene photos. I saw a young man, probably about my age at the time, slumped over the steering wheel of his car. He had a gunshot wound to his forehead, a small red circle. His eyes were open. I felt a wrenching feeling in my stomach, a feeling I have never felt before and have fortunately never felt since. At that point I realized that regardless of the hundreds, if not thousands, of violent acts I had seen in movies and television, none could come close to this. I had never seen the horrific simplicity of a wound like that one, never seen the true absence of expression in a person's face. No actor I had ever seen was able to truly "do death" right, I realized. It became clear that I knew nothing about violence for the most part. Yes, I have read the research, but that knowledge was just academic; this was real.

This is not to say that violent media do not create real emotional responses. Good storytelling can create sadness and fear, and depending on the context violence can even be humorous (like the *Three Stooges* or other slapstick comedy). Media violence may elicit no emotional response—but this does not necessarily mean someone is desensitized or uncaring when real violence happens in our lives. It may mean that a script was mediocre and that the audience doesn't care about its characters. But it could be because media violence is not real and most of us, even children, know it. Sociologist Todd Gitlin calls media violence a way of getting "safe thrills."[45] Viewing media violence is a way of dealing with the most frightening aspect of life in a safe setting, like riding a roller-coaster while knowing that you will get off and walk away in a few minutes.

Fueled by news reports of studies that seem to be very compelling, many people fear that kids can't really distinguish between real violence and media violence. An unpublished study of eight children made news across the United States and Canada. "Kids may say they know the difference between real violence and the kind they see on television and video, but new research shows their brains don't," announced Montreal's *Gazette*.[46] This research, conducted by John Murray, a developmental psychologist at Kansas State University, involved MRIs of eight children, aged eight to thirteen. As the kids watched an eighteen-minute fight scene from *Rocky IV,* their brains showed activity in areas that are commonly activated in response to threats and emotional arousal. This should come as no surprise, since entertainment often elicits emotional response; if film and television had no emotional payoff, why would people watch?

But the press took this small study as proof of what we already think we know: Kids can't tell the difference between fantasy and reality. A *Kansas City Star* reporter described this as "a frightening new insight," and the study's author stated the children "were treating *Rocky IV* violence as real violence."[47] And while Yale psychologist Dorothy Singer warned that the size of the study was too small to draw any solid conclusions, she also said that the study is "very important."[48] We want research to support our fear so badly that even a minor, unpublished study will nonetheless circulate throughout the news media. The dangerous content that grabs headlines presumes players are blank slates, easily influenced with no clear distinction between right and wrong.

The results of most research this small might be able to get a researcher some grant money for further investigation, but nearly never make the news. But instead, this study was treated as another piece to the puzzle, and clearly made headlines because of its dramatic elements: a popular movie, medical technology, and children viewing violence. In any case, there are big problems with the interpretation offered by the study's author. First, this study actually discredits the idea of desensitization. The children's brains clearly showed some sort of emotional reaction to the violence they saw. They were not emotionally deadened, as we are often told to fear. But kids can't win either way within the media-violence fear, since feeling too little or too much are both interpreted as proof that media violence is harmful to children.

Second, by focusing on children, the study and subsequent reports make it appear as though children's thoughts are completely different from adults'. Somehow, by virtue of children being children, their brains can know things that they don't. But in all likelihood adult brains would likely react in much the same way. Do an MRI on adults while they watch pornography and their brains will probably show arousal. Does that mean the person would think that he or she just had actual sex? The neurological reaction would probably be extremely similar, if not identical, but we can't read brainwaves and infer meaning. That's what makes humans human: the ability to create meaning from our experiences. And adults are not the only ones capable of making sense of their lives.

Professor Murray's comments imply that researchers can read children's minds and know things about their thoughts that the kids themselves cannot, a rather troubling presumption. Violence has meanings that cannot simply be measured in brainwaves, MRIs, or CAT scans. No matter what these high-tech tools may tell researchers, experiencing real violence is fundamentally different from experiencing media violence. It is adults, not kids, who seem to have trouble grasping this idea.

In an ABC *World News Tonight* broadcast, a thirteen-year-old boy described how his "palms get sweaty," he gets nervous, and he feels "an adrenaline rush" while playing video games.[49] Reporter Michele Norris interpreted this reaction as an admission "that the line between fantasy and reality is not always clear." But physiological changes are not indicators of a shift from reality. As sports fans will tell you, the

Hail Mary pass, the bottom of the ninth inning, and any action with the game on the line can lead to very real changes in heart rate and blood pressure without the fan believing that they are really playing.

If we want to learn about what causes kids to commit real acts of violence, depictions of media violence won't help us much—talking with people who have experienced both will. For several years in the mid-1990s, I worked with criminologists on a broad study of juvenile violence to understand the causes and correlates of youth violence in Los Angeles.[50] We wanted to understand the full context of violence in order to help develop conflict management programs with community members. Usually when we talk about violence and media, it is common to defer to people who have studied media effects—but most of these researchers haven't studied violence itself much, if at all.[51] However, truly knowing about both violence and media comes from experiencing them *both* firsthand, something I fortunately have not. But we knew there were many young people in Los Angeles who had and that they were real violence experts. To interview them, we went to the areas with the highest violent arrest rates (not to those with the most video gamers). Initially, we conducted a survey to ascertain the level of violence in each neighborhood. We then did follow-up in-depth interviews with fifty-six males, aged twelve to eighteen, who had experienced violence as victims or offenders (or both) to understand how they made sense of both real and media violence.[52] Our interviewees clearly described the differences between media violence and actually experiencing violence firsthand.

Above all, their stories tell us that the meaning of violence is made within particular social contexts. For most of those interviewed, poverty and neighborhood violence were overwhelming influences in their lives, shaping their interactions and their understanding of their futures. More than three-quarters of respondents (77 percent) noted that gang activity was prominent in their neighborhoods. Slightly less than half (48 percent) reported feeling tremendous pressure to join gangs, but less than one in ten (9 percent) claimed gang member-ship. Eighty-eight percent heard guns being fired on a regular basis, and nearly one-third (30 percent) had seen someone get shot. More than one-quarter (27 percent) had seen a dead body, and 14 percent had been threatened with a gun themselves. Almost one-quarter (23 percent) had been attacked with some sort of weapon.

Through interviewing these young people, we found that the line between victim and offender is hard to draw and that violent incidents occur within murky contexts. The people we call violent offenders are not necessarily predators, looking to swoop down on the weak and in-nocent. Instead, we see that violent incidents often happen within a larger context of fear, intimidation, despair, and hopelessness. These kids were trying to survive in destroyed communities as best they could. Unfortunately, violence was often a part of their survival.

Public discussions about violence often ignore these violence experts, who clarified several key differences between their actual experiences with violence and media violence. For one, many described media vio-lence as gorier, with over-the-top special effects. Over and over the boys described how fear in their lives comes not from seeing blood on or off screen but from the uncertainty about when violence will next occur. In post–September 11 America, with threats of terrorism and ongoing military conflicts, this is something most Americans can now relate to. One seventeen-year-old stated that because violence in his neighbor-hood was so pervasive, media violence was strangely comforting: He said at least when it occurred on television, he knew he was safe.

Another key difference in meaning is the clear distinction between good and evil in media depictions of violence. "It's more pumped-up like, [a] heroic thing," an eighteen-year-old informant told us. "Like most of violence on TV is like a heroic thing. Like a cop does some-thing amazing. Like somebody like a bad guy, the violence is usually like pin-pointed toward a bad person." Other boys described the lack of punishment in their experiences compared with media violence; law enforcement to them was not as effective as it may appear on police dramas. A seventeen-year-old compared his experiences with the *Jerry Springer* show, saying, "They have security that break it up if something happens. [Nobody] is really going to get hurt that much because there probably will be two or three blows and security will hop on stage and grab the people." He went on to describe how, in his experience, the police were not concerned with who the good guy was, that there is no discussion, and often no real resolution. Ironically, one of the central complaints about media violence is that often there are no consequences, but our informants told us that in reality things are even worse.

A major concern about media violence is that it creates unfounded fear that the world is a dangerous place. Communications scholar George Gerbner describes this as the "mean-world" syndrome: By watching so much television violence, people mistakenly believe that the world is a violent place. But what about people who do live in dangerous communities? With the boys we interviewed, poverty and hopelessness gnaw away at them on a daily basis. "It's just poverty," an eighteen-year-old told us. "I wouldn't recommend nobody comin' here. . . . I just wouldn't recommend it." Not surprisingly, the majority of boys we interviewed did not find media violence to be a big source of fear. In fact, some boys said they enjoyed watching violence to point out how producers got it wrong. As experts, they can detect the artificiality of media violence.

The boys also expressed resentment when their neighborhoods are used in stereotypical portrayals. "The people that make the movies, I'm pretty sure they never lived where we live at, you know, went to the schools we went to," explained a seventeen-year-old we interviewed. "They were, most of 'em were born in you know, the upper-class whatever, you know? I don't think they really have experienced how we live so that's why I don't think they really know how it is out here." Others explained how movies, violent or otherwise, were a luxury they could rarely afford. Besides, impoverished communities often have no movie theaters. One boy told us he never went to movies because it wasn't safe to be out at night or to go to other neighborhoods and possibly be mistaken for a rival gang member.

Some of the boys did say that media violence made them more afraid, based on the violent realities of their communities. "If you watch a gangster movie and you live in a neighborhood with gangsters, you think you'll be killed," an informant said. Another respondent, who said he had to carry a knife for protection, told us, "It makes you fear going outside. It makes you think twice about going outside. I mean, how can you go outside after watching someone get shot on TV? You know, [my friend] was just walking outside of his house and got shot. And you think to yourself, damn, what if I walked out of my house and got shot?" In both cases the fear that stemmed from media violence was rooted in their real-life experiences.

Violence exists within specific social contexts; people make meaning of both real violence and media violence in the context of their lives. It is clear from these examples that neighborhood violence and poverty are important factors necessary to understand the meanings these young people give to media violence. Other contexts would certainly be different, but when researchers or critics focus on media violence, real-life circumstances are often overlooked.

The public hears little about research that challenges the conventional wisdom or the studies that seek to understand how young people make sense of media violence. The American news media is rarely interested in covering media-violence research without a cause-effect result. British scholar David Buckingham writes that Americans "persist in asking simplistic questions about complex social issues" to avoid talking about controversial issues such as gun control.[53] We have been held hostage by denial, while European and Australian media scholars in particular study media in a much more complex fashion.

For example, a British study found that children's definitions of violent television differed by gender, telling us that masculinity claims are made by boys "tough enough" to not be scared by media violence.[54] The genre and context of the story contribute to whether or not kids consider a program violent.[55] Like adults, children tend to think media violence is harmful, just not for them—kids younger than them may be affected, they tell researchers.[56] A study of children's emotional responses to horror films found that they did sometimes have nightmares (parents' biggest concern for their children), but chose to watch scary films so they could conquer their fears and toughen up.[57] Horror films helped the children experience fear and deal with anxiety in a safe setting. The study's author concluded that watching media violence might be a way for children to prepare themselves to face their fears more directly. While parents may hope to prevent their children from ever being scared or having a bad dream, nightmares are a normal way for children (and adults) to deal with fear and anxiety.

British researchers Garry Crawford and Victoria Gosling interviewed video gamers and found that it is a central source of male bonding for players. Computer games let people temporarily adopt different identities, and also enjoy a sense of mastery upon improving their performance in the games. Participants playing sports-related games also gain specific knowledge about the sport, which for males in particular can enhance social standing among peers.[58]

Studies like the ones described above are absent from American news reports about media and violence, so we are encouraged to keep thinking about children as potential victims of popular culture. American researchers are quick to discount children's abilities as media audience members, as is evident in traditional media-effects research in which children's ideas are missing. And by overlooking adults' use of the same media we ignore the widespread and varied uses of video games and other media.

Watching media violence is obviously different from experiencing actual violence, yet media phobics have repeatedly used the two modes of experience interchangeably. Clearly media violence can be interpreted in many ways: as frightening, as cathartic, as funny, or absurd. We can't make assumptions about meaning no matter what the age of the audience.

We also need to acknowledge the meaning of violence in American media and American culture. It's too easy to say that media only reflect society or that producers are just giving the public what it wants, but violence sells. Violence is dramatic, a simple cinematic tool and easy to sell to domestic and overseas markets, since action-adventure movies present few translation problems for overseas distributors. But in truth, violence and aggression are very central facets of American society. We reward violence in many contexts outside of popular culture. Aggressive personalities tend to thrive in capitalism: Risk-takers, people who are not afraid to go for it, are highly prized within business culture. We celebrate sports heroes for being aggressive, not passive. The best hits of the day make the football highlights on ESPN, and winning means "decimating" and "destroying" in broadcast lingo.

We also value violence, or its softer-sounding equivalent, the use of force, to resolve conflict. On local, national, and international levels violence is largely considered acceptable. Whether this is right or wrong is the subject for a different book, but the truth is that in the United States the social order has traditionally been created and maintained through violence. We can't honestly address media violence until we recognize that in part our media culture is violent because we, as a society, are.

Assumption #4: Research Conclusively Demonstrates the Link between Media and Violent Behavior

But what about all the research done on media and violence? While this is probably one of the most researched issues in social science, the research is not nearly as conclusive as we are told. Many researchers have built their careers on investigating a variety of potentially harmful effects that television, movies, music, video games, and other forms of popular culture might have. Two things are interesting about this body of research: First, it concentrates heavily on children, presuming that effects are strong on children and perhaps unimportant with adults; and second, that researchers almost always test for *negative* effects of popular culture. Even when crime rates drop, as they generally have in the U.S. over the past decade, these studies don't investigate whether media could explain *positive* events. We might want to ask why many researchers are so committed to finding reasons to blame media for social problems and use popular culture as the central variable of analysis—rather than violence itself.

Many people now view the media explanation as a common sense explanation. While most of the general public has never actually read the research, we frequently hear reports on it in the news, allegedly demonstrating a clear connection. Headlines like "Survey Connects Graphic TV Fare, Child Behavior" (*Boston Globe*), "Cutting Back on Kids' TV Use May Reduce Aggressive Acts" (*Denver Post*), "Doctors Link Kids' Violence to Media" (*Arizona Republic*), and "Study Ties Aggression to Violence in Games" (*USA Today*) are commonplace. The media-violence connection seems very real, with studies and experts to verify the alleged danger in story after story. But the popular press often provides no critical scrutiny and fails to challenge the conceptual problems much of the research contains.

In 2004, the *Dallas Morning News* published a story titled "Link Between Media and Aggression Clear, Experts Say."[59] The article reports on claims from a recently published article without any critique. While the researchers quoted concede that most people who consume violent media will not become violent, they suggest that *anyone* could possibly be triggered by media violence and that we have no way of predicting this beforehand. The article does not mention any other predictors of violence, by omission implying that media is the biggest contributor.

Stories like this run in newspapers across the country. The *Los Angeles Times* ran a story called "In a Wired World, TV Still Has Grip on Kids."[60] The article provides the reader the impression that research provides overwhelming evidence of negative media effects: Only three sentences out of a thousand-plus words offered any refuting information. Just two quoted experts argued against the conventional wisdom, while six offered favorable comments. Several studies' claims drew no challenge, in spite of serious shortcomings.

For example, researchers considered responses to a "hostility questionnaire" or children's aggressive play as evidence that media violence can lead to real-life violence. But aggression is not the same as violence, although in some cases it may be a precursor to violence. There is a big difference between rough play at recess, being involved in an occasional schoolyard brawl, and becoming a serious violent criminal. Nor is it clear that these effects are anything but immediate. And aggression is not necessarily a pathological condition; we all have aggression that we need to learn to deal with and channel appropriately. Second, several of the studies use correlation statistics as proof of causation. Correlation indicates the existence of relationships, but cannot measure cause and effect. Reporters may not recognize this, and some researchers may forget this, but in either case journalists have the responsibility to provide some critical context.

This pattern repeats in story after story. A *Denver Post* article described a 1999 study that claimed that limiting TV and video use reduced children's aggression.[61] The story prefaced the report by stating that "numerous studies have indicated a connection between exposure to violence and aggressive behavior in children," thus making this new report appear part of a large body of convincing evidence. The only quasi challenge to this study came from psychologist James Garbarino, who noted that the real causes of violence are complex, although his list of factors began with "television, video games, and movies." He did cite guns, child abuse, and economic inequality as important factors, but the story failed to address any of these other problems.

The reporter doesn't mention the study's other shortcomings. First is the assumption that the television and videos kids watch contain violence at all. The statement we hear all the time in various forms—"the typical American child will be exposed to 200,000 acts of violence on television by age eighteen"—is based on the estimated time kids spend watching television, but tells us nothing about what they have actually watched.[62] Second, in these studies, aggression in play serves as a proxy for violence. Author Gerard Jones points out that play is a powerful way by which kids can deal with feelings of fear.[63] Thus, watching the Power Rangers and then play fighting is not necessarily an indicator of violence, it is part of how children fantasize about being powerful without actually intending to harm anyone. Finally, the researchers presumed that reducing television and video use explained changes in behavior, when in fact aggression and violence are complex responses to specific circumstances created by a variety of environmental factors. Nonetheless, the study's author stated that "if you . . . reduce their exposure to media you'll see a reduction in aggressive behavior."

A spring 2003 study claiming to have long-term evidence that children who watch television violence become violent adults ironically made news the week that American troops entered Iraq. This study is unique in that it tracked 329 respondents for fifteen years, but it contains several serious shortcomings that prevent us from concluding that television creates violence later in life.[64] First, the study measures aggression, not violence. The researchers defined aggression rather broadly; they constructed an "aggression composite" that includes such antisocial behavior as having angry thoughts, talking rudely to or about others, and having moving violations on one's driving record. Violence is a big jump from getting lots of speeding tickets. But beyond this composite, the connection between television viewing and physical aggression for males, perhaps the most interesting measure, is relatively weak. Television viewing explains only 3 percent of what led to physical aggression in the men studied.[65] Although some subjects did report getting into physical altercations, fewer than 10 of the 329 participants had ever been convicted of a crime, too small a sample to make any predictions about serious violent offenders.

Other long-term studies used correlation analysis to isolate television from other factors to attempt to connect watching television with violence later in life. A 2002 study published in *Science* considered important issues like childhood neglect, family income, and neighborhood violence, parental education, and psychiatric disorders. They found that these issues are positively correlated to both more television viewing and to aggressive behavior.[66] The authors concede that no causal connection can be made—it is very likely the factors that lead people to watch more television are the same factors that contribute to aggression and violence. For instance, someone who watches a lot of television may have less parental involvement, less participation in other recreational activities like sports or extracurricular programs at school, or for older teens a job. And of course we have no idea *what* they are watching on television in studies like these, despite the authors' blanket statement that "violent acts are depicted frequently on television."

While television has been under the microscope for the last forty years, video games are a relatively new target for media violence researchers. While critics traditionally considered television and movies passive mediums, video games are more interactive. Because of their interactivity, we might presume that video games would create even more potential for real violence. Yes, the violent content of many of these games is shocking, and it's worth exploring why simulated killing is frequently a young male pastime. Many of the gamers are adults; according to industry estimates, the average video game player is thirty-five, the average video game purchaser is forty, and nearly a quarter of players are over fifty.[67]

And as with television, media violence researchers mostly begin with the expectation that playing violent video games causes aggression in children. Articles like "Video Games and Real-Life Aggression" (2001), "Video Games: Benign or Malignant" (1992), and "Is Mr. Pac-Man Eating Our Children?" (1997) are just a few examples of a flurry of studies that have appeared in professional journals since the 1980s, all assessing that one outcome.[68] We might wonder why researchers conduct so many studies on the same issue if the findings really are as conclusive as the authors sometimes suggest. A 2007 review in the journal *Aggression and Violent Behavior* found a clear case of publication bias, where studies about video games testing for negative effects are far more likely to be published than other possible links.[69] As much as social scientists claim they can be completely objective, even scholars have preconceived beliefs and agendas that color the research questions they ask, the way their studies are designed, and the interpretations that follow. In fairness, nearly all professional researchers are up front about the shortcomings of their findings and point out that their results are preliminary or that they cannot truly state that popular culture like video games *cause* violence. But when a journal article hits the news wires, cautious science tends to fly out the window. Serious problems in conception or method rarely make it into press reports because they complicate the story. This is not entirely the researcher's fault, but reports ultimately lead the public to believe that a preponderance of evidence against video games exists, when instead it is a preponderance of *studies* that have been done to try to prove that our fear of video games is rational.

The main problem with many of these video game studies is how they define and measure aggression. For instance, a 1987 study had subjects impose fake money fines on opponents as an indicator of aggression.[70] A pretty big stretch, but equally questionable measures are often used to suggest that video game users will become aggressive, and even violent. A 2000 study by psychologists Craig Anderson and

Karen Dill is a case in point. "Video Games and Aggressive Thoughts, Feelings and Behavior in the Laboratory and Life" was published in the *Journal of Personality and Social Psychology* and quickly made international news.[71] Newspapers, magazines, and other professional journals reported on their study as definitive evidence that video games can increase aggressive behavior. *Time* magazine concluded that "playing violent video games can contribute to aggressive and violent behavior in real life," in May 2000.[72] There's just one problem: Upon close inspection, the studies the article based its conclusions on are riddled with both conceptual and methodological problems. Let's take a closer look to better understand why.

The Anderson and Dill results are based on two studies done with their introductory psychology students, so the sample is not representative. Part of their study looks at whether past video game use is associated with delinquency, but the most serious delinquent youth rarely make it to college, let alone show up for an appointment to participate in a study for their psychology class. Further, their first study used nearly twice as many female students as males. But males are more likely to play video games and are much more likely to commit serious acts of violence. In the first study, the students completed a questionnaire that asked about their favorite video games as teens, how violent they thought the games were, how much time they spent playing, and then their history of aggression and delinquency. Students were asked to think back and recall information from four to ten years prior, depending on their age. From this survey, researchers claimed they found a correlation between time spent playing video games and their aggressive and/or delinquent behavior.

But this study was not designed to assess causality, just the existence of a relationship between time spent playing games and rating higher on irritability and aggression questionnaires.[73] Nonetheless, the authors claim that video games "contribute to [the] creation of aggressive personality," a conclusion that is a clear leap in logic.[74] Because correlation measures association, not cause and effect, it is equally possible that those with aggressive personalities are more likely to enjoy aggressive video game playing.

Anderson and Dill conducted a second study in a laboratory; in this experiment, students played a video game for fifteen minutes. Some played a violent game and others played a nonviolent educational game. When they finished, the students were asked to read "aggressive words" (like "murder") on a computer screen and were timed to see how fast they said the words aloud. Because the violent game players repeated the words faster, they were deemed to have "aggressive thoughts" and perhaps be more prone to violence. Another leap in logic and questionable interpretation, as the words they read on the screen were not indeed their own thoughts, nor are aggressive thoughts necessarily dangerous. It is what we do with our hostility that is important. The researchers have stumbled onto something interesting: Even a short time spent playing computer-generated games appear to quicken visual reflexes.

Other studies have supported this finding: A 2005 review published by the National Swedish Public Health Institute found no reliable link with violence, but instead found spatial abilities of players improved.[75] While video games strengthen hand-eye coordination and improve reflexes, the claim that video games *create* the desire to actually kill a live human is not supported by evidence. If this were the case we would see far more of the millions of video game users become violent instead of an extreme minority. It seems we're less interested in learning about actual effects of video games than we are in trying to justify our anxieties about media and violence.

The Anderson and Dill study also included a follow-up one week later. Students returned to the lab and played another game for fifteen minutes. If they won, they were allowed to blast their opponent with noise (unbeknownst to the subjects, they played against a computer and their opponent wasn't real). The violent-game players blasted their perceived opponents slightly louder and longer, and this was taken as the indicator of increased aggression caused by video games. We have to seriously question whether making noise is a good proxy for aggression, and if this form of aggression is in any way linked with violence. Making loud noises one day, murder the next?

The authors admit in their report that "the existence of a violent video game effect cannot be unequivocally established" from their research.[76] Nonetheless, an Alberta, Canada, newspaper reported that this study is proof that "even small doses of violent video games are harmful to children," even though children were not the subjects of the study.[77] The article skillfully used preexisting fears to prime readers before presenting the findings of this study. The *Alberta Report* article titled "Mortal Konsequences" begins by introducing Jane Baker, a regular "Calgary mom" who doesn't like video games. The story goes on to proclaim that this study "discover[ed] what some parents have always suspected" and then presents claims of the Anderson and Dill study.

Apparently Calgary mom Jane Baker will now never allow video games in her house; the message here is no other parent should either. But it's not just a small Canadian newspaper reporting on these findings as fact. *Time* magazine concurred: "None of this should be surprising," the author stated, listing the violent nature of games like Doom and Mortal Kombat.[78] Even the British medical journal *The Lancet* reported on this story without critical scrutiny.[79] It doesn't matter how weak a study may be; it can still gather international attention as long as it tells us what we think we already know.

The results of studies that challenge the video game–violence connection don't make headlines, but there are plenty of them, dating back at least to 1993. Psychologist Guy Cumberbatch found that children may become frustrated by their failure to win at video games, as most games are designed to be increasingly difficult, but this anger does not necessarily translate to the outside world. Cumberbatch concluded, "We may be appalled by something and think it's disgusting, but they know its conventions and see humor in things that others wouldn't."[80] In 1995, psychologist Derek Scott concluded that "one should not overgeneralize the negative side of computer games playing" after his study found no evidence that violent video games led to more aggression.[81]

Beyond individual studies, reviews of research appear regularly in scholarly journals, and their findings are often contradictory. Although a 1998 review in the journal *Aggressive and Violent Behavior* declared that a "preponderance of evidence" suggests video games lead to aggression, a review the next year in the same journal argued that methodological problems and a lack of conclusive evidence do not enable us to conclude that video games lead to aggression. In 2004, the same journal published another review, which noted that "there is little evidence in favor of focusing on media violence as a means of remedying our violent crime problem."[82] A 2001 review in *Psychological Science* concluded that video games "will increase aggressive behavior," while another 2001 analysis in *Journal of Adolescent Health* declared that it is "not possible to determine whether video game violence affects aggressive behavior."[83]

Clearly, the research on the effects of video games and other violent media cannot allow us to conclude they are a significant cause of real violence. But fear persists for other reasons. Video games represent the digital age, where play and much of our daily routine is mediated by a microchip. Video games, a strange new world to many older adults, seem easy to blame for creating violence, alienation, and disconnection. Politicians and policy makers can conveniently overlook other factors that explain America's violence problem.

The Politics of Blaming Media for Violence

Many of the Columbine victims' families, robbed of their day in court when the killers committed suicide, filed lawsuits against those who

seemed like the next in line of responsibility, the video game manufacturers. Claiming that the games led to the shootings by "making
violence pleasurable and disconnected from reality," a $5 billion law-
suit was filed against Eidos, maker of games like "Sword of Berserk"
and "Urban Chaos."[84] Another suit alleged that the creators were responsible because they knew that violence would result from playing
the games. Both suits were thrown out and never went to trial, and
to date no court has found popular culture liable for causing violence.[85]
Curiously, the same fervor was never directed against gun manufacturers, whose products will clearly kill or maim when used correctly.
On the contrary, a bill breezed through Congress in early 2000 that
made it more difficult to sue gun manufacturers, a victory for the powerful gun lobby. Are joysticks really more dangerous than guns?

Video game fears are not just reinforced by news reports and lawsuits, but by the involvement of elected officials. In 1993, the Senate
Judiciary and Government Affairs Committee met to discuss video
games, which resulted in the industry's agreement for more self-
regulation in the form of ratings. Calls for self-regulation are just
about all the government can do, since the First Amendment generally prohibits intervention.

But that hasn't stopped politicians from appearing to take on the
video game industry. For the most part politicians are limited to meetings with industry leaders and making speeches expressing their disdain for video games, which resonates with their constituents. They
cite the problematic research discussed above and tell their constituents that the video game violence/real violence connection has
been scientifically proven and can lead to tragedies like the Columbine
massacre. Chances are good none of them had ever played a video
game or seen more than a few of the most shocking clips.

There is no shortage of witnesses to testify at hearings like these.
During July 2000 hearings, physician Michael Brody told the Senate
that video games are "Darwinian, paranoid and controlled," and en-

courage players to lack empathy.[86] He declared that they are "not toys or even games in the traditional sense," arguing that they "do little to act as catalysts for the telling of a child's own stories, as real toys do." He also charged they do nothing to "promote imagination" or "develop strategies for problem solving." Of course, the same might be said of coloring books, and reading a book doesn't necessarily help children tell their own story either. But should the government decide what qualifies as a toy?

"This is one of the vehicles by which politicians try to be famous," complained a video game distributor in Tampa, Florida.[87] A few of his state's members of Congress proposed new legal restrictions that would prevent minors from purchasing or renting M-rated games. In late 2001, Representative Doug Wiles (R-FL) spoke of making violent video games "on par with . . . the rental or purchase of adult movies."[88] M-rated video games would be displayed in a separate room like pornography, according to this plan, which Representative Joe Baca (D-CA) introduced as the "Protect Children from Video Sex and Violence Act of 2002" in May of that year. Baca claimed this bill was necessary since video games are allegedly "brainwashing and conditioning our kids to violence."[89] Selling or renting violent video games to minors would become a federal crime. First-time offenders would be fined $1,000, and repeat offenders could be fined up to $5,000 and serve a possible ninety-day jail term.

Although the bill eventually died in the subcommittee on crime, terrorism, and homeland security, criminalizing video rental clerks is hardly realistic in the Netflix era. In any case, *Forbes* estimates that 90 percent of video game purchases are made by adults, not "two year-old[s] with a bunch of money," as the *Tampa Tribune* hyperbolically warned.[90] It's likely that parents make many of these purchases and rentals; *Forbes* reported that of the adult game buyers, nearly two-thirds have children in their households. In spite of congressional attempts to regulate retailers, it appears that many parents have not bought into the video game menace and are the main purchasers of video games.

Several states have also tried to restrict video game sales. California, Illinois, and Michigan have all passed laws making it illegal for minors to purchase video games considered violent or sexually explicit— and courts have ruled each of these states' laws to be unconstitutional violations of the First Amendment.[91] (Ironically, the California statute was signed into law by a former movie action hero, Governor Arnold Schwarzenegger.) The federal judge who struck down the California law determined that the claims of psychological harm rationalizing the law had not been proven.

If retailers aren't constructed as the problem, then parents are. When politicians run out of ways to try to restrict game makers and distributors, they then blame parents for not policing their children as much as the government may wish it legally could. A Chicago *Sun-Times* headline, "Parents Cautioned to Heed Ratings," is an example of calls for parents to restrict their kids' video game use.[92] An *ABC World News Tonight* report on video games in July 2002 featured a parent who felt her son was mature enough to play Grand Theft Auto III. The reporter described her decision as "giving in" to her son, which an expert called "irresponsible."[93]

In spite of politicians and well-meaning experts' attempts to act as super-parents, there is no clear and consistent age boundary between maturity and immaturity. Any attempt to make such decisions should be made by those who know a young person best, not the government acting like a punitive parent. Politicians who try to micromanage childhood and adolescence will fail on several counts: They miss the big-picture issues that could explain why some young people may spend so much time playing video games and what else could be done instead (like providing more extracurricular activities or job training programs). Of course there is nothing wrong with kids having leisure time and fun too. Politicians who fail to understand the pleasure in popular culture alienate young people, who may feel more like pawns of the political system than true constituents. Government attempts to regulate what video games kids play simply won't work in a digitized era. And yet attempts to crack down on popular culture generate bipartisan support from across the political spectrum.

While some fear that the content of video games and other violent entertainment may be harmful, we also need to consider the harm of diversion from the issues that politicians could be exploring instead of leading the media phobia brigade. We might ask why so many parents are afraid for their kids to play outside in their communities, and why many neighborhoods have few spaces for teens to safely congregate. We could also consider using video gaming to build other skills and interests. The army has created a game to promote enlistment—ironically this is a nonviolent game, while real military service is often anything but nonviolent.[94] We should see through the games politicians play too, and avoid falling into the culture-blaming trap we are so often led into.

Violence elicits fear because it sometimes may seem to defy prediction, as the Columbine shootings and the September 11th attacks exemplify. We look to find predictors so we can know better for the future. In the face of something so horrific we are open to lots of explanations, including the role that video games may have played. After the high-profile shootings of the 1990s, the FBI conducted a study to produce a profile of school shooters. In the end, they couldn't—school shootings are so rare and they shared many characteristics with nonviolent kids—like playing video games.

This is not to say that we cannot predict what leads to violence. The majority of young people who turn to violence have a number of other risk factors that we need to focus on more: violence in the home and/or neighborhood, a personal and/or family history of substance abuse, and a sense of hopelessness due to extreme poverty. Specific contexts also must not be ignored; for instance, in the study of youth violence in Los Angeles I noted earlier, we found that the vast majority of homicides involving young offenders are gang-related, drawing on the aforementioned problems, not video games. If kids in impoverished communities actually had video games there may even be a reduction in violence, not because of any cathartic effect, but because they would have something else to do other than congregate in dangerous places. I say this only semiseriously, but to understand why people become violent we need to start by looking at garden-variety violence rather than the headline-grabbing exception.

Politicians, researchers, and the news media may be fascinated by media violence, but the everyday causes of actual violence often receive little attention from policy makers. Yes, media violence may be a small link in a long chain, but certainly it's not the central link. Much as the Beatles' song "Helter Skelter" allegedly sent Charles Manson the message to start a race riot or J. D. Salinger's *Catcher in the Rye* inspired John Lennon's killer, for people who view the world through violent lenses, violence in popular culture may reinforce their perception. The media-violence story, the research, and its emotional baggage make open debate next to impossible. Those who fear media violence police the boundaries of this dogma to avoid challenging their intuitive belief that popular culture is dangerous. But taste and influence are two very different things: Media researchers are often media critics in disguise. There's nothing wrong with media criticism—we could probably use more of it—but when media criticism takes the place of understanding the roots of violence we have a problem. Dissent is dismissed as Hollywood propaganda, reinforced when the press quotes a studio executive as the only person refuting popular culture's alleged danger.

To hear that "Washington [is] again taking on Hollywood" may feel good to the public and make it appear as though lawmakers are onto something, but real violence remains off the agenda.[95] This tactic appeals to many middle-class constituents whose experience with violence is often limited. Economically disadvantaged people are most likely to experience real violence, but least likely to appear on politicians' radar. A national focus on media rather than real violence draws on existing fears and reinforces the view that popular culture, not the decades-long neglect of whole communities, leads to violence.

Unfortunately many children are exposed to real violence, not only in their communities, but sometimes in their own homes. We should not deny this and use the illusion that childhood is always carefree until the media gets to them to shield ourselves from this reality.

Notes

1. John Leo, "When Life Imitates Video," *U.S. News and World Report,* May 3, 1999, p. 14.

2. Ibid.

3. Max B. Baker, "Armey Urges Reunion to Rethink Planned Marilyn Manson Concert," Fort Worth *Star-Telegram,* March 20, 1999, p. 3.

4. Scott Mervis, "Devil's Advocate: Marilyn Manson Is a Panty-Wearing Soldier in the Battle for the First Amendment," Pittsburgh *Post-Gazette,* May 2, 1997, p. 20.

5. James H. Burnett III, "Detractors, Fans Greet Marilyn Manson Here," Milwaukee *Journal Sentinel,* April 26, 1999, p. 1.

6. Marilyn Manson, "Columbine: Whose Fault is it?" *Rolling Stone,* June 24, 1999, p. 23.

7. See Jonathan L. Freedman, *Media Violence and Its Effect on Aggression* (Toronto: University of Toronto Press, 2002), p. 43.

8. Dorothy Dimitre, Letter to the editor, San Francisco *Chronicle,* September 18, 2000, p. A16.

9. Ibid.

10. Richard Saltus, "Survey Connects Graphic TV Fare, Child Behavior," *Boston Globe,* March 21, 2001, p. A1.

11. Ibid.; Rosie Mestel, "Triggers of Violence Still Elusive," *Los Angeles Times,* 7 March 2001, p. A1.

12. "A Poisonous Pleasure," editorial, St. Louis *Post-Dispatch,* July 30, 2000, p. B2. Psychologist Jonathan Freedman suggests that the claim of 1000 studies is inflated, and that there have been more like 200 studies conducted. Freedman, *Media Violence,* p. 24.

13. "A Poisonous Pleasure," p. B2.

14. Freedman, *Media Violence,* p. 200.

15. Todd Gitlin, *Media Unlimited: How the Torrent of Images and Sounds Overwhelms Our Lives* (New York: Metropolitan Books, 2001), p. 145.

16. Jim Sullinger, "Forum Examines Media Violence," *Kansas City Star*, August 29, 2001, p. B5.

17. Kathy McCabe, "Taking Aim at Youth Violence," *Boston Globe*, March 12, 2006, p. 1.

18. Jennifer Blanton, "Media, Single Parents Blamed for Spurt in Teen Violence," Pittsburgh *Post-Gazette*, August 2, 2001, A1.

19. Federal Bureau of Investigation, *Ten-Year Arrest Trends, Uniform Crime Reports for the United States, 2006* (Washington, DC: U.S. Department of Justice, 2007), http://www.fbi.gov/ucr/cius2006/data/table_32.html.

20. James Alan Fox and Marianne W. Zawitz, *Homicide Trends in the United States* (Washington, DC: U.S. Department of Justice, 2000).

21. Federal Bureau of Investigation, *Arrests by Age, Uniform Crime Reports for the United States, 2006* (Washington, DC: U.S. Department of Justice, 2007), http://www.fbi.gov/ucr/cius2006/data/table_38.html; Population estimate from U.S. Census Bureau, *Population Division, Annual Estimates of the Population by Selected Age Groups and Sex for the United States: April 1, 2000 to July 1, 2006* (Washington, DC: U.S. Bureau of the Census, 2007).

22. Federal Bureau of Investigation, *Uniform Crime Reports for the United States, 1964–1999* (Washington, DC: U.S. Department of Justice, 2000).

23. Lori Dorfman, et al., "Youth and Violence on Local Television News in California," *American Journal of Public Health* 87 (1997): 1311–1316.

24. Los Angeles Police Department, Statistical Digest 2007, Information Technology Division, http://www.lapdonline.org/get_involved/pdf_view/40457.

25. E. Britt Patterson, "Poverty, Income Inequality and Community Crime Rates," in *Juvenile Delinquency: Historical, Theoretical and Societal Reactions to Youth*, 2nd ed., ed. Paul M. Sharp and Barry W. Hancock (Upper Saddle River, NJ: Prentice Hall, 1998), pp. 135–150.

26. Wayne Wooden and Randy Blazak, *Renegade Kids, Suburban Outlaws: From Youth Culture to Delinquency*, 2nd ed. (Belmont, CA: Wadsworth, 2001).

27. Howard N. Snyder and Melissa Sickmund, *Juvenile Offenders and Victims: 2006 National Report* (Washington, DC: U.S. Department of Justice, Office of Justice Programs, Office of Juvenile Justice and Delinquency Prevention, 2006), p. 67, http://ojjdp.ncjrs.gov/ojstatbb/nr2006/downloads/chapter3.pdf.

28. Cited in Glenn Gaslin, "Lessons Born of Virtual Violence," *Los Angeles Times*, October 3, 2001, p. E1.

29. Ronald K. Fitten, "Trial to Begin for Teen Charged in Triple Slaying," *Seattle Times*, August 24, 1997, p. B1.

30. Ronald K. Fitten, "Loukaitis Jurors Hear Parents, See Pearl Jam Video," *Seattle Times*, September 9, 1997, p. B3.

31. Ibid.

32. Alex Fryer, "School Violence Pervades Films, Books and Music," *Seattle Times*, April 25, 1999, p. A1.

33. Caroline J. Keough, "Young Killer Wrestles Again in Broward Jail," *Miami Herald*, February 17, 2001, p. A1; Michael Browning, et al., "Boy, 14, Gets Life in

TV Wrestling Death," *Chicago Sun-Times,* March 10, 2001, p. A1; "Wrestle Slay-Boy Faces Life," *Daily News,* January 26, 2001, p. 34.

34. "13 Year-Old Convicted of First-Degree Murder," *Atlanta Journal and Constitution,* January 26, 2001, p. 1B.

35. Caroline Keough, "Teen Killer Described as Lonely, Pouty, Disruptive," *Miami Herald,* February 5, 2001, p. A1.

36. Tamara Lush, "Once Again, Trouble Finds Lionel Tate," *St. Petersburg Times,* May 25, 2005, p. 1B.

37. "Murder Defendant, 13, Claims He Was Imitating Pro Wrestlers on TV," *Los Angeles Times,* January 14, 2001, p. A24. Later in media interviews, Lionel said that Tiffany was lying down on the stairs and he accidentally crushed her when he came bounding down the steps.

38. Tamara Lush, "Once Again, Trouble Finds Lionel Tate," *St. Petersburg Times,* May 25, 2005, p. 1B.

39. Abby Goodnough, "Ruling on Young Killer is Postponed for Psychiatric Exam," *New York Times,* December 6, 2005, p. 25.

40. Tom Farmer, "Out of Control; Child Stabbing Puts Focus on Violent Movies," *Boston Herald,* February 6, 2001, p. A1.

41. Ibid.

42. Jessica Heslan, "Stab Victim's Classmates Counseled," *Boston Herald,* February 8, 2001, p. 14.

43. "Tackling Violence Puzzle," editorial, *Boston Herald,* February 7, 2001, p. 24.

44. Quoted in M. B. Hanson, "The Violent World of Video Games," *Insight on the News,* June 28, 1999, p. 14.

45. Todd Gitlin, *Media Unlimited: How the Torrent of Images and Sounds Overwhelms Our Lives* (New York: Metropolitan Books, 2001), p. 92.

46. Chris Zdeb, "Violent TV Affects Kids' Brains Just as Real Trauma Does," *The Gazette (Montreal),* June 5, 2001, p. C5.

47. Jim Sullinger, "Forum Examines Media Violence," *Kansas City Star,* August 29, 2001, p. B5.

48. Marilyn Elias, "Beaten Unconsciously: Violent Images May Alter Kids' Brain Activity, Spark Hostility," *USA Today,* April 19, 2001, p. 8D.

49. Michele Norris, "Child's Play? Grand Theft Auto III Provides Video Gamers with a Virtual World of Extreme Violence," *ABC World News Tonight,* July 2, 2002.

50. I would like to thank Cheryl Maxson and Malcolm Klein for including measures in their study, "Juvenile Violence in Los Angeles," sponsored by the Office of Juvenile Justice and Delinquency Prevention, grants #95-JN-CX-0015, 96-JN-FX-0004, and 97-JD-FX-0002, Office of Justice Programs, U.S. Department of Justice. The points of view or opinions in this book are my own and do not necessarily represent the official position or policies of the U.S. Department of Justice. All interviews were conducted in 1998. The content of the interviews involved the youths' descriptions of a selection of the violent incidents that the youths had experienced, the major focus of the study. At the end of each interview, youths were asked whether they thought television and movies contained a lot of violence. This question was posed

to ascertain their perceptions of the levels of violence in media. Following this, respondents were asked whether they thought that viewing violence in media made them more afraid in their neighborhoods and why or why not they felt the way they did. This topic helped respondents begin to compare the two types of violence and consider the role of media violence in their everyday lives. Finally, respondents were asked to name a film or television program that they felt contained violence, and compare the violence in that film or program to the violence they experienced and had described in the interview earlier. This question solicited direct comparison between the two modes of experience (lived and media violence). The subjects were able to define media violence themselves, as they first chose the medium, and then the television program or film that they wished to discuss. Definitions of media violence were not imposed on the respondents. The interviews were tape-recorded and transcribed. Data were later coded using qualitative data analysis software to sort and categorize the respondents' answers. Data were collected by random selection by obtaining a sample of addresses from a marketing organization, and households were then enumerated to determine whether a male between the ages of twelve to seventeen lived in the residence for at least six months. (Interviewees were sometimes eighteen at the time of follow-up.) It was determined that if youths had lived in the neighborhood for less than six months, their experiences might not accurately reflect activity within that particular area. They were excluded in the original sampling process.

51. But not necessarily—researchers who study media violence often have backgrounds in communications, psychology, or medicine.

52. No females were included because primary investigators concluded from previous research that males were more likely to have been involved in violent incidents.

53. David Buckingham, *After the Death of Childhood: Growing Up in the Age of Electronic Media* (London: Polity, 2000), p. 130.

54. David Buckingham and Julian Wood, "Repeatable Pleasures: Notes on Young People's Use of Video," in *Reading Audiences: Young People and the Media,* ed. David Buckingham (Manchester, UK: Manchester University Press, 1993).

55. Ibid., p. 132.

56. Ibid.

57. Ibid., p. 137.

58. Garry Crawford and Victoria Gosling, "Toys for Boys? Marginalization and Participation as Digital Gamers," *Sociological Research Online 10*, no. 1 (March 31, 2005); Garry Crawford, "The Cult of the Champ Man: The Cultural Pleasures of Championship Manager/Football Manager Games," *Information, Communication & Society* 9 (2006): 523–540.

59. Karen Patterson, "Link Between Media and Aggression Clear, Experts Say," *Dallas Morning News,* April 19, 2004.

60. Rosie Mestel, "In A Wired World, TV Still Has Grip on Kids," *Los Angeles Times,* September 18, 2000, p. F1. The same article also appeared in Montreal's *Gazette* as "The Great Debate: Experts Disagree Over the Extent of the Effects of Media Violence on Children" on September 30, 2000.

61. Susan FitzGerald, "Cutting Back on Kids' TV Use May Reduce Aggressive Acts," *Denver Post*, January 15, 2001, p. A2.

62. Ibid.

63. See Gerard Jones, *Killing Monsters: Why Children Need Fantasy, Super Heroes, and Make-Believe Violence* (New York: Basic Books, 2002).

64. L. Rowell Huesman, et al., "Longitudinal Relations Between Children's Exposure to TV Violence and Their Aggressive and Violent Behavior in Young Adulthood: 1977–1992," *Developmental Psychology* 39, no. 2 (2003): 201–221. Kids who regularly watched shows like *Starsky and Hutch, The Six Million Dollar Man*, and *Road Runner* cartoons in 1977 were regarded as high violence viewers.

65. Based on r=.17.

66. Jeffrey G. Johnson, et al., "Television Viewing and Aggressive Behavior During Adolescence and Adulthood," *Science* 29 (March 2002): 2468–2471.

67. Statistics from industry group Entertainment Software Association, http://www.theesa.com/facts/index.asp, accessed on November 24, 2008.

68. Lillian Bensley and Juliet Van Eenwyk, "Video Games and Real-Life Aggression: Review of the Literature," *Journal of Adolescent Health* 29 (2001): 244–257; Jeanne B. Funk, "Video Games: Benign or Malignant?" *Journal of Developmental and Behavioral Pediatrics* 13 (1992): 53–54; C. E. Emes, "Is Mr. Pac Man Eating Our Children? A Review of the Effect of Video Games on Children," *The Canadian Journal of Psychiatry* (1997): 409–414.

69. C. J. Ferguson, "Evidence for Publication Bias in Video Game Violence Effects Literature: A Meta-Analytic Review," *Aggression and Violent Behavior* (2007): 470–482.

70. M. Winkel, D. M. Novak, and H. Hopson, "Personality Factors, Subject Gender, and the Effects of Aggressive Video Games on Aggression in Adolescents," *Journal of Research in Personality* 21 (1987): 211–223.

71. Craig Anderson and Karen Dill, "Video Games and Aggressive Thoughts, Feelings and Behavior in the Laboratory and Life," *Journal of Personality and Social Psychology* 78 (2000): 772–790.

72. Amy Dickinson, "Video Playground: New Studies Link Violent Video Games to Violent Behavior," *Time*, May 8, 2000, p. 100.

73. For further problems with this study, see Guy Cumberbatch, "Only a Game?" *New Scientist*, June 10, 2000, p. 44.

74. Anderson and Dill, "Video Games," p. 22.

75. A. Lager, A. and S. Bremberg, "Health Effects of Video and Computer Game Playing—A Systematic Review of Scientific Studies," National Swedish Public Health Institute, 2005.

76. Anderson and Dill, "Video Games," p. 33.

77. Marnie Ko, "Mortal Konsequences," *Alberta Report*, May 22, 2000.

78. Dickinson, "Video Playground," p. 100.

79. Marilynn Larkin, "Violent Video Games Increase Aggression," *The Lancet*, April 29, 2000, p. 1525.

80. Quoted in Charles Arthur, "How Kids Cope with Video Games," *New Scientist,* December 4, 1993, p. 5.

81. Derek Scott, "The Effect of Video Games on Feelings of Aggression," *The Journal of Psychology* 129 (1995): 121–133.

82. Joanne Savage, "Does Viewing Violent Media Really Cause Criminal Violence? A Methodological Review," *Aggression and Violent Behavior* 10 (2004): 99–128.

83. Karen E. Dill and Jody C. Dill, "Video Game Violence: A Review of the Emperical Literature," *Aggression and Violent Behavior* 3 (1998): 407–428; Mark Griffiths, "Violent Video Games and Aggression: A Review of the Literature," *Aggression and Violent Behavior* 4 (1999): 203–212; Lillian Bensley and Juliet Van Eenwyk, "Video Games and Real-Life Aggression: Review of the Literature," *Journal of Adolescent Health* 29 (2002): 244–257; Craig A. Anderson and Brad J. Bushman, "Effects of Violent Video Games on Aggressive Behavior, Aggressive Cognition, Aggressive Affect, Physiological Arousal, and Prosocial Behavior: A Meta-Analytic Review of the Scientific Literature," *Psychological Science* 12 (2001): 353–359.

84. Ashling O'Connor, "Eidos Faces U.S. Shooting Lawsuit," *Financial Times,* June 6, 2001, p. 24.

85. "Ending the Blame Game," *Denver Post,* March 6, 2002, p. B6; Leo, "When Life Imitates Video," p. 14.

86. Michael Brody, "Playing With Death," *The Brown University Child and Adolescent Behavior Letter,* November 2000, p. 8.

87. Joe Follick, "Lawmakers: Restrict Sale of Violent Video Games," *Tampa Tribune,* December 25, 2001, p. 1.

88. Ibid.

89. Accessible online at http://www.house.gov/baca/hotissues/video_factsheet.htm.

90. Follick, "Lawmakers."

91. Declan McCullagh, "Judge Blocks California Video Game Law," *CNET News,* December 22, 2005, http://www.news.com/Judge-blocks-California-video-game-law/2100-1043_3-6005835.html.

92. Jim Ritter, "Parents Cautioned to Heed Ratings," *Chicago Sun-Times,* May 12, 2002, p. 11.

93. Norris, *ABC World News Tonight.*

94. Alex Pham, "Army's New Message to Attract Recruits: Uncle 'Sim' Wants You," *Los Angeles Times,* May 22, 2001, p. A1.

95. Megan Garvey, "Washington Again Taking on Hollywood," *Los Angeles Times,* June 2, 2001, p. A1.

Popular Culture Promotes Teen Sex

We live in a time when virtually nothing is off-limits in pop culture, and the most private information about celebrities' love lives becomes tabloid fodder. In 2007, when Nickelodeon star Jamie Lynn Spears became pregnant at sixteen, critics took her story as proof positive that being part of the pop culture machine was the root of the problem. "Hollywood . . . appears to be embracing teenage pregnancy," a *Washington Times* story claimed.[1] "Doesn't anybody remember the old sequence of events of how this was supposed to happen?" a pop culture critic asked, adding that his children were no longer permitted to watch Spears' show, *Zoey 101.*[2] This comment highlights what a lot of adults believe and parents fear: Sex is no longer a big deal to kids, and young teens are casually "hooking up" and "growing up faster than ever." Books like *Teaching True Love to a Sex-at-13-Generation* suggest that today's entire generation of kids are sexually active before high school. Their evidence? They look to the media; pop culture is full of sex, the harbingers of Sodom and Gomorrah argue, and therefore so must be kids.

As we will see in this chapter, while popular culture may be awash in sex, young people are not nearly as sexually active as many fear. It may seem like a given that teens think sex is just another way of saying hello, thanks to news about racy Facebook or MySpace pages, and articles like "Good Girls Do," which details the oral sex exploits of a few young Canadian teens.[3] A *Boston Globe* article describes a group of local thirteen-year-olds dressed as prostitutes for Halloween, and pretty soon it seems like a trend.[4] Daytime talk shows have long featured promiscuous teens as problems that their parents can't handle. Topics like "My teen is going on a date" might be more applicable to regular kids, but probably not a big ratings grabber. Horror stories of teen promiscuity make the news and demonstrate the popular hypothesis that kids now are morally depraved and imply the media are at fault. Note that stories about promiscuous *adults* aren't considered newsworthy, but headlines like "Don't Let TV Be Your Teenager's Main Source of Sex Education," "Grappling with Teen Sex on Television," and "Racy Content Rising on TV" help create an atmosphere of anxiety amongst adults who fear that the rules have changed and that young people are becoming more promiscuous than ever.[5]

"Kids pick up on—and all too often act on—the messages they see and hear around them," wrote sex educator Deborah Roffman in a *Washington Post* article titled "Dangerous Games: A Sex Video Broke the Rules, But for Kids the Rules Have Changed."[6] Interesting that we don't level the same charges against adults, who are more likely to be sexually active, more likely to be rapists and sex offenders than teenagers. Roffman's article featured the story of a teenage boy from the Baltimore area who videotaped himself having sex with a classmate and then showed the tape to his friends. Certainly this story is troubling, but also troubling is the supposition that this incident is representative of all young people, whose rules of proper conduct have allegedly changed. We wouldn't dare make the same sweeping generalizations about equally appalling adult behavior.

But Roffman is not surprised: "What else do we expect in a culture where by the age of nineteen a child will have spent nearly 19,000 hours in front of the television . . . where nearly two-thirds of all television programming has sexual content?"[7] There are several things wrong with the assumption that sexual content from television led to this sex video. First, if our television culture is so sex-laden and causes such inappropriate behavior, we would expect even more incidents like this, but this case was enough of an anomaly that it made headlines. Clearly the story received media attention based on its shock value and its rarity. Second, the 19,000 hours is an average, and perhaps a dubious one at that. How many hours of television did you watch last week? Last night? I'm here to tell you I have no idea, and neither do lots of people who respond to surveys that statistics like these are derived from. The amount of viewing tells us nothing about the content itself. Besides, we have no idea if this kid even watches television—typically television viewing declines in adolescence, and adults tend to watch more television than young people do.[8] Finally, "sexual content" in such studies is often broadly defined to include flirting, hand-holding, kissing, and talk about sex so the "two-thirds of all television programming" estimate is questionable at best. Roffman compared the incident to the 1999 film *American Pie,* where the lead character broadcast a sexual encounter over the Internet. However, there is no proof the Maryland boy even saw this movie. This is a common media-blaming technique: Draw a parallel with a similar scene from a movie without knowing for certain if the perpetrator actually saw it.

It is far too simplistic to blame raunchy movie scenes for changes in sexual behavior. This chapter challenges this media fear by examining why sexual attitudes have changed over the past century. The way we think about sex has changed much more than the actual behavior. We will see that youth of today are not nearly as promiscuous as some might think. Rather than being blindly influenced by sex in media, teens are actively involved in trying to figure out who they are in a culture that might offer a lot of sexual imagery but little actual information about intimacy, sex, and sexuality.

Though it may seem like media culture has created a sex-crazed generation, this chapter critically assesses common beliefs about media, youth, and sex. The relationship between the three is more complex than we are often told. As we will see, changes in economics and demographic shifts during the past century have driven changes in sexual attitudes and behavior. But sexuality has always been part of coming of age, and parents have always felt anxious about this passage. Adults' declining ability to control children's sexual knowledge has created a high level of fear, and popular culture—the source of what seemed like secret information in the past—is often blamed instead of other social changes. When we take a closer look at how young people make sense of sexuality in media, we see that they are not simply influenced by popular culture, but use sexual representations to create identity and status within their peer groups.

Sexual Revolution: As Seen on TV?

Not too long after the motion picture camera was invented, someone filmed the first sex scene. Contrast this Victorian Era development with the era's Comstock laws, which made any reference to birth control sent through the mail legally obscene and a violation of federal law. Now you have a basic understanding of the way in which concerns about sex in media have always existed—and have always been contradictory.

In spite of the common belief that sexually laden popular culture is something new to recent decades, film content in the 1920s featured stars like Rudolph Valentino's passionate kissing, occasional female nudity, and sometimes even orgies. Because most of these films were not preserved and are rarely screened we can easily forget they existed. And like today, Hollywood's early stars engaged in sometimes scandalous behavior, including wild parties, frequent failed marriages, and sex scandals. Most notably, Roscoe "Fatty" Arbuckle was tried for rape and murder when a woman died after visiting his hotel room in San Francisco. While the cause of death was later determined *not* to be homicide, Arbuckle's notoriety made conservative groups concerned about the impact this growing industry would have on American society. Movies were a new source of influence that religious leaders feared would bypass the family, school, and religion in importance in young people's lives. If this sounds familiar, it is because things haven't changed as much as we might think.

Politicians and the Catholic Legion of Decency called for government censorship. Instead, the new film industry guaranteed self-regulation by creating a special organization to monitor movie content and ensure it met what were deemed acceptable moral standards. The new code, formally implemented in 1934, was led by prominent political figure Will Hays. What came to be known as "The Code" restricted film content to what the Hays Office deemed "wholesome entertainment" as the country took a more conservative turn at the end of the 1920s.[9] But the code censored much more than just sex. Films that critiqued corporations and capitalism were deemed un-American; content that seemed to criticize "natural or human" laws could potentially incite "the lower and baser element" of American society.[10] Rules governing film production were overtly racist—no interracial relationships were allowed—and any criticism of the status quo was interpreted as a violation of the "moral obligation" of the entertainment establishment. The Hays Office justified extremely rigid boundaries of filmmaking in the name of preserving children's "morality."

The Code dominated film production until 1966. With competition from television cutting into box office revenues, films started presenting sexuality more frankly beginning in the 1960s, particularly as European New Wave films by directors like Federico Fellini and Jean Luc Godard helped redefine movies as art. Twenty years later, cable television and the VCR brought more sexually explicit programming directly to consumers, bypassing network television standards and practices. In order to keep dwindling market share, networks have had to compete by offering content that keeps our attention when so many other things might tempt us to look elsewhere.

Why is there so much sexual imagery in media culture today? Market forces.

Sex has become another product of contemporary society, circulating more rapidly and difficult to control and regulate because highly sexualized images attract attention and profit. Adults now have less control over what young people know about sex, which blurs the perceived distinction between adults and children.

Popular culture may be different today than in the past—yes, Lucille Ball couldn't say the word "pregnant" on her 1950s television show. But it does not explain social changes. We didn't arrive here on the coattails of television or movies; popular culture incorporates and reflects societal issues and values, many of which some people find objectionable. Instead of targeting attention solely on popular culture, we need to first understand the social context of sex in twentieth and twenty-first century America.

Our concerns about sexually active young people are by no means new—during the 1920s adults were horrified by the short dresses young women wore and the "petting parties" young people attended, as well as what was going on in the backseats of the new horseless carriages. So why the often rose-colored view of sex in the past?

Many older adults today came of age between the 1930s and 1950s, and were not entirely chaste as teens themselves. But the movies and television of their era were, and this is what we mostly think of when we think of the middle of the twentieth century. Chances are, if history is any indicator, in about fifty years people will look back at today as an age of innocence too. When it comes to young people and sexuality, the past has always seemed more innocent because it is viewed through the lens of nostalgia.

Rarely does a history book mention teen sex as a major concern of the day, nor do our grandparents typically discuss this aspect of their lives when recalling their youth. But rather than significant differences in behavior, what has seriously changed is the *expectation* of who teens are. Until the twentieth century, most teens were likely to be regarded as near-adults with full familial and economic responsibilities. They worked, married, and raised children—siblings or their own—at much earlier ages than many of us do today. The experience of adolescence, a middle period between childhood and adulthood, emerged as the outcome of industrialization and the diminished necessity for people in their teen years to join the labor force. The time before adulthood steadily lengthened throughout the twentieth century, as did the gap between sexual maturity and marriage. Socially and sexually we expect teenagers today to function partially as adults and partially as children. The roles and expectations of adolescents today are far different from their counterparts a hundred years ago, and even from their grandparents' at midcentury, when many young people married right after high school. Teen sex was very common: It just took place after a wedding (or precipitated one). Yet today we hope that people who are sexually mature don't engage in sexual behavior before socially defined adulthood, despite the fact that children—particularly girls—reach physical maturation earlier than in midcentury.

Along with changes in the experiences and meaning of adolescence came different beliefs about courtship and dating. During the "good old days" adults shared many of the same fears that today's parents have, that young people were engaging in behavior they never did at their age, and that kids had too much freedom and not enough sexual restraint. Rather than the "revolution" we are so often told happened in the 1960s, young peoples' sexual behavior steadily changed throughout the twentieth century, as have perceptions of how parents should deal with the coming of age issues of dating and sexuality.[11] Yes, birth control became much more widely discussed with the advent and distribution of the birth control pill, but it was mostly only available to married women at this time. And in states like Connecticut, any use of birth control was illegal until the 1965 Supreme Court's ruling in *Griswold v. Connecticut*.

It is nearly impossible to understand these changes without considering the economic context. Courtship began to change with the rise of industrialization and marked the gradual decrease of adult control. Before World War II, American child-rearing practices reflected the belief that controlling children's behavior could prevent any untoward sexual exploration later in life. Additionally, parental supervision of courtship was much simpler in rural life, where work was more likely to be closer to the home. A suitor might call on a potential mate at her home with parents or chaperones very close by. Industrialization led to the growth of cities and took adults away from the home for longer periods of time. The possibility for supervision decreased, as did the amount of space a family might have had in which courtship could take place. Dating moved from the parlor to the public sphere, and progressively became more of an independent pursuit with less family intervention, particularly as marriage became more about romantic connections and less tied to making good economic matches between families.[12] Factor in that the widespread availability of electricity at the beginning of the twentieth century enabled nightlife to emerge away from the family home, and the automobile became an important part of American dating. Having a car provided more privacy, and the ability to travel even farther from parental supervision. Drive-in restaurants and movies as well as lovers' lanes are examples of semiprivate settings where teens went to be away from parental supervision.

Highly populated cities offered more anonymity, and the expansion of suburbs following World War II created even more space for young people to congregate away from adults. The 1950s economic boom created the possibility for many people to experience youth as a time of leisure, while the previous generation was much more likely to be in the labor force. Young people likely had fewer responsibilities than their parents had before them, and childhood and adolescence were increasingly seen as time for fun.[13] Dating became associated with recreation rather than procreation, as the search for a spouse became a more distant concern. Historian Beth L. Bailey describes how remaining chaste before marriage gradually lost its economic value in the marriage market, particularly as women had more opportunities to become self-supporting.[14] The new affluence of the postwar era led to higher rates of high school and college attendance, which increased the physical distance between adults and young people, as well as increasing the opportunities for couples to be alone. The influence of Sigmund Freud and Benjamin Spock in the postwar era also altered perceptions about sexuality and childhood. Both Freud and Spock considered children inherently sexual, so sexual curiosity was natural, even necessary for healthy development. Unlike the prewar notion that control created a well-adjusted child, postwar advice urged parents to avoid shaming their children. Parents were encouraged to provide information about sex, a major shift from prewar practices.

Contrary to our collective nostalgia suggesting otherwise, premarital sex did occur before the so-called sexual revolution of the 1960s; it was the *reaction* to premarital sex that changed. In midcentury, for instance, if sex resulted in pregnancy, it was more likely to remain secret through a quick marriage, a forced adoption, or in some situations, an abortion disguised as another medical procedure.[15] The main difference now is that we are more likely to acknowledge both premarital sex and teen pregnancy than in the past. Teenage girls today are less likely to be pressured into early marriage and more likely to have access to birth control and information about sex.

Starting in the early 1970s a backlash against the new openness began.[16] This new sexual openness led to fears that a more accepting approach to childhood sexuality had gone too far, that the lack of discouragement in early childhood led to less restraint against premarital sex. But think back to your own facts of life talk, if your parents had one with you. If it was anything like mine, it was tense and embarrassing for all parties involved—certainly not a pep talk. Concerns about parents' being too open blamed behavioral changes on the availability of information and did not take into account the demographic, economic, and political changes of the twentieth century. Our contemporary ambivalence about sexuality was born, as were complaints that the media make them do it. Today American adults want young people to be both psychologically healthy and sexually restrained, which is why we are at best ambivalent about providing children with information about sex. In many schools, sex education now is often just abstinence education.

Rather than a secret shame, sex today is out in the open. It's on talk shows, in newspaper stories, and blogged about online. Talking about sex and sexuality was once taboo; we do a lot of it now. But talk is not the same as action.

More Promiscuous Than Ever?

Just as sexuality seems like a new invention for each generation of teens, the fear of teen sexuality is renewed in each adult generation. When I was in high school, my peers were sure that my sister's class, just three years behind us, had completely different morals than we did. Rumors flew of who was doing what with whom, and next came the generalizations and laments that the teens coming after us were promiscuous, to put it kindly.

Teenage sex is by now a cliché associated with irresponsibility, disease, promiscuity, and unwanted pregnancy. We claim that teens have trouble controlling themselves due to raging hormones, implying that promiscuity is somehow natural and inevitable. Ironically, while we blame biology for shaping teen behavior, we condemn young people for doing what allegedly comes naturally. Meanwhile, we ignore the majority of teens who are responsible or do not engage in sex, and we don't stereotype promiscuous adults as hormone-crazed animals. The Centers for Disease Control and Prevention (CDC) studies teen's sexual behavior in its "Youth *Risk* Behavior Surveillance System" (YRBSS) (emphasis mine), but rarely do we study *adults'* sexual behavior as risky. When it comes to young people and sex, we tend to hear only the negative side of the story. We hear about the kid who makes a sex video and shows all of his friends. The teens frequently on tabloid-style talk shows speak freely of their ample sexual experience. Let's face it, these kids make the news and the talk shows because their stories are lascivious and sensational. Chastity just isn't dramatic. Sometimes a young star proclaims their intent to remain a virgin until marriage, which also makes news, appearing to be a notable exception. But this too reflects the public fascination about teen sex.

Consequently, a false impression exists—created in part by media culture—that young people are sexually out of control at earlier and earlier ages. Even teens themselves think their peers are having sex more than they really are. A survey conducted by the National Campaign to Prevent Teen Pregnancy found that more than half of teens overestimated the percentage of their classmates who are sexually active.[17] So what does the CDC's YRBSS study and other data tell us about teens and sex today?

- The rate of high school students who have ever had sexual intercourse declined from 54 percent in 1991 to 48 percent in 2008.[18]
- For those sexually active, condom use increased from 46 percent in 1991 to 62 percent in 2007; 82 percent of sexually active males and 74 percent of females reported using some form of contraception during first intercourse.[19]
- The birth rate for teens fifteen to seventeen fell to 21 per thousand in 2005, the lowest rate in the nation's history.
- Teen abortion rates dropped 46 percent between 1990 and 2002 (the latest year data is available for teens alone), attributed mainly to increased contraceptive use and declines in sexual activity.[20] Abortion rates continue to drop for women of all ages.

- In spite of the so-called "oral sex epidemic," just 10 percent of teen females and 12 percent of males report having had heterosexual oral sex but not intercourse.[21]

While media critics tend to focus on popular culture, the decisions to have sex, use contraception, and, if pregnant, have a baby or an abortion are complicated ones. But some clear patterns exist. Regardless of ethnicity, males are more likely to claim sexual experience, which may tell us more about their perceptions of masculinity than their actual behavior. African American males are significantly more likely to report being sexually active than any other group.

As sociologist Mike A. Males points out in his book, *The Scapegoat Generation: America's War on Adolescents,* this does not necessarily mean they really are having sex, but may feel pressure to report that they are. African American males are significantly more likely to report that their first sexual encounter took place before they were thirteen; in 2005, 27 percent claimed early sexual activity.[22] This seems highly unlikely, considering that among females only 7 percent of African American, 4 percent of Latina, and 3 percent of white females report the same early sexual onset. By contrast, 11 percent of Latino boys and 5 percent of white boys claim to have had sex before age thirteen.

Before we start fearing that kids are having sex earlier and earlier, overall less than 4 percent of girls and just under 9 percent of boys said they had sex before thirteen in 2005, compared with 11 percent of boys and 8 percent of girls in 1995, according to the National Center for Health Statistics.[23]

Live births, however, are real and reflect measurable racial/ethnic differences. The birthrate for African American teens is nearly triple, and the birthrate for Latina adolescents is four times higher than for white teens.[24] At the same time the bulk of the drop in teen birthrates is due to a dramatic decline in African American teen births from eighty-two per thousand in 1990 to thirty-five per thousand in 2005.[25] Births to very young teens, aged ten to fourteen, have also fallen for African Americans and Latinas, from five and two births per thousand in 1990, respectively, to just over one per thousand in 2005.[26] (I discuss teen pregnancy more in the next chapter.) But as a 2006 study found, just one-third of sexually active African American males and less than half of African American females had information about contraception before they had sex.[27] Regardless of race, fewer teens today learn about birth control at school, thanks to the political support of abstinence-only education; according to the study noted above, while 72 percent of females had been given information about contraception in 1995, only 62 percent were in 2002.[28]

Poverty is also a risk factor for sexual activity; this might seem counterintuitive, because early births also aggravate the experience of poverty, but for those who see little hope of college or a career ahead, a baby may seem less of an imposition than for middle-class or affluent teens who have aspirations that may feel more realistic. Sociologist Mike A. Males analyzed teen birth trends and found that we can best predict the teen birthrate by tracking adult birth rates and poverty rates; teen birthrates mirror similar adults' rates, not changes in media or abstinence education.[29] Simply charging poor people with personal failure helps us avoid examining why the link between teen motherhood and poverty is so strong, to be discussed in Chapter 5.[30]

In order to understand teen sex we need to consider the role that adults play. Males points out in *Scapegoat Generation* that adult men aged nineteen to twenty-four are far more likely than teen boys to father children born to teenaged girls, and adult men, not teenaged boys, are most responsible for spreading HIV and other sexually transmitted diseases to girls.[31] According to a 1994 Guttmacher Institute report, for 40 percent of girls under fifteen who reported being sexually active, their only sexual experience was rape, often by someone described as "significantly older."[32]

This reality highlights the inadequacy of the term "teenage sex." We overlook the role adults, particularly adult men, play in teen pregnancy and the spread of sexually transmitted diseases. Adult men are responsible for seven out of ten births to girls eighteen and younger.[33] Also, because the HIV infection rate for teen girls is so much higher than for teen boys (a whopping disparity of eight to one), it is unlikely that teen boys are responsible for a large proportion of new cases.[34]

In a way, our society enables adult sexual involvement with teens. South Carolina's age of consent is just fourteen for girls, but sixteen for boys. If this seems very young, English common law, on which American laws are based, originally set the age of consent as young as ten. In most states, the age of sexual consent is now sixteen. Some states, like South Carolina, even have separate ages for males and females, making it legal for an adult to have sex with a sixteen-year-old girl but not a boy of the same age. In these states teens cannot vote or purchase alcohol, but adults can have sex with them without legal recourse. Now passing laws certainly does not make people have sex or not, but it tells us about what age lawmakers think that it is okay for adults to engage in sex with teen girls. The numbers indicate that adults are very much a part of the "teenage" sex equation.

Nonetheless, politicians and public health officials try to steer this conversation away from adults and onto teens. We are all too eager to point out the bad behavior of a few teenagers and hold them up as symbolic of an entire generation. Imagine if we saw a story on the news about a child molester followed by a commentary on how the middle-aged generation is completely without moral grounding. Of course this would never happen—we would say the molester was a sick individual, different from the rest of us. Yet we never afford young people this same explanation. Teens are accused of participating in risky sexual behavior, allegedly coaxed by sex in media. Adults tend to ignore the fact that a large proportion of young people report very little or no sexual experience, and instead focus only on those who report otherwise.[35]

Finally, and perhaps most significantly, we overlook the role of sexual abuse in the discussion about teens and sex. For many young people, sex is not a choice they have made, but was forced upon them. Adolescents who have been sexually abused as children are also far more likely to engage in riskier sexual practices in the future.[36] Rather than focus so heavily on popular culture leading to sexual activity, adult behavior must be taken to task. We need to pay more attention to adults who impregnate, infect, and sexually abuse children and adolescents, as well as to those who would limit the information young people get about sexual health even further. They are the problem here, not the media. Yet much of our research on sex continues to focus on popular culture, ignoring the complex roles politics, race, and poverty play in the teen sex equation.

Studying Sex

In addition to violence, American media-effects researchers also attempt to find negative connections between teen's sexual behavior and media. Using correlation studies, which measure relationships but cannot assess cause and effect, several studies have claimed that watching sexual content leads to actual sex by teens.[37] One very interesting study, published in the journal *Pediatrics*, interviewed nearly 1,800 young people ages twelve through seventeen about their sexual experiences, television viewing, and other factors that may lead to earlier sexual behavior. They then reinterviewed them one year later to see what factors were most associated with sexual advancement. While they found that watching sexual situations on television is associated with more sexual behavior, other important factors, like age, parents' education, and scoring high on a "sensation seeking" scale were actually stronger factors in predicting sexual behavior. Other important predictors, including having many older friends and engaging in other risky behaviors, are included in the analysis but the authors don't discuss these issues in their recommendations. The authors acknowledge that they cannot really assess cause and effect here; teens thinking about having sex may be more likely to watch sexual situations on television. Nonetheless, they conclude that reducing sexual content on television would delay teen sex.[38]

Researchers' continued focus on television as the main problem, even when their own research offers more important findings, reinforces the public's belief that television and media are the keys to change. Likewise, the Kaiser Family Foundation (KFF) has conducted several studies of sex on television, mostly looking for reasons to attribute risky and dangerous teen sexual behavior to popular culture. Examination of studies like these reveals our tendency to underestimate youth and overstate the power of popular culture.

While the authors of the most recent KFF study, published in 2005, note the importance of peers, parents, and schools in sexual socialization, television is the main focus of their study. Researchers analyzed over a thousand television programs, counting incidents they deemed sexual in nature.[39] By using content analysis, researchers determined the meaning of sexual messages of these programs, yet they interviewed no young people to ascertain how teens actually interpret these messages. This method isolates meaning from the context of both the program and the audience, a problem the researchers don't seem to be worried about. Additionally, this study broadly defines sexual messages to include seductive gestures, flirting, alluding to sex, touching, kissing, and implication of intercourse. When the incidents get boiled down into statistics, hugs and hand-holding can appear the same as more explicit representations of sex. Their biggest finding: 70 percent of the shows they included in the 2005 study had some form of sexual content, up from 64 percent in 2002 and 56 percent in 1998.[40]

The authors surmise that "Televised portrayals of intercourse play a role in socializing young viewers to the patterns of behavior that are normative in our culture."[41] But the study never tests its assumptions about youth empirically in this or their previous studies. The researchers seem to presume that young viewers will be heavily influenced by television, completely negating young peoples' ability to interpret media images on their own, or the role of other factors in deciding whether or not to have sex.[42] The authors note that media are an important source of information about sex for teens, but media sources are not where young people get most of their knowledge. Within their 2001 report, authors noted that only 23 percent of teens say they learn "a lot" about pregnancy and birth control from television, while 40 percent have "gotten ideas on how to talk to their boyfriend or girlfriend about sexual issues" from media.[43]

In the third paragraph of the 2001 KFF report the authors note almost as an aside that many teens feel they do not get enough information about sex from parents or teachers. Rather than focusing on this point, they continue to study the media issue. Many Americans fear that popular culture is filling the void that nervous adults have created and beg Hollywood to teach kids about sex more responsibly. Adults should focus on enriching, rather than restricting young people's knowledge about sex and start by dealing with what they do know. Media gets flak for leaking what we like to think of as adult information, which we are either too embarrassed or unwilling to share ourselves.

The authors of the 2005 study cite the risky sexual behaviors some adolescents engage in to support the need for their research. Although they preface their findings by acknowledging that teen pregnancy has declined, they go on to emphasize negative behaviors: the percent who do get pregnant (including young adults eighteen and nineteen) or who contract sexually transmitted diseases. As I noted in the previous section, most sexually active teens reported using condoms, yet the authors of the KFF report chose to invert these statistics to tell the negative story, focusing on how many teens did *not* use a condom during their last sexual encounter.[44] Dangerous behavior is of course important to examine, but perhaps the biggest problem here is that we focus on adolescent risk and fail to put it in the context of adult behavior. For instance, the 2000 General Social Survey found that just under 20 percent of adults used condoms during their last sexual encounters.[45] By ignoring adults within the media-sex panic we pathologize teen behavior even if it is consistent with (or better than) that of adults.[46]

In sum, this study found that sexual content (as the researchers define it) on television rose from a similar study three years before, but so what? We are left with no information about how young people actually interpret and make sense of these programs. It is important that we find out how young people interpret sexual images in advertising, music, and television in their context, and in their own words. If we are so concerned about teen sexuality we need to talk with them, not just about them, to learn more.

A British study did just that, yet received none of the media attention the KFF study did. "Talking Dirty: Children, Sexual Knowledge, and Television" critically examined how children make sense of representations of sexuality and romance on television.[47] Yes, initiating conversations about sex with children is difficult; it is considered morally questionable in some situations. Likewise, providing sex education in schools is frequently the subject of fierce debate. Maybe that's why studies conducted by the Kaiser Family Foundation only focus on television. Talking about sex is considered indecent where children are concerned, enabling us to maintain the illusion that they can be separated from the rest of the world.

No doubt, this is why the British authors chose a provocative title for their study, which takes a rather different perspective on media and young people than the KFF study. "Talking Dirty: Children, Sexual Knowledge, and Television" was published in the journal *Childhood* in spring 1999 with no American fanfare. Not surprising, considering that the authors challenge our assumptions about childhood and sexuality at every turn. First, the authors critique the belief that television is responsible for the loss of childhood innocence and argue it is best to find out what children think rather than continue to focus on what adults wish they didn't know. The researchers sought to find out how the children they studied made sense of the programs they watched, and how they understood the content in the context of their own lives. Unlike the KFF study, which presumed heavy influence, these researchers were interested in how children negotiated their social roles as children dealing with a subject that is regarded off-limits for them. The research team sought to find out what the children knew and how they made sense of it on their own terms, avoiding value judgments in the process.

Secondly, in contrast with traditional views that we need only pay attention to teenagers when it comes to sex, these researchers talked with six-, seven-, ten-, and eleven-year-olds in small groups, asking them to talk about what programs they liked and disliked. Children were then asked to sort a list of program titles into categories, which enabled researchers to see how the children defined adult content. They then compared these shows with programs that the kids considered appropriate for children, teens, or general audiences. The researchers never brought up the topic of sex themselves but the children occasionally did when defining what made a program "for adults."

Researchers found that although most children felt that programs with romantic themes were "adult" shows (like daytime talk and dating shows), the ten- and eleven-year-olds were quite familiar with these programs and others like them. Kids reported that adult shows were appealing because they knew that they were supposed to be off-limits. Gender was also a factor here: Younger boys were likely to deny any interest in shows with kissing or romantic themes. That was "girl stuff," which they wanted no part of. The authors also observed that children feigned shock or disgust about romantic scenes, as the kids properly performed the role of children, supposedly ignorant about all things romantic or sexual.

Rather than advance the narrow view that sexual content does something *to* children, the researchers also found that children use talk about sex in popular culture to build peer connections and to make sense of sexuality from a safe distance. Children use adult themes from television to try to demonstrate adult-level competence and knowledge. The researchers concluded that neither television nor audiences "hold anything approaching absolute power. Television obviously makes available particular representations and identities. . . . In defining and debating the meanings of television, readers also claim and construct identities of their own."[48] Young people may borrow ideas from popular culture as part of an interactive negotiation process where children seek acceptance and status from their peers. While popular culture is an important part of this undertaking, it is not the all-powerful force many adults fear.

Several American studies also demonstrate the importance of sexuality within elementary and middle school children's peer groups. For instance, sociologists Patricia and Peter Adler studied children's peer groups for eight years and concluded that we need to understand the process of how preadolescents navigate peer cultures. Rather than simply negative sources of peer pressure, the Adlers found that children negotiate individual identities while striving to maintain status amongst peers, and sexual themes are interwoven into this process. Adults somehow fail to acknowledge (or remember) that curiosity about sexuality is a big part of growing up.[49]

Similarly, in her study of elementary school students, sociologist Barrie Thorne discusses how games like "kiss and chase" demonstrate that children actively construct meanings of heterosexuality through play.[50] We might deem this sort of behavior innocent child's play, but that would ignore how children themselves define their experiences. How many of us played chasing games like this, where girls and boys excitedly try to catch and kiss each other? Thorne details how children's play incorporates heterosexual meanings into everyday occurrences and shapes male-female interactions. She found that kids accused peers of "liking" a student of the other sex in order to police gender boundaries and sanction crossover behavior from time to time. Think of how popular rhymes ("Susie and Bobby sitting in a tree, K-I-S-S-I-N-G") among girls highlight the importance of romantic connections within children's games.

Obviously, as kids get older, sexual content takes on different meanings. In a study of middle school students, researchers found that boys often recounted sexually explicit scenes from movies for their peers in order for the storyteller to solidify his or her rank in the group.[51] For example, researchers observed a group of boys talking about a scene from the 1982 movie *Quest for Fire,* a sci-fi adventure they saw on video, which the authors had coincidentally also seen. The boys discussed the female characters as passive sexual objects (in much the same way they discussed their female classmates), but the authors' interpretation of the same scene was somewhat different. Yes, the boys' discussion about women was very troubling, but popular culture is not solely responsible for their frame of reference. This is the sticking point: While the boys used the movie to reinforce their perspective of women, we must also consider the broader context of the sexual objectification of women and male dominance, which of course predates film and television. So to change their frame of reference we have to address the full social context in which the film itself was created, not to mention the boys' lives more generally. For many boys, reinforcing male dominance and objectifying women leads to popularity. Boys learn to at least appear to uphold these views to avoid rejection by their peers.

This example demonstrates that young people are not simply influenced by popular culture, they negotiate meaning within the context of their friends and within the larger structure of social power.

There *is* a problem when boys must adopt very narrow versions of masculinity to fit in with one another. But if we were to somehow totally succeed in keeping children away from these sorts of films, or even do away with all such representations of sexuality in popular culture, we will have done nothing to address the real issue. The media did not initiate women's objectification, but we see it most clearly there. Popular culture is often where we see reflections of power and inequality. It is naïve to think that the next generation *only* reproduces this shallow form of sexuality because they see it in movies or on TV. They are part of a society where gender inequality is replicated in many social institutions, including education, religion, government, and in the workforce. Our popular culture shows us some of the ugly realities of our society but is not where these realities originate.

In my own research with high school students, I found that teens discuss sexuality in media differently depending on the context: In groups comprised of mostly males, they collectively celebrated sexual images of women in advertising, while mainly female groups tended to challenge the objectification of women.[52] One male student in my study (whom I'll call Scott) stood out the most. Scott appeared to be sixteen, slender, and perhaps the class intellectual. After viewing an Evian commercial with a young, attractive woman swimming in a pool, Scott eagerly announced that he wanted to "buy this girl." In truth, it seemed his intention was to fit in with his more athletic male peers than it was to demean women. As his male classmates laughed, he continued, saying, "I just want to go buy Evian with that girl swimming in it . . . I just like her commercial!" His peers met Scott's comments with supportive amusement. Interestingly, boys in predominantly female groups tended to agree with their female classmates that the ad's use of a scantily clad woman offended them. The teens I studied clearly demonstrate how the meaning of popular culture is created collectively in the context of peer culture, a negotiation process that goes way beyond simple cause and effect.

As this example demonstrates, sometimes young people talk about sexuality in order to bolster their status among their friends. Rather than only criticize the quantity of sexual images in the media, providing more opportunities for young people to critically discuss these images is a way to better understand underlying beliefs about sex and gender. Sexuality, as much as adults may like to convince themselves otherwise, is not only a part of adulthood and adolescence but also a part of childhood. We often dismiss things like childhood crushes as puppy love, but the reality is that the development of sexual identity is an important component of childhood. Instead of young people simply learning about sex in the media and then acting on what they watch, preteens and teens try to make sense of what they see in the context of their other experiences. Seeing all these images of sex does not necessarily mean that children interpret them by having sexual intercourse.

Coming to terms with sexuality in popular culture and their lives is a major part of adolescence and preadolescence as well. While many adults are concerned that kids are becoming sexually aware too early, we cannot place all of the blame on media. While this is tempting, we must realize that sexuality is not just a consequence of media culture, but also a part of growing up. As if they were on a shopping trip, young people try on new identities to see how they fit, to see if they feel right, and how others respond to them. Some identities young people try on bear resemblance to adult identities. If we want to change the identities young people experiment with, we must provide more, not fewer, choices for them. They also try to fit into the larger society, where issues of sex, gender, and power are deep-seated.

The Power of Innocence

It is difficult to think of sexuality as anything but personal and individual, but the way we *understand* sex is socially constructed. Sexuality is a central site where struggles over social power take place.[53] So while sexuality is personal, the uses and meanings attached to the practice are decidedly social and linked with broader systems of power.

Speaking of power, controlling information about sex has historically been used in order to maintain dominance over others. Withholding knowledge about birth control keeps many women in developing countries in poverty, and withholding information about sex from children is a way to maintain adult authority.

An ongoing and unresolved political debate, whether and when children should have comprehensive information about sex, reflects this conflict. And while it may seem like keeping information from kids protects them, it can be more dangerous than we might think. As several studies have found, abstinence-only education does not effectively delay teen sexual onset. Teens who take virginity pledges are less likely to use condoms when they do have sex, and are just as likely to contract STDs as their peers.[54] By trying to keep information about sexual health from young people, adults are actually putting them at greater risk.

Second, maintaining the myth of childhood innocence is not simply a benign fantasy, it can be a dangerous one. Sexually curious or sexually knowledgeable kids are defined as lesser children, or, as media studies professor Valerie Walkerdine put it, "Virgins who might be whores."[55] A child with knowledge of sex is considered damaged, spoiled, and robbed of his or her childhood, when in fact their knowledge may stem from sexual abuse.[56] Most importantly, clinging to the notion of childhood innocence serves to further entice those who exploit children. Defining children as pure and powerless ironically sets some children up for abuse. Abusers are often titillated by innocence, which our cultural construction of childhood unconsciously supports. Instead of only focusing on perpetrators who take advantage of children, we must also reevaluate how our culture unwittingly contributes to this eroticized definition of childhood innocence, particularly in regards to girls and women.[57]

Virginity has served as a sexual commodity for centuries, increasing female value on the marriage market in the past and fueling male fantasies in the present. Cultural critic Henry Giroux described a film called *Kids* in which the hypersexual male character is called the "virgin surgeon," and for this he is a hero among his male peers.[58] Innocence serves as a sexual marker denoting increased desirability, reflecting the traditional gender order where women's passivity and lack of experience are prized and reproduce patriarchal power. Beauty pageants are a good example of the contradictions between innocence and sexuality projected onto the female child's body. While young girls in pageants are made to look like women, women are encouraged to look like young girls.[59] The teenage female body is fetishized as the ideal against which adult women are measured.

In fact, the majority of concerns about teens and sex are really about teenage *girls*. Historically, abstinence has been a female burden, with girls and women supposedly responsible for regulating male sexuality. The social control of women has been secured in recent history by policing female sexuality. Even within the confines of marriage, at the turn of the twentieth century femininity meant not taking too much pleasure from sex. Clinics provided treatment to women who suffered from such unnatural urges. Authorities viewed women who enjoyed sex as deviant and considered them dangerous. Even when women's desire ceased to be considered a medical problem, sexual gratification was defined as a socially undesirable quality, one that might reduce a woman's chances for marriage. This was of course a serious threat in a time when women's wages rarely enabled them to live independently. The need for male financial support, as well as the fear of unplanned pregnancy, socially and economically constrained women in the recent past.

The threat of rape has also historically been used to keep women from public spaces, supported by the practice of humiliating rape victims in court (and in the news media) which sometimes continues despite rape shield laws. Women's sexuality has been a double-edged sword: A woman's worth has been tied to her appeal to men, yet rape has historically been blamed on women for being too appealing. The threat of sexual violence, even if not carried out, serves to limit women's movement and freedom.

In recent decades the widespread availability of birth control and declines in the wage gap between men and women have created more personal freedom for women. But the old sexual double standards, that male sexuality is natural and female sexuality is a threat, are still alive in our fears about teens and sex. Concerns about teens' sexual activity reflect shifts in the gender order: Attempts to control teen sexuality tend to leave male sexuality out of the conversation. A *New York Times* article even suggested that earlier onset of puberty for girls might be due to overstimulation from sex in media.[60] Interestingly, this hypothesis would not apply to boys, since their physical maturation has remained relatively stable over the last century. So why is female sexuality so frightening?

Teenage girls are considered a threat when they seek to become more than just sexual objects—when they act as sexual agents we worry. American culture still promotes the idea that only girls hold the keys to chastity, but at the same time they are held up as the ideal form of female desire. Open any fashion magazine and chances are good a teenage girl will be pouting back at you. We see this representation of teenage girls in many forms of popular culture, but it certainly does not originate there: Its history lies in our tendency to value women who are young and sexually available for men. Rather than only blaming media culture for this representation of teenage girls, we need to take a closer look at the nature of power, sex, and gender in contemporary American society. Underneath fears of teens having sex are concerns about the changing meaning of gender.

Girls are not the only objects of concern: Historically the sexual and reproductive practices of disempowered groups like immigrants, racial ethnic minorities, gays and lesbians, and the poor have been subject to greater surveillance and control. When groups are considered a danger to themselves or to others, restricting their freedom seems justifiable. We rationalize social control of young people based on the few who are held up as promiscuous bad examples, insisting that these teens prove most adolescents are incapable of making responsible decisions or are too easily influenced by media.

Historically, fears that the population is becoming less Protestant and less white have led to attempts to control the reproduction of immigrant and nonwhite groups. This has been accomplished by policies promoting sterilization, removing girls from their families if juvenile courts believed they were likely to engage in sex, and, more recently, demonizing mothers of color.[61] Due to this fear, during the early part of the twentieth century white women's pregnancies were encouraged, and their access to birth control and abortion was restricted. The sexuality of groups perceived to be a threat is labeled dangerous and serves to legitimate public policies that restrict members' behavior. Many African American men were lynched by whites allegedly protecting white women's virtue; black male sexuality came to be defined as a threat to the racial order. States enacted miscegenation laws for much the same reason—to prevent a union of a nonwhite man and a white woman—but they were certainly not enforced when slave owners fathered the children of black slave women. This double standard reveals how the dominant group maintains power by controlling the sexuality of others. Concerns about promiscuity, pregnancy, and disease have served as a way for powerful groups to assert control over those whom they feel threatened by, whether the threat is real or imagined.

Realities of Teens, Popular Culture, and Sex

Societal shifts spurred by economic changes have altered American life, which has made it more difficult to monitor teens. No matter how hard adults may try, the illusion of innocence cannot be sustained—nor is it as beneficial to young people as we might think: Censoring media will not work, nor will less than complete and honest sex education.[62] This includes understanding how young media audiences use and make sense of sexual content in popular culture. No matter how much we may want to turn back the clock, we can't. In some ways teen sexuality *is* a threat: It destroys the unsustainable myth that adults can fully control young people's knowledge or their actions. Sex on TV, in movies, and on the Internet understandably makes many parents uncomfortable and embarrassed. Representations of sex in media expose the reality that childhood does not and cannot exist in a separate sphere from adulthood. Ironically, we use sex as the ultimate dividing line between childhood and adulthood, the line in the sand that adults try so hard to maintain and young people try so hard to cross. We define sex as a ticket to adulthood, so we should not be surprised when teens do, too. Sex in popular culture reminds us that we cannot sustain the lengthened version of childhood we have idealized since the mid-twentieth century. The realities of sex dispel myths about childhood, and media remind us that such myths cannot be upheld. The media are an easy target, but they are not the root cause of the changes in the attitudes and practice of sexuality in the twenty-first century.

As we have seen, changes throughout the twentieth century have provided young people with the means to become more independent from their parents, rendering their behavior far harder to control. We often associate changes in sexual behavior with changes in media. Historical shifts are difficult to see and understand, while media are by nature visible and always trying to grab our attention. And yes, frank exploration of sexuality is more prominent in popular culture now than it was at midcentury. But sexuality within popular culture has changed in conjunction with other social changes. Media are not the sole cause, but a messenger, jumping into the social conversation about sex, not starting it. To paraphrase Syracuse University's Robert Thompson's explanation, media do not push the envelope, they merely open the envelope that has been sitting under our noses.[63]

That said, we should not ignore representations of sexuality in media. They provide useful clues about power and privilege and can launch greater exploration of contested meanings of both sexuality and gender. Rather than seek to censor, we should study media representations to analyze the taken-for-granted nature of relationships and sexuality in our culture. But instead of using these representations for cultural criticism, we often condemn the images and fail to critically challenge what they represent. If we are really concerned about the meanings young people make from such images, we ought to encourage people to critically address them.

This doesn't mean we encourage young people to have sex. So what are the main issues we *should* focus on, if not the media? First, as researchers Debra Boyer and David Fine found in their comprehensive study of teens who became pregnant, 55 percent of their respondents had been molested, and 44 percent had been raped prior to their pregnancy. The authors noted that, "sexually victimized teenagers began intercourse a year earlier, were more likely to use drugs and alcohol and were less likely to practice contraception."[64] While popular culture provides some titillating explanations for teen sex, others are decidedly more mundane. Family monitoring, support, and communication are also important predictors of teens likely to hold off on having sex.[65] Using drugs and alcohol is also associated with early sexual initiation.[66] And as we saw earlier in this chapter, there are significant racial/ethnic disparities in sexual behavior. A 2008 study found that African American males experienced a rise in self-concept after becoming sexually active.[67] Clearly the reasons teens have sex are complex and cannot be boiled down to what's on TV.

In sum, we need to reverse course away from only teaching abstinence and using scare tactics about sex in favor of education that helps young people deal with the realities of sexuality. Most centrally, adults need to let go of the illusion that childhood innocence can be maintained through ignorance—teenagers' or our own.

Notes

1. Jennifer Kabbany, "A Quandary Is Born; Starlet's Pregnancy Expands National Debate," *The Washington Times,* January 1, 2008, p. A2.

2. Ibid.

3. Sara Wilson, "Good Girls Do," *The Globe and Mail,* February 7, 2004, p. F4.

4. Bella English, "The Disappearing Teen Years," *The Boston Globe,* March 12, 2005, p. C1.

5. Kathleen Kelleher, "Birds and Bees: Don't Let TV Be Your Teenager's Main Source of Sex Education," *Los Angeles Times,* April 30, 2001, p. E2; Brian Lowry, "Grappling With Teen Sex," *Los Angeles Times,* February 20, 1999, p. A1; Marla Matzer, "Racy Content Rising on TV," *Daily News,* February 10, 1999, p. N1; Deborah M. Roffman, "Dangerous Games; A Sex Video Broke the Rules. But for Kids the Rules Have Changed," *Washington Post,* April 15, 2001, p. B1.

6. Roffman, "Dangerous Games," p. B1.

7. Ibid.

8. Barrie Gunter and Jill L. McAleer, *Children and Television: The One Eyed Monster?* (New York: Routledge, 1990).

9. Lyn Gorman and David McLean, *Media and Society in the Twentieth Century: A Historical Introduction* (New York: Blackwell, 2003), pp. 36–40.

10. The Motion Picture Production Code, 1930, http://www.media-accountability .org/library/USA_-_Hays_code_1930.doc.

11. Henry Jenkins, "The Sensuous Child: Benjamin Spock and the Sexual Revolution," in *The Children's Culture Reader,* ed. Henry Jenkins (New York: New York University Press, 1998), p. 209.

12. Stephanie Coontz, *Marriage, a History: From Obedience to Intimacy, or How Love Conquered Marriage* (New York: Viking, 2005).

13. For further discussion see Martha Wolfenstein, "Fun Morality: An Analysis of Recent American Child-Training Literature," in *The Children's Culture Reader,* ed. Henry Jenkins (New York: New York University Press, 1998), p. 199.

14. Beth L. Bailey, *From Front Porch to Back Seat: Courtship in Twentieth-Century America* (Baltimore: Johns Hopkins University Press, 1989).

15. Rickie Solinger, "Race and 'Value': Black and White Illegitimate Babies, 1945–1965," in *Feminist Frontiers,* 4th ed., eds. Laurel Richardson, Verta Taylor, and Nancy Whittier (New York: McGraw-Hill, 1997), p. 282.

16. Jenkins, "The Sensuous Child," p. 225.

17. Results of the National Campaign to Prevent Teen Pregnancy as reported by Lisa Mascaro, "Sex Survey: Teach Teens To Just Say No," *Daily News,* April 25, 2001, p. N1.

18. Department of Health and Human Services, "Trends in the Prevalence of Sexual Behaviors," *National Youth Risk Behavior Survey: 1991–2007* (Washington, DC: Centers for Disease Control and Prevention, 2008), http://www.cdc.gov/ HealthyYouth/yrbs/pdf/yrbs07_us_sexual_behaviors_trend.pdf.

19. J. C. Abma, et al., "Teenagers in the United States: Sexual Activity, Contraceptive use, and Childbearing, 2002," *Vital and Health Statistics*, 2004, Series 23, No. 24; Guttmacher Institute, *Facts on American Teens' Sexual and Reproductive Health* (New York: Guttmacher Institute, 2006), http://www.guttmacher.org/pubs/fb_ ATSRH.html#n11.

20. Stephanie J. Ventura, et al., *Recent Trends in Teenage Pregnancy in the United States, 1990–2002* (Hyattsville, MD: National Center for Health Statistics, December 13, 2006), http://www.cdc.gov/nchs/products/pubs/pubd/hestats/teenpreg 1990-2002/teenpreg1990-2002.htm.

21. W. D. Mosher, et al., "Sexual Behavior and Selected Health Measures: Men and Women 15–44 years of age, United States, 2002," *Advance Data from Vital and Health Statistics*, 2005, No. 362, http://www.cdc.gov/nchs/data/ad/ad362.pdf.

22. Danice K. Eaton, et al., "Percentage of High School Students Who Engaged in Sexual Behaviors, by Sex, Race/Ethnicity, and Grade, United States, 2005," Youth Risk Behavior Surveillance Summaries (Atlanta: Centers for Disease Control and Prevention, 2006), http://www.cdc.gov/mmwr/preview/mmwrhtml/ ss5505a1.htm#tab44.

23. Abma, et al., "Teenagers in the United States."

24. National Center for Health Statistics, National Vital Statistics System, "Birth Rates for Females Ages 15–17 by Race and Hispanic Origin, 1980–2005," *America's Children: Key National Indicators of Well-Being, 2007* (Atlanta: Centers for Disease Control and Prevention, 2007), http://www.childstats.gov/americas children/famsoc6.asp.

25. J. A. Martin, et al., "Adolescent Births: Birth Rates by Mother's Age, and Race and Hispanic Origin, 1980–2006," Centers for Disease Control and Prevention, National Center for Health Statistics, National Vital Statistics System; J. A. Martin, et al., "Births: Final data for 2005," *National Vital Statistics Reports, 56* (6), (Hyattsville, MD: National Center for Health Statistics, 2007), http://www.childstats .gov/americaschildren/tables/fam6.asp?popup=true.

26. Martin, et al., "Births."

27. Guttmacher Institute, *Facts on Sex Education in the United States* (New York: Guttmacher Institute, 2006), http://www.guttmacher.org/pubs/fb_sexEd2006.html#9.

28. L. D. Lindberg, "Changes in Formal Sex Education: 1995–2002," *Perspectives on Sexual and Reproductive Health*, 38 (2006): pp. 182–189.

29. Mike A. Males, *The Scapegoat Generation: America's War on Adolescents* (Monroe, ME: Common Courage Press, 1996), pp. 214–215.

30. In *Framing Youth: Ten Myths About the Next Generation* (Monroe, ME: Common Courage Press, 1999), pp. 182–188, Males discusses the connections between poverty and early pregnancy. He argues that underlying fears of teenage pregnancy is fear of young people of color, and that focusing only on pregnancy enables us to

avoid talking about race and class. He concludes it is easier to demonize teen mothers and popular culture than to understand why teen pregnancy is so much more likely among the poor. The middle-class privileges many Americans take for granted often do not apply to this disadvantaged group, who are less likely to benefit from public education and whose economic prospects, even without children, are rather grim. In sum, Males argues that the teens most at risk of becoming pregnant are the same ones we demonize as we refuse to acknowledge the economic and social challenges they face prior to becoming parents.

31. Males, *The Scapegoat Generation*, pp. 47–48, 52.

32. Guttmacher Institute, *Sex and America's Teenagers*.

33. Males, *The Scapegoat Generation*, p. 48.

34. Ibid., p. 51.

35. Statistics supporting this point from the Centers for Disease Control and Prevention can be found in the introduction of: Dale Kunkel, et al., *Sex on TV: A Biennial Report to the Kaiser Family Foundation 2001* (Menlo Park, CA: Kaiser Family Foundation, 2001).

36. See Debra Boyer and David Fine, "Sexual Abuse as a Factor in Adolescent Pregnancy and Child Maltreatment," *Family Planning Perspectives* 24 (1992): 4–11.

37. J. D. Brown and S. F. Newcomer, "Television Viewing and Adolescents' Sexual Behavior," *Journal of Homosexuality* 21 (1991): 77–91; J. Bryant and S. C. Rockwell, "Effects of Massive Exposure to Sexually Oriented Prime-Time Television Programming on Adolescents' Moral Judgment," in *Media, Children, and the Family: Social Scientific, Psychodynamic, and Clinical Perspectives*; D. Zillman, J. Bryant, and A. C. Huston, eds. (Hilldsale, NJ: Lawrence Erlbaum, 1994), pp. 183–195; Rebecca L. Collins, et al., "Watching Sex on Television Predicts Adolescent Initiation of Sexual Behavior," *Pediatrics* 114 (2004): e280–e289.

38. Collins, et al., "Watching Sex on Television."

39. D. Kunkel, K. Eyal, K. Finnerty, E. Biely, and E. Donnerstein, "Sex on TV 4" (Washington, DC: Henry J. Kaiser Foundation, 2005), http://www.kff.org/entmedia/upload/Sex-on-TV-4-Report-Methodology.pdf. This study is the foundation's fourth study of sex on television, which analyzed 1,154 programs from the 2004–2005 season. Authors sought to address whether the frequency of what they defined as sexual messages were increasing, how sexual messages are presented, and whether the risks and responsibilities of sex are portrayed.

40. Accessible online at http://www.kff.org/entmedia/upload/Sex-on-TV-4-Report-Findings.pdf.

41. Kaiser Family Foundation, "Sex on TV 4," p. 42.

42. For discussion about how audiences create varying meanings from texts and are not simply manipulated by messages, see: David Morley, *Television, Audiences and Cultural Studies* (New York: Routledge, 1992); John Fiske, *Understanding Popular Culture* (London: Routledge, 1989); and Ien Ang, *Living Room Wars: Rethinking Audiences for a Postmodern World* (London: Routledge, 1996).

43. Kaiser Family Foundation, "Sex on TV 4," p. 1.

44. Ibid., p. 2.

45. John E. Anderson, "Condom Use and HIV Risk Among U.S. Adults," *American Journal of Public Health* 93 (2003): 912–914, http://www.ajph.org/cgi/reprint/93/6/912.pdf.

46. For more discussion see Mike Males, *Framing Youth: Ten Myths About the Next Generation* (Monroe, ME: Common Courage Press, 1999), chapter 6.

47. Peter Kelley, David Buckingham, and Hannah Davies, "Talking Dirty: Children, Sexual Knowledge and Television," *Childhood* 6, no. 22 (1999): 221–242.

48. Ibid., p. 238.

49. Patricia A. Adler and Peter Adler, *Peer Power: Preadolescent Culture and Identity* (New Brunswick, NJ: Rutgers University Press, 1998).

50. Barrie Thorne, *Gender Play: Girls and Boys in School* (New Brunswick, NJ: Rutgers University Press, 1993).

51. Donna Eder, Catherine Colleen Evans, and Stephen Parker, *School Talk: Gender and Adolescent Culture* (New Brunswick, NJ: Rutgers University Press, 1995), pp. 83–102.

52. Karen Sternheimer, "A Media Literate Generation? Adolescents as Active, Critical Viewers: A Cultural Studies Approach" (Ph.D. dissertation, University of Southern California, 1998).

53. See Michel Foucault, *The History of Sexuality Volume 1: An Introduction* (New York: Vintage, 1980).

54. Sexuality Information and Education Council of the United States, Public Policy Fact Sheet (Washington, DC: SIECUS, October 2007), http://www.siecus.org/policy/research_says.pdf; Hannah Brückner and Peter Bearman, "After the Promise: The Consequences of Adolescent Virginity Pledges," *Journal of Adolescent Health* 36 (2005): 271–278.

55. Valerie Walkerdine, "Popular Culture and the Eroticization of Little Girls," in *The Children's Culture Reader,* ed. Henry Jenkins (New York: New York University Press, 1998), p. 257.

56. Jenny Kitzinger, "Who Are You Kidding? Children, Power, and the Struggle Against Sexual Abuse," in *Constructing and Reconstructing Childhood,* eds. Allison James and Alan Prout (London: Falmer Press, 1997), pp. 165–189.

57. For further discussion see James R. Kincaid's provocative book, *Child-Loving: The Erotic Child in Victorian Literature* (New York: Routledge, 1992).

58. Henry Giroux, "Teenage Sexuality, Body Politics, and the Pedagogy of Display," in *Youth Culture: Identity in a Postmodern World,* ed. Jonathon S. Epstein (Malden, Mass.: Blackwell Publishers, 1998), p. 28. Also see Naomi Wolf's discussion of the virginity fetish in *The Beauty Myth: How Images of Beauty Are Used Against Women* (New York: Anchor Books, 1991), p. 14.

59. Giroux discusses beauty pageants in "Stealing Innocence: The Politics of Child Beauty Pageants," in *The Children's Culture Reader,* ed. Henry Jenkins (New York: New York University Press, 1998), p. 277.

60. Lisa Belkin, "The Making of an Eight-Year-Old Woman," *New York Times Magazine,* December 24, 2001, p. 38.

61. For a discussion of this practice in the beginning of the twentieth century see Steven Schlossman and Stephanie Wallach, "The Crime of Precocious Sexuality," in *Juvenile Delinquency: Historical, Theoretical and Societal Reaction to Youth*, 2nd ed., eds. Paul M. Sharp and Barry W. Hancock (Englewood Cliffs, NJ: Prentice-Hall, 1998), pp. 41–62. Immigrant girls were often considered delinquent if juvenile courts believed they were likely to engage in sex—no proof of actual behavior was necessary.

62. See Debra Haffner, *Beyond the Big Talk: Every Parent's Guide to Raising Sexually Healthy Teens* (New York: Newmarket Press, 2001). Also see Deborah Roffman, *Sex and Sensibility: The Thinking Parent's Guide to Talking Sense About Sex* (Reading, MA: Perseus, 2001).

63. Closing speech delivered at the National Media Education Conference in Colorado Springs, Colorado, 1998. Thompson noted that television programs tend to be at least a decade behind in terms of presenting social changes. For instance, in spite of the social turbulence of the 1960s, television programs did not reflect the changing social climate until the 1970s.

64. Debra Boyer and David Fine, "Sexual Abuse as a Factor in Adolescent Pregnancy and Child Maltreatment," *Family Planning Perspectives* 24 (1992): 4–19.

65. Maria C. Velez-Pastrana, Rafael A. Gonzalez-Rodriguez, Adalisse Borges-Hernandez, "Family Functioning and Early Onset of Sexual Intercourse in Latino Adolescents," *Adolescence* 40 (2005): 777–791.

66. Emily Rosenbaum and Denise B. Kandel, "Early Onset of Adolescent Sexual Behavior and Drug Involvement," *Journal of Marriage and the Family* 52, no. 3 (1990): 783–798.

67. Amy E. Houlihan, et al., "Sex and the Self: The Impact of Early Sexual Onset on the Self-Concept and Subsequent Risky Behavior of African American Adolescents," *The Journal of Early Adolescence* 28, no. 1 (2008): 70–91.

Popular Culture Promotes Teen Pregnancy and Single Parenthood

In the 2007–2008 school year, seventeen girls from a high school in Gloucester, Massachusetts, became pregnant. Their story became national news when the school's principal told *Time* magazine that many of the girls wanted to get pregnant, and in fact created a pact to do so.[1] As of this writing there has been no confirmation from any of the girls involved that they actually made any sort of pre-pregnancy pact—one pregnant teen from the school denied that such a pact exists—yet the story sparked a national debate about what caused these teens to get pregnant. There is a simple answer, the one you probably learned about in health class. But much of the debate focused on celebrities and representations in popular culture. *Juno*, the 2007 dark comedy about a flippant teen who becomes pregnant and decides to give her baby up for adoption, was a prime target of focus on *Good Morning America, The Today Show*, and other outlets across the media spectrum.[2] Did *Juno* make pregnancy cool? And what about Jamie Lynn Spears, the star of the tween Nickelodeon show *Zoey 101*, who became pregnant at sixteen? Was coverage of her pregnancy and subsequent delivery an inspiration to her young fans?

Regardless of what causes these and other teens to get pregnant, popular culture is capitalizing on the issue. In 2008, an NBC "reality" show, *Baby Borrowers*, featured teen couples who want to become parents babysitting for children as the children's parents watch from next door. An ABC Family program, *The Secret Life of the American Teenager*, is about a wholesome, fifteen-year-old girl-next-door type who gets pregnant. The show could have been called "The Secret Life of *an* American Teenager," but by generalizing to "the" American teenager, the show implies that this teen, in fact, could be anyone.[3]

Teen pregnancy and single parenthood are important issues in the United States; American teens are more likely to become pregnant than their counterparts in other industrialized nations.[4] Children are now much more likely to live in single parent families in the U.S. compared with past generations. These changes are significant, but what has caused them? What about celebrities who seem to glamorize single parenthood or having children outside of marriage? Do television shows featuring kids that mouth off to their parents mock the importance of families? Can movies make divorce seem like a liberating experience? While all of these issues help us raise questions about the state of relationships and families today, there are other factors that are not as visible (or frankly, as fun to talk about) that are behind the major shifts in families. Economic changes are the most central factor in the rise in single parent families, and are the best predictors of teen pregnancy. In this chapter we will explore both the cultural and structural changes that have created major shifts in how families form in the United States today, looking beyond popular culture.

Pop Culture Under Assault: The 1990s

During the decade of the 1990s, "family values" became a potent political tool. The phrase became a shortcut for particular political positions, indicating support for traditional gender roles, where women's main focus is on mothering, men's on earning, and marriage is stable, the fulcrum upon which family life rests. The family values platform was also used as a label for issues dear to many evangelical Christians, including challenges to abortion and gay and lesbian rights. Challenging an opponent's family values became a powerful weapon to cast someone as antifamily, a charge that could derail a candidate who didn't seem to at least pay lip service to family values. Criticizing popular culture is an easy way to do just that, and television and movies became a target for those from across the political spectrum.

Some of the first shots were lobbed at *The Simpsons,* the cartoon family that debuted on Fox, first as part of *The Tracey Ullman Show* in 1987, and then on its own in 1989. It has since become a widely celebrated series, but when the show first became popular critics complained that the show was a blatant assault on families. During a 1992 speech, former President George H. W. Bush stated, "We need a nation closer to the Waltons than the Simpsons."[5] Parents and educators expressed their disapproval of Bart, fearing that children would revere him as a role model. A school in South Carolina was to be named "Springfield Elementary" until someone discovered that Springfield was the name of Bart Simpson's school.[6] At that time, the Simpson family was considered the prime example of everything wrong with American families at the century's end. The kids talked back to their parents and teachers and challenged authority. Critic Frank McConnell noted that *The Simpsons* "deconstruct the myth of the happy family."[7] If we take a closer look at the Simpsons, we see a two-parent family where the mother stays home with the kids while the father works in the paid labor force. Isn't this the family values proponents' dream?

Not exactly. *The Simpsons* contains elements of family life usually left hidden from the public eye. Father Homer is often portrayed as an overweight slob who rejoices in his own laziness. We assume that the parents "parent" the children and impart their values and wisdom. However, *The Simpsons* expose the reality that sometimes children hold wisdom that their parents do not. Lisa typically knows more than both of her parents, and Bart frequently outwits them, revealing that moms and dads aren't always in charge. It is clear why parents would be uneasy with this instability, which exposes how tenuous parental power over children really is. This and other 1990s television shows, most notably *Married . . . with Children*, served as powerful critiques of family life in sharp contrast to television families of mid-century like *Leave it to Beaver*, *Father Knows Best*, and the former president's example, *The Waltons*, all of which idealize two-parent families. While these families likely bore little resemblance to most people's experiences, they seemed to provide a cultural reference that maintained the illusion of the ideal family, something that the 1990s television families did not. In any case, it is very interesting that mere *representations* of families have the power to elicit public outcry, presuming that the representations themselves are behind challenges real families face.

Were blended families more harmonious because *The Brady Bunch* seemed to forget that they were a step family? Could interracial adoptive families solve their problems in 22 minutes like the Drummonds of *Diff'rent Strokes*? Probably not, but these shows and others like them reinforced traditional paternal authority, something that became harder to do as divorce rates rose. In 1970, 3.2 percent of the population over eighteen was divorced; this number nearly doubled to 6.2 in 1980 and continued its rise to just under 9 percent in 1990.[8] The divorce rate began its steep ascent around 1960, tripling by 1980, although after 1979 the actual rate of divorce began to decline modestly.[9] Popular culture was a bit late on the scene; divorce was rarely portrayed in movies until the late 1970s with films like *An Unmarried Woman* (1978) and *Kramer vs. Kramer* (1979). On television, *Maude* (1972–1978) featured a divorced (and extremely controversial) Bea Arthur, yet this show was about a woman in middle age, with an adult daughter only a marginal character on the show. *One Day at a Time* (1975–1984) featured a divorced mother of two daughters. Rather than preceding or encouraging the divorce trend, these

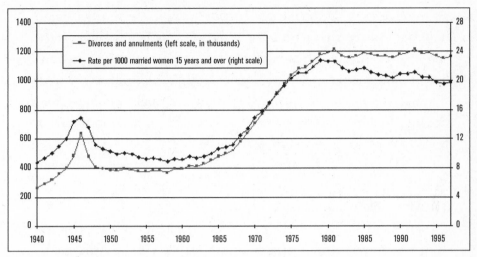

Divorces and Divorce Rates, 1940–1997.
Source: U.S. Census Bureau.

shows appeared closer to the peak of divorce rates, which subsequently leveled off.

During this time, between 1975 and 1995 particularly, birth rates to unmarried women rose significantly. In 1970, about one in ten births involved an unmarried mother. By the late 1990s the number rose to nearly one in three.[10] When unmarried television character Murphy Brown had a baby in a 1992 episode, she became the target of political ire. Former Vice President Dan Quayle accused Murphy of "mocking the importance of fathers" by having a baby without being married, which he argued contributed to the causes of the civil unrest in Los Angeles following the acquittal of the police officers accused of beating Rodney King. Quayle noted that the fact that the character was an "intelligent, highly paid professional woman" only made matters worse, since it appeared to be a "life-style choice."[11]

I suspect that Quayle was not a regular viewer of the sitcom about a clever yet complicated news anchor. If he was, he would know that the father of Murphy's baby—her ex-husband—left her upon learning of the pregnancy, which was unplanned. The choice she made to go through with the pregnancy rather than have an abortion might have been interpreted positively by those in the family values camp. But instead she embodied family values proponents' anger, not only because of her single parenthood, but likely because she symbolized the successful career woman. Murphy Brown might not have had a baby to thumb her nose at men, but her fictional fame in the traditionally male world of political journalism did challenge images of the gender order. In response, the show began the next season with Murphy suffering from sleep deprivation and struggling to cope with a newborn, hardly glamorizing single motherhood.

Beyond the debates over families remains an interesting question: Why do representations of families in popular culture strike such a nerve? Whether it be the sitcom characters of the past, or the celebrities we gossip about today, pop culture figures might not always be real, but they provide real touchstones that we can point to and all know about. Unlike individual families, which are by nature private and typically not subject to public scrutiny, fictional families and celebrity gossip are open targets. They might symbolize, and yes, sometimes help normalize issues currently undergoing societal shifts. And yet they are not the sources of change, but typically representations of larger social forces at work.

A "Murphy" Effect?
Trends in Teen and Unmarried Births

Since the *Murphy Brown* controversy we have witnessed two significant changes: many more births to unmarried women, and far *fewer* births to teenagers. In 1991, the birthrate for teens aged fifteen to nineteen was just under 62 per thousand. By 2006, this rate fell 34 percent to about 42 births per thousand. The rate had been falling annually until 2006, when it increased from 40.5 in 2005 to 41.9 births per thousand teens. For the youngest teens aged ten to fourteen, the birthrate fell more than 50 percent, from 1.4 births per thousand to .6 births per thousand. The majority of teen births are to eighteen- and nineteen-year-olds: 73 per thousand in 2006 (down 26 percent from 1991).[12] Compare these rates to the 1950s, when births to teens fifteen to nineteen peaked near *one hundred* per thousand—in other words about 10 percent of women had a baby by the time they were twenty.[13] By contrast, in 2006 just over 4 percent of women had their first child in their teen years.

There are also notable disparities by race and ethnicity. In 2006, African American teens aged fifteen to nineteen were more than twice as likely to give birth as their white counterparts (63.7 per thousand compared with 26.6 per thousand). Native Americans of the same age were about twice as likely as whites to have a baby (54.7 per thousand). Latinas are the most likely to have a baby during this time, with rates at 83.0 per thousand. By contrast, Asian American teens were the least likely to give birth, with just 16.7 per thousand having a baby in 2006.[14] Despite these differences, it is important to note that much of the decline in overall teen birthrates is due to a drastic drop in births to African American teens, from 115.5 per thousand in 1991 to 63.7 per thousand in 2006.[15]

Besides race and ethnicity, one of the best predictors of higher fertility is poverty. When the perceived loss of opportunity a baby brings is lowest, the chances of a pregnancy and birth increase.[16] For those who do not see a clear-cut path to college, for instance, or a lucrative profession that a baby might potentially disrupt, pregnancy becomes more likely. For many teens in this category, becoming a mother is a rite of passage into adulthood, a way of establishing a sense of status when few other pathways appear available. Yes, this often continues the cycle of poverty, both in the U.S. and globally. This could help explain why the U.S. has higher teen pregnancy rates than other industrialized nations do, since we also have significantly higher poverty rates here that are associated with race (I will talk more about this in Chapter 9).

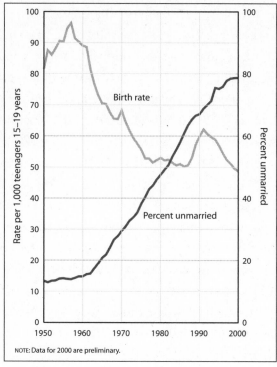

Birth Rate for Teenagers 15–19 Years and Percent of Teenage Births to Unmarried Teenagers, 1950–2000. *Source*: S. J. Ventura, T. J. Mathews, B. E. Hamilton, *National Vital Statistics Reports* 49, no 10 (Hyattsville, MD: National Center for Health Statistics, 2001), http://www .cdc.gov/nchs/data/nvsr/ nvsr49/nvsr49_10.pdf.

And yet stories about the pregnant Gloucester teens help us think that teen motherhood is a relatively new problem, rather than one in decline. Reports that Gloucester High School already has a day-care center at school made many observers shake their heads, wondering if we have grown too accepting of teens having babies. The pregnancies are not new, as noted in the figure above, where the major change is in the rise of *unmarried* teen mothers. In the 1980s we saw a turning point, where the majority of teens who had given birth did not get married first. Perhaps it is not an accident that this is the time when teen pregnancy became viewed as a major social problem. Yes, teen birth rates did rise after years of decline or stability. But what really changed was the view of marriage itself, which gradually has been detaching from parenthood.

Pregnant teens are more visible now than in midcentury, when girls were often sent away or got married; either way they were likely to drop out of school, whereas now school districts have made efforts to encourage graduation. Declines in teen marriage rates are not necessarily a bad thing: These marriages are among the most likely to end in divorce. According to a 2002 CDC report, those who marry before the age of twenty are significantly more likely to divorce than couples who are older: 48 percent of marriages with a partner under eighteen end in divorce within ten years, compared with 29 percent when the couple is over twenty-five at the time of marriage.[17] The report also concludes that marriages that come after or soon before the birth of the couple's first child are more likely to end.[18]

In any case, marriage no longer assures economic survival, particularly a marriage to a man with less education in a low-income occupation. The CDC report found that marriages in low-income communities are more likely to end: 44 percent compared with just 33 percent in middle-income communities and 23 percent in high-income areas. This percentage is especially high for African American couples in low-income areas, where 56 percent of marriages end in divorce.[19] This instability could also explain why more women are having children outside of marriage. In 2005, nearly 37 percent of all births in the United States were to unmarried women, an increase from 28 percent in 1990 and 18 percent in 1980.[20] In 2005, unmarried birth rates were highest for women in their twenties; as noted above, birth rates for teens declined between 1990 and 2005. Birthrates for unmarried women in their thirties also increased, more than doubling since 1980.[21] Births to unmarried women in their forties, like fictional character Murphy Brown, also increased from 12 percent in 1980 to 19 percent in 2005, although birth rates for this age group are lower than any other.[22]

Like Murphy, some women likely did not intend to become single mothers. And many women classified as single are not necessarily alone. According to the National Survey of Family Growth, in 2002 about 40 percent of so-called "single mothers" were cohabiting with a partner that they were not married to.[23] Others may be like Murphy in some respects: successful, unmarried, professional women, who decide to become mothers anyway.

There are significant racial/ethnic differences in unmarried mothers. Unlike Murphy and high-profile white celebrities who might have children without being married, Latinas have the highest rates, with more than one hundred births per thousand to unmarried Latina women in 2003. By contrast, nearly sixty-eight per thousand births to African American women, thirty per thousand births to white women, and twenty-five per thousand births to Asian/Pacific Islander women were unmarried. [24] And in contrast to single parent celebrities, the majority of unmarried mothers are low earners, with less education than their married counterparts.[25] So while we might see professional women with healthy incomes decide to go it alone on shows like *Oprah* and *Entertainment Tonight,* most unmarried mothers' lives are far less glamorous. Yet some, like movie critic Michael Medved, charge that celebrities who have children outside of marriage make illegitimacy "chic."[26] Have the lifestyles of actors like Angelina Jolie and Brad Pitt helped normalize what was once deviant behavior?

What Changed American Families?

While popular culture might help us get used to the idea of single parent families or having children outside of marriage, there are other major factors behind the shifts we have witnessed in the past half-century. The causes of large-scale changes to families are complex, and individual families are even more complicated. In this section I will explore four key issues that have contributed to the increase in single parent families and the rise in divorce rates since the mid-twentieth century. First, economic changes have created the need for most adults to work in the paid labor force, and have affected families in other ways that I will discuss. Second, legal changes have altered marriage, divorce, and single parenthood and are also important to consider. Third, these shifts have led to new expectations for marriage itself, leading people to marry later, and sometimes walk away from marriages. Finally, I will conclude by looking at how all of these served to create new cultural meanings and norms for families and marriage. This is where popular culture comes back into the picture.

Money Matters

We have all heard that arguments over money are a major contributor to divorce. Couples with financial problems experience more stress and interpersonal friction. But macro economic changes are important to consider as well. One of the most significant shifts has been the rise and fall of the so-called "family wage" in the twentieth century. Starting in the 1920s and accelerating after the end of World War II in 1945, real wages rose, meaning that a single (male) earner could typically support a family and an increasingly higher standard of living. This made what we often think of as the traditional family possible, and meant that for many during this time, marriage afforded substantial economic benefits to women. By contrast, being unmarried would create serious financial hardships for women, particularly if they had children. Few occupations were open to women, and those that were rarely paid enough to support a family.

Bear in mind, the low divorce rates of midcentury did not necessarily mean marriages were always happy. For some women who had worked in the labor force during World War II, the return to domesticity was not necessarily their choice, and divorce rates spiked during the war years of the 1940s. The growth of the suburbs meant that fewer extended families lived together and shared child rearing and household tasks, placing more pressure on mothers who sometimes felt isolated in new tract homes, as Betty Friedan detailed in her 1963 book *The Feminine Mystique*.

Yet the main reason many women entered the paid labor force in the last decades of the twentieth century was not personal fulfillment, but necessity. Declines in men's real wages, or the purchasing power of men's earnings, meant that many more families required a second earner. Low-income women had always worked in the labor force, but gradually the need for dual incomes trickled up class lines. This middle-class squeeze, as we have come to call it, put pressure on families in two important ways. First, it introduced new time pressures on families and challenged the traditional gender order by shifting family responsibilities. Second, as women gained economically, they had choices that their mothers likely did not. With the passage of the Equal Credit Opportunity Act, signed into law in 1974, unmarried women were able to get credit cards in their own name. This, coupled with the gradual decline in the wage gap between men and women, meant that women were no longer as economically beholden to marriage as they had been in the past. Many women no longer had to choose between staying in an unhappy marriage and becoming homeless.

Critics blamed feminism for undermining marriage, but in truth the need for women to enter the labor force in large numbers had more to do with other economic factors of the 1970s: skyrocketing inflation, led in part by high energy costs, the beginning of deindustrialization, which bled manufacturing jobs from many cities, and the decline in unions and the family wage and benefits that accompany unionized jobs. Yes, for some women getting a job meant personal fulfillment, but for the majority it was not simply a matter of choice.

Legal Changes

The divorce rate dipped after World War II and remained relatively flat until the mid-1960s, when there was a big jump. Not only did the economic circumstances create changes within families, but laws changed as well.

One such change came with the 1965 Supreme Court decision *Griswold v. Connecticut,* which overturned a state law banning the use of contraception and effectively ended the "Comstock Laws," originally passed in 1873, which made distributing information about birth control illegal and classified as obscene. This decision made birth control more widely available, and helped weaken the chain linking sex and marriage, a change that some decry and others celebrate. Just three years later in 1968, another significant decision, *Levy v. Louisiana,* gave so-called "illegitimate" children the same rights as children born to married parents. Prior to this decision, children born outside of marriage had few inheritance rights, and in this case the children born to Louise Levy were initially denied the right to sue a doctor for malpractice after their mother died, since they were not considered legitimate. Following this decision, the term "illegitimacy" no longer had legal bearing on family law, and eventually the word itself fell into disfavor.

Perhaps the biggest legal change affecting divorce rates came in 1970, with the introduction of the first no-fault divorce law in California. This meant that spouses no longer had to prove to a judge that they deserved a divorce, and it became easier if one party wanted out—with or without their spouse's agreement. Keep in mind this didn't necessarily *cause* people to get divorced; rates had been on the rise already. Instead, this served to streamline the process and reduce the need to spend significant time in the already burdened family courts. Still, critics insist that this made divorce too easy, although most people who go through a divorce will likely disagree that it is ever easy, even if the legal process has been simplified. Calls for "covenant marriage" in many states seek to allow couples to choose a form of marriage that would essentially opt them out of no-fault divorce. Ironically, these laws are often promoted by evangelical Christians, who actually have higher divorce rates than non-evangelicals.[27] To limit divorce, public policies are better served by addressing the factors that contribute to a marriage's dissolution, rather than *how* it is done legally.

The Meaning of Marriage

As marriage no longer guaranteed financial stability and courts made it easier to dissolve unhappy marriages, the meaning of marriage itself changed. In the course of a century, women gained property inheritance rights and the ability to maintain custody of children. Few divorces occurred prior to the twentieth century largely because women nearly always lost any parental rights and had no claims on any property or wealth from the marriage. As legal changes—particularly voting rights—made women full citizens, eventually with all the same rights as men, they were no longer as dependent on men for economic survival.

Marriage evolved to become less of an economic arrangement and more about personal fulfillment, although certainly a financial factor remains. As historian Stephanie Coontz writes in *Marriage, A History*, nineteenth-century observers were very concerned that marriages based on love alone would become unstable. They were correct, although from our twenty-first-century vantage point marriage based on partnership and emotional fulfillment seems superior to marriage based on maintaining family reputation, consolidating power, or the transfer of property. But as Coontz notes, "love conquered marriage." As marriage became linked with romance at the end of the nineteenth and into the twentieth century, it became more unstable, and overloaded with expectation. Instead of roles of servitude, clear-cut and unambiguous, changes in the economic structure have made marital roles more equal. I and many others would agree that this is a change for the better. By today's standards, a marriage based on having no place else to go is not much of a marriage at all.

For others, they see the effect and overlook the cause of change. Movements to reinstate patriarchal marriage that encourage women to view their husbands as the leader of the family might work in some families, but we no longer have an economic structure that supports female dependence in the manner it did in previous generations on a large scale. Not only is it impossible to roll back the clock to the preindustrial age when marriage was a vital economic arrangement, but as women entered the labor force in larger numbers the United States experienced tremendous economic growth. If somehow families could afford to live on one income (and not rely on children's labor, as many families did before the 1930s), the country's productivity would decline and the economy would shrink. Women's participation in the paid labor force is necessary on both personal and societal levels, and many women find that their contributions in the workforce are a source of fulfillment. According to the General Social Survey, a nationally representative survey conducted by the University of Michigan, in 2006 women were slightly more likely to report being highly satisfied with their work than men (52 versus 49 percent).[28]

At the same time, money has not completely separated itself from marriage. A 2006 Gallup Poll found that while married people tended to be happier than unmarried respondents, 67 percent of those with higher incomes were happy, compared with 56 percent of those married and in the lowest income group.[29]

Perhaps our expectations for marriage do not live up to the reality: According to the General Social Survey, slightly fewer married people report being very happily married today than in the 1970s, when divorce rates were skyrocketing. In 1972, 67 percent reported being very happy in their marriage, and that percentage remained in the upper sixties for most of the 1970s. In 2006, the most recent year data are available, just under 61 percent reported that their marriage was very happy, a percentage relatively representative of the responses in the 2000s. By contrast, the percent reporting that they were "not too happy" in their marriage has remained relatively stable and low: just under 3 percent in 1972, and about 2 percent in 2006.[30] This could also reflect the changing expectations people have about marriage being a source of total emotional fulfillment. But a 2007 British poll found that nearly a quarter of respondents regretted marrying their spouse, and 15 percent had reservations about getting married at the time of their wedding.[31] The survey also notes that some respondents admitted to getting married for the party and social aspects of the wedding itself.

Just as the meaning of marriage has changed, weddings have become a multibillion dollar industry. Ironically, the emphasis on elaborate weddings began as marriage itself became less stable. From relatively simple affairs for most mid-twentieth century couples to big-budget extravaganzas for many now, the wedding itself has taken on more importance. As Chrys Ingraham writes in her book *White Weddings: Romancing Heterosexuality in Popular Culture*, the "wedding-industrial complex" encourages couples to focus on throwing the most elaborate party, spending an average of nearly $28,000 per affair.[32] From the gown to the invitations, favors, food, musicians, flowers, attendants, and the honeymoon, wedding planners focus a tremendous amount of attention onto consuming the *fantasy* of marriage at the very time when the real meaning of marriage is unclear and in flux. This practice has become a part of the romantic idea of marriage, and is embedded in popular culture from movies and television shows to books, magazines, Web sites, and toys (mostly for girls). Even as women have other means to carve out a sense of identity, the wedding remains predominant—brides-to-be often describe it as "my day" or the chance to feel like a princess for a day. Of course in America, princesses exist only in fairy tales, but marriages exist in the real world. When fantasy meets reality, disappointment is likely. What impact does popular culture have on this misperception of marriage?

Happily Ever After?

While the happily-ever-after fantasy is clearly a mainstay in celebrity gossip, which fawns over weddings and babies, and in romantic comedies where love conquers all, an equally powerful part of our culture broods over marriage's demise. Critics like Michael Medved argue that movies and television often demean the importance of marriage, making divorce appear liberating and families constraining.[33] He and others look to the real lives of movie stars, particularly those who have children outside of marriage, and fear that they are setting a bad example for the rest of us. Are they negatively influencing Americans' values?

Cohabitation has become more common in American society—U.S. Census Bureau estimates suggest that just over 1.5 million heterosexual couples cohabited in 1980, rising to about 5.2 million couples by 2005.[34] Rather than simply a cultural shift, this trend in part reflects the economic changes discussed above, where marriage offers less financial stability now than in the past. Those most likely to cohabitate are those among the least likely to derive financial benefits through marriage. In a 2005 poll of young adults age eighteen to twenty-four, 59 percent agreed that it was acceptable for a couple to live together without being married, and yet 57 percent agreed that people who want children should be married.

While this might seem like young people aren't as committed to marriage, 67 percent of those polled agreed that marriages should only end in "extreme circumstances," and that it should be a lifetime commitment.[35] A 2006 *Washington Post*/Kaiser Family Foundation/Harvard University poll of American adults of all ages found that 76 percent of adults believed that marriage is very or somewhat important.[36] And most people do eventually marry—even if the union does not last. Approximately 96 percent of Americans have married at least once by the age of 65.[37] According to the U.S. Census Bureau, in 2006 half of Americans over fifteen were married, and just under 11 percent were divorced.[38]

Although much has been made recently of the declining proportion of married women, Census data indicate that in 2000 the percentage of never-married women over fifteen was *lower* than it was during the first four decades of the twentieth century. Between 1900 and 1940 the percentage of women who had not married ranged from 31 to 26 percent, compared with 24 percent in 2000. While the percentage of widowed women has remained virtually the same since 1900, the percentage of divorced women increased from 0.5 to 11 percent. Compared with the turn of the last century, more women had gotten married—and subsequently divorced—than their great-grandmothers' generation.[39] Marriage still matters and most people intend to get married. The importance of marriage can be underscored by the gay rights movement's push to be included in this still-hallowed institution.

Just because people value marriage doesn't mean it's easy to maintain. In a Pew Research Center Poll, 66 percent of respondents felt that it was hard to have a good marriage (by contrast, 21 percent said it was easy, and 9 percent said "probably impossible").[40] It is important to keep in mind that the economic pressures that make marriage more challenging, rather than the lack of values, is likely behind the break-up of many marriages. The stressors associated with economic difficulties place tremendous strain on families, stressors that often override the best intentions of wedding vows.

Popular culture is contradictory on this matter: It both celebrates marriage and increasingly supports alternatives. While it may seem as though it is leading these trends, pop culture is instead serving as an echo chamber, both reflecting back and amplifying the changing nature of personal relationships and families. Yes, celebrity gossip and entertainment no longer demonize single mothers to the extent that they might have in the past. The morality codes enforced within the film industry in Hollywood's early days have gone the way of the double feature, and television shows certainly are not as genteel as they were in the days of Ricky and Lucy Ricardo's separate beds and being "in a family way." But it is a mistake to overlook the overarching changes that have altered families—probably permanently. Popular culture may make these changes most visible, and sometimes draw criticism when we take notice. Understanding the rise in single parenthood, divorce, and changes in marriage requires more than understanding changes in the media, which often leave out the less-than-entertaining details.

Notes

1. Kathleen Kingsbury, "Pregnancy Boom at Gloucester High," *Time,* June 18, 2008, http://www.time.com/time/world/article/0,8599,1815845,00.html.

2. Ann-Marie Dorning, "Teen Baby Boom in One Mass. High School," *Good Morning America,* June 20, 2008, http://abcnews.go.com/GMA/OnCall/Story?id=5210525; "Teen 'Pregnancy Pact' has 17 Girls Expecting," *msnbc.com News Services,* June 20, 2008, http://www.msnbc.msn.com/id/25272678/.

3. ABC Family homepage for "The Secret Life of the American Teenager," http://abcfamily.go.com/abcfamily/path/section_Shows+Secret-Life-Of-The-American-Teenager/page_Season-1-Episode-1.

4. Guttmacher Institute, "Teenagers Sexual and Reproductive Health" (Washington, DC: Guttmacher Institute, 2002). Accessible online at http://www.guttmacher.org/pubs/fb_teens.pdf.

5. "Bush Barks Up Wrong Tree When He Slams Simpsons," *TV Guide,* May 23, 1992, p. 31.

6. "A Rascal Cartoon Character Sets Off Controversy in S.C.," *Los Angeles Times,* March 1, 1994, p. A5.

7. Frank McConnell, "'Real' Cartoon Characters: The Simpsons," *Commonweal,* June 15, 1990, p. 389.

8. U.S. Bureau of the Census, Table 58, *Marital Status of the Population, by Sex, Race, and Hispanic Origin: 1970 to 1994* (Washington, DC: Government Printing Office, various years).

9. U.S. Department of Health and Human Services, Underlying Population Trends, "Divorces and Divorce Rates, 1940–1997" (Washington, DC: Government Printing Office, 2000), http://www.acf.hhs.gov/programs/cse/pubs/reports/projections/ch04.html.

10. U.S. Department of Health and Human Services, Underlying Population Trends, "Nonmarital Births, 1970-1998" (Washington, DC: Government Printing Office, 2000), http://www.acf.hhs.gov/programs/cse/pubs/reports/projections/ch04.html.

11. Editorial, "Dan Quayle vs. Murphy Brown," *Time,* June 1, 1992, http://www.time.com/time/magazine/article/0,9171,975627,00.html.

12. Brady E. Hamilton, Joyce A. Martin, and Stephanie J. Ventura, "Births: Preliminary Data for 2006," *National Vital Statistics Reports* 56, no. 7 (Hyattsville, MD: National Center for Health Statistics, 2007), p. 8, http://www.cdc.gov/nchs/data/nvsr/nvsr56/nvsr56_07.pdf.

13. Stephanie J. Ventura, T. J. Mathews, and Brady E. Hamilton, "Births to Teenagers in the United States, 1940–2000," *National Vital Statistics Reports* 49, no. 10 (Hyattsville, MD: National Center for Health Statistics, 2001), figure 2, http://www.cdc.gov/nchs/data/nvsr/nvsr49/nvsr49_10.pdf, figure 2.

14. Hamilton, Martin, and Ventura, "Births," see Table 2; Births and Birth Rates, by Age, Race, and Hispanic Origin of Mother: United States.

15. Ventura, Mathews, and Hamilton, "Births to Teenagers," http://www.cdc.gov/nchs/data/nvsr/nvsr49/nvsr49_10.pdf.

16. For more discussion see Karen Sternheimer, "The Gloucester Pregnancy 'Pact': When Gossip Goes Global," *Everyday Sociology Blog,* June 30, 2008, http://nortonbooks.typepad.com/everydaysociology/2008/06/the-gloucester.html.

17. M. D. Bramlett and W. D. Mosher, "Cohabitation, Marriage, Divorce, and Remarriage in the United States," National Center for Health Statistics, *Vital Health Statistics* 23, no. 22 (2002), fig. 19, p. 18.

18. Ibid., fig. 23, p. 19.

19. Ibid., fig. 27, p. 20.

20. Hamilton, Martin, and Ventura, "Births." See Table C, "Rates for Unmarried Women, and Birth Rate for Married Women, United States, 1980 and 1985–2005," page 12.

21. Hamilton, Martin, and Ventura, "Births," fig. 7.

22. Forum on Child and Family Statistics, "Percentage of all Births to Unmarried Women by Age of Mother, 1980–2005," *America's Children: Key National Indicators of Well-Being, 2007* (Washington, DC: Government Printing Office, 2008), http://www.childstats.gov/americaschildren/famsoc2.asp.

23. Hamilton, Martin, and Ventura, "Births," p. 11.

24. Ibid.

25. Forum on Child and Family Statistics, "Percentage of all Births , 1980–2005."

26. Michael Medved, *Hollywood vs. America: Popular Culture and the War on Traditional Values* (New York: HarperCollins, 1992).

27. Christine Wicker, "Dumbfounded by Divorce," *Dallas Morning News,* June 17, 2000, http://www.adherents.com/largecom/baptist_divorce.html; Bramlett and Mosher, "Cohabitation," table 15, p. 49.

28. Tom W. Smith, "Job Satisfaction in America: Trends and Socio-Demographic Correlates," *General Social Survey* (Chicago: National Opinion Research Center, 2007), http://www-news.uchicago.edu/releases/07/pdf/070827.jobs.pdf.

29. "Poll: Marriage + money = happiness," *United Press International,* January 12, 2007, http://www.physorg.com/news87830140.html.

30. General Social Survey, *Happiness of Marriage, 1972–2006* (Chicago: National Opinion Research Center, 2007).

31. "Almost a Quarter of Britons Regret Marriage," *Reuters*, April 12, 2007, http://www.reuters.com/article/gc08/idUSL1235270420070412.

32. Chrys Ingraham, *White Weddings: Romancing Heterosexuality in Popular Culture*, 2nd ed. (New York: Routledge, 2008), p. 9.

33. Medved, *Hollywood vs. America*.

34. U.S. Census Bureau, Current Population Reports, "Table 52: Unmarried Couples by Selected Characteristic: 1980 to 1999," *Statistical Abstract of the United States: 2001 (120th Edition)* (Washington, DC, 2007), http://www.census.gov/prod/2002pubs/01statab/pop.pdf; U.S. Census Bureau, Current Population Reports, "Table 62: Unmarried-Partner Households by Sex of Partners and Type of Household: 2005," *Statistical Abstract of the United States: 2008 (127th Edition)* (Washington, DC, 2007), http://www.census.gov/compendia/statab/tables/08s0062.pdf.

35. Greenberg Quinlin Rosner Research telephone poll conducted with 892 adults age eighteen to twenty-four throughout the United States, August 10–17, 2005.

36. Telephone poll conducted by the Washington Post, Kaiser Family Foundation, and Harvard University of 2,864 American adults March 20–April 29, 2006.

37. U.S. Census Bureau, Current Population Survey, 2006 Annual Social and Economic Supplement, "Table A1: Marital Status of People 15 Years and Over, by Age, Sex, Personal Earnings, Race, and Hispanic Origin, 2006" (Washington, DC: Government Printing Office, 2007), http://www.census.gov/population/socdemo/hh-fam/cps2006/tabA1-all.xls.

38. U.S. Census Bureau, American Community Survey 2006, "Table S1201: Marital Status" (Washington, DC: Government Printing Office, 2007), http://www.factfinder.census.gov/servlet/STTable?_bm=y&-geo_id=01000US&-qr_name=ACS_2006_EST_G00_S1201&-ds_name=ACS_2006_EST_G00_ .

39. U.S. Census Bureau, U.S. Census of Population 1900–1950, 1960, 1970, 1980, 1990, "General Population Characteristics" (Washington, DC: Government Printing Office, various years), http://www.census.gov/population/www/socdemo/hh-fam.html.

40. Telephone poll conducted by Pew Research Center for the People and the Press, 1,501 American adults surveyed September 5–October 2, 2006.

Popular Culture Makes Kids More Materialistic Than Ever

Would you become a living advertisement for the right price? College students like Shawn Taylor of Toronto, Canada, would. In 2006, the twenty-seven-year-old journalism student told the *Toronto Sun* that he would gladly exchange the blank space on his clothing for corporate logos to help with tuition.[1] I'm not sure if Shawn found a sponsor, but his idea is not without precedent. In 2001, two New Jersey teens put themselves on the market to be walking advertisements to fellow college students in exchange for tuition dollars. And it worked—a credit card company bit and paid for their services.[2] Their plan led to massive media coverage and discussion about how branding has crept into just about every aspect of young Americans' lives, even education.[3]

It would be hard to argue that consumption is not a central facet in young peoples' lives today, mostly because it is a central defining feature of American life in general. For many Americans across the age spectrum, how much you have and what brand of stuff you buy contributes to the production of an individual's status. Our things help us acquire membership in "status communities," formal or informal groups that we try to appear to belong to based on displays of material goods. For better or for worse, our things have real implications about how others define us socially, and this process is certainly worthy of critical scrutiny.

However, most (although not all) criticism of materialism and consumerism is laid at the feet of children and teens. Concerns that young people have misguided priorities, want things they don't need that their parents can't afford, and are overly focused on material goods apply just as much to their older counterparts. Observers cite surveys that show incoming college freshmen are more likely to value their income potential than college students of the past were.[4] Television shows like MTV's *My Super Sweet 16* feature young people whose demands for high-end everything make the word "spoiled" seem like a modest understatement. A Harris Interactive Survey of eight- to eighteen-year-olds conducted in 2007 found that the majority—74 percent of teens and 66 percent of preteens—agreed that they "would be happier if I had more money to buy more things for myself."[5] A *Chicago Tribune* article that same year described tweens and teens as "the most brand-oriented and materialistic generation in history."[6]

Children and teens' increasing consumer knowledge and power clearly make some adults uneasy. In November 2004, the *Washington Post* ran a front-page article about DC area teens who do not just know about designer labels, but insist on wearing Dolce & Gabbana, Coach, Burberry, Gucci, and other high-priced brands. Cast as shallow spendthrifts whose poor parents struggle in "modest townhome[s]," the article highlights a few teens whose only sense of caution is in "sticking with Coach and Kate Spade" since "Prada is really expensive."[7]

Sometimes media coverage portrays young people not just as superficial dupes of marketers but dangerous. A 2001 *Time* magazine article titled "Who's in Charge Here?" cautioned that materialistic youth could be deadly.[8] The story starts by describing how an overindulged seventeen-year-old crashed her Mercedes into another teenager while driving drunk, killing the other teen. Anecdotes about spoiled kids abound in stories such as these, portraying marketplace knowledge as a sign of overindulgence; the *Time* article describes a preschooler who told her teacher she was wearing a Calvin Klein dress. "Kids shouldn't know about designers by age four," the teacher laments. "They should be oblivious to this stuff." I'm guessing the child was aware of designer names because they are important to her parents. Yet the problem here is cast as the child's, not the adults'.

Children continue to be the focus of our fears of hyperconsumption, especially when it appears that children's consumer knowledge is greater than that of their parents. Kids are thought to be especially influential when parents are purchasing computers or other technology products, and estimates of the amount of purchases children influence range from $100 billion to $300 billion annually.[9] A July 2001 *U.S. News & World Report* article uses the term "kidfluence" to describe the power children have to influence their parents' purchasing decisions. Kidfluence challenges the conventional notion that children are either too influential or easy prey who need protection from "premature consumerism."[10] So perhaps the power of persuasion held by advertisers is not nearly as important as children's power to persuade adults. This power threatens traditional notions of adult-child relations and repositions children as sources of knowledge. Adults are often reluctant to acknowledge the degree to which children influence us—we are more accustomed to thinking of children as learners and adults as teachers, but it also works the other way around.

A *Boston Herald* article described a child's influence on her grandfather.[11] "Grandfather . . . is putty in her seven-year-old hands," the article chided. "She knows what she wants; she works me," Grandpa admitted. According to a 2007 *Senior Journal* report, grandparents spend an estimated $27.5 billion annually on their grandchildren.[12] Presumably this is mostly by choice, not coercion. The *Herald* story went on to describe how parents can combat their persuasive kids— by using "the ultimate weapon: the word 'no.'" A mother interviewed for the piece was described as such an example, as a mom who "doesn't fall prey to pressure from her son." The language here is that of battle; words like "weapon" and "falling prey" connote a rather antagonistic relationship between children and parents in the "war" of consumption. A *Los Angeles Times* article described advertising's "blitz upon us" as a menace to unprepared adults, who must learn to "combat the effects of advertisements."[13]

Who is the battle really between? While many adults outwardly claim that the conflict is between powerful advertisers and vulnerable kids, it appears the real struggle is between adults and children, and parents don't exactly know what to do. That's probably because they are fighting a battle that might be seen instead as an opportunity to teach and learn about setting limits. Perhaps advertising creates a sense of inadequacy in parents because many can't possibly meet all of their children's material desires. As products of a consumerist society themselves, many believe that they should.

Could the temptation of an ever-increasing number of gadgets, like cell phones, iPods, flat-screen TVs, or the variety of other goods on the marketplace today be luring young people away from things that really matter? While that may be the case, focusing exclusively on young people as easily persuaded into the world of consumer goods leaves the rest of us off the hook.

Approximately two-thirds of the economic growth in the United States can be attributed to consumer purchases, meaning that consumers are the engine driving the economy. In times of trouble, be it after the attacks of September 11, 2001, or recent economic downturns, we were told by government leaders to shop our way back to good times. While excessive buying certainly has its downside including personal debt, environmental costs, and diverting us from addressing both deeper personal and social issues, our economy is predicated on consumption fervor. If we are to look critically at children and teens, we must consider adults' role in materialism as well.

Typically parents are portrayed as overwhelmed by their children's unrelenting requests for more, rather than active participants in hyperconsumption themselves.

Stories of out-of-control adult shoppers are common when the holiday buying season starts, but concerns about consumption and advertising usually focus exclusively on children and teens, because many believe that they are easily influenced. But are young people really the naïve consumers we often presume them to be? This chapter explores how and why we deflect concern about advertising and consumption onto children and teens, as well as the relationship between consumption and social problems more generally. Materialism is an issue that has real environmental effects, but by only focusing on children's materialism we do little to address what problems it might cause. In contrast to complaints that today's children are excessively materialistic as the result of advertising, this chapter considers other factors that create the tendency to view having more stuff as both personally fulfilling and socially advantageous. Complaints about children's consumption reflect ambivalence about our consumer-driven culture.

Child Consumers in Context

The fear that children are lured into our hyperconsumerist society too soon draws on romantic notions of childhood innocence, in which children are somehow untainted by consumer culture until advertisers enter their allegedly pure space. In reality, consumption often precedes birth. Parents with the means to do so spend thousands on branded nursery furniture, the right stroller, car seat, and brand-name clothes. But while blaming affluent parents for our culture of consumption may seem like the answer, the truth is our highly consumerist society has been created and sustained by a large shift in the American economy following World War II. Economist Daniel Bell described this as a "postindustrial" economy based on surplus and driven by consumption.[14] We live in a consumption-oriented society not simply because parents can't say no, but because our economy has been built on consuming abundance. Instead of recognizing how these broad economic forces shape our buying habits, we tend to blame individual consumers, and usually other peoples' consumption at that.

Some charge that parents now spend "guilt money" on children to make up for the time they can no longer spend with them because they are so busy working to buy more stuff. But Ellen Galinsky, director of the Families and Work Institute, challenged the common belief that "selfish, greedy parents . . . sacrifice their children at the altar of their own materialism." In her book *Ask the Children: What America's Children Really Think about Working Parents*, Galinsky notes that parents are in fact making family time an important priority. Suzanne Bianchi, a University of Maryland sociologist, supports this contention. In her 1998 study, Bianchi found that on average parents spend more time with children than in the past.[15] Mothers spent an average of 5.8 hours with their kids each day in 1998 (compared with 5.6 hours in 1965), and fathers spent an average of 4 hours a day with children in 1998, a sharp rise from 2.7 hours in 1965.[16]

Nonetheless, other people's parenting skills remain an easy target. Blaming other parents enables the rest of us to avoid looking at the broader economic system, which has created a culture of consumption. For example, in a *Chicago Sun-Times* op-ed article, Betsy Hart facetiously wrote that she and her husband would like to be reincarnated as their own children "because of all the neat stuff they have."[17] But she insisted that it is other parents who cross the line: "our kids' stuff pales when compared with the indulgences enjoyed by many children and teens," she explained. Others would agree with her: In December 2007, Reuters reported on an online poll where 94 percent of parents think that kids today are spoiled, but only 55 percent think their own kids are.[18]

A *San Diego Union-Tribune* headline warned parents, "Don't Give Your Kids Too Much," and claimed that overindulgence is a problem in "any income bracket."[19] By this logic, *all* children have too much—it's not just a handful of colorful examples, but allegedly a problem impacting even poor children. In a Time/CNN poll conducted in the summer of 2001, 80 percent of parents agreed with the statement that kids are more spoiled than ten to fifteen years ago.[20] For many adults, materialism appears to be a widespread problem among today's youth. A 1997 PBS special supports this belief, warning parents that "affluenza" has become a national "epidemic."[21] An anti-advertising group blames childhood affluenza on advertisers, proposing that "no advertising [should be] directed at kids that promotes an ethic of selfishness."[22] Betsy Hart concurred in her *Chicago Sun-Times* piece: "We have a serious problem of a generation of kids who don't know what it means to be told 'no.'"[23]

A whole generation? While this is quite a sweeping generalization, Hart's opinion is clearly shared by many. Each generation tends to believe that the next is worse than their own, but this is more than benign age-centrism.

In reality, the number of children in middle-income families has declined, while the proportion of children whose families earn at least four times the poverty level have increased. According to the U.S. Census Bureau, in 1980, 21 percent of children lived in high-income households, 41 percent were part of medium-income families, and 41 percent were in low-income households. By contrast, in 2006, 44 percent of children were in high-income families, 32 percent in medium, and 39 percent in low-income families.[24]

Often called the "middle class squeeze," more children are growing up affluent than a generation before, but the number of children in low-income families has not declined as significantly. This growing divide makes those at the top highly visible, but those at the bottom remain relatively invisible. By continuing to believe that greed is

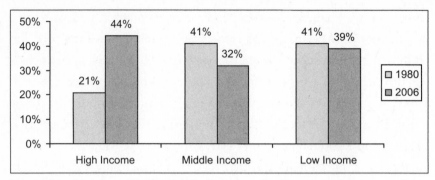

Percentage of American Children by Family Income Levels, 1980 and 2006.
Source: U.S. Census.

a characteristic of youth today, we can overlook that an estimated 1 million children suffer from neglect each year and that in any given year about one in five American children is living in poverty. Is affluenza really their biggest problem? Probably not, but believing that children are categorically overindulged diverts our attention from funding programs to assist those in need. After all, if kids have so much, why give any more money, say for public education?

We can learn more about young people's actual relationship with consumption. Sociologist Viviana Zelizer challenges the sentimentalized notion of children as helpless consumers in her analysis of children's economic roles. Her ethnographic research with children reveals that they are not just shoppers, but engage in significant economic negotiations with both adults and their peers in their everyday lives.[25]

In interviews with elementary school children and their parents, cultural anthropologist Cindy Dell Clark found that money left by the "tooth fairy" serves as an important rite of passage.[26] A child may begin to earn an allowance at this age, and thus they learn to become consumers in their own right. Clark notes that this time is often difficult for parents, who must come to terms with the fact that their child's "babyhood" has ended. So while the step towards independence is important, parents may indeed feel a powerful sense of loss that accompanies a child's entrée into the world of consumer culture. Critics may blame advertisers for luring children out into the world, but within a consumerist society this is an inevitable and necessary step toward learning to make choices in the economic world. Anxiety about young children's consumption coincides with their first steps towards independence.

Participating in consumer culture doesn't necessarily mean that children (or adults) are inordinately materialistic. In a study of pre-school children, researcher Ellen Seiter found that children use consumption to create both group and individual identity.[27] The children wore T-shirts with recognizable logos and carried lunch boxes with Disney characters to create a shared culture and let their peers know that they were "in on" kid culture. Children use consumption to begin to assert their independence from their parents, as being a consumer in American society is a step towards maturity.

Consumption is a social act: Buying may be an individual activity, but the types of purchases we make can create a sense of shared identity. Children's play with particular toys or knowing about the latest fad is a way of creating a shared culture. Adults use consumption in the same way, of course, buying cars, gadgets, and clothes that indicate we are members of various groups.

Maybe we should question why consumption is so much a part of fitting in with other kids, but we rarely ask the same question about our own behavior, like why so many adults desire a $50,000 car when the $20,000 one works just as well or better. Or why, as of July 2008, the average American household had more than $8,000 in credit card debt.[28] It's too simple to say we are all just fodder for advertising genius. We consume what we do for a number of reasons: We need things, we are making statements about who we are as individuals, and we are affiliating ourselves with certain groups, making status distinctions. Children are no different in this regard.

So we should be cautious when we criticize children for exhibiting buying habits similar to adults'. The key difference between children's consumption and our own is that as adults we tend to be outsiders in the world of children's culture. Their consumption is an easy target for us because their culture may not hold meaning for us and may even seem silly. Some parents cite the fervor over fads like Pogs or Pokemon (I confess that I once bought a pet rock as a child in the 1970s) as proof that children are easily duped into throwing money away on items adults find useless. Often adults judge children's culture based on our own tastes. When adults view children's tastes pejoratively it is easy to proclaim that slick advertisers have hoodwinked kids, rather than recognize that children may enjoy things we adults don't get.

Of course an identity only based on consumption is rather empty, and concerns about advertising often stem from the fear that consumption is making this generation more superficial than children of the past. Learning to be a responsible consumer means we all need to realize that having things will not fill all of our needs. This may be a hard lesson to teach, in part because advertisers insist their products will cure what ails us, but more importantly because lots of us have yet to master this lesson ourselves. *Los Angeles Times* fashion writer Valli Herman-Cohen gushed that she "love[s] [her] insanely expensive purse . . . and everything it says about me."[29] Although tongue-in-cheek, the author explained how good it made her feel to buy the deeply discounted bag (marked down from $2,000 to the bargain price of $1,500). At the same time we need to recognize that consumption can be pleasurable—who am I to judge how a person spends $1,500 of her own money? My point here is that we adults haven't done a great job resisting advertisers' claims that a newer new car is the answer or that we can lose ten pounds this weekend by swallowing some magic powder.

These are all serious issues to address in a consumer-oriented society, where we are told by government leaders that if we stop consuming people will lose their jobs, where interest rates are lowered to discourage saving, and we receive stimulus checks to encourage us to go shopping. We show people we love them with material goods, reward children with gifts and teach them that holidays means shopping, even if you must go into debt in the process. Consumption is the building block of a capitalist society and has become the hallmark of American culture.

Yet public discussion seldom turns a critical eye on adults. In fact, if adults do question capitalism or our culture of consumption, they tend to be viewed as extremists. But adults can safely charge the next generation for being overly materialistic or pawns of advertisers without challenging the status quo. Rather than address consumption head-on, we deflect our concerns onto children and their consumption.

If people have a problem with capitalism and consumption, fine. Just don't leave yourself out of the circle of responsibility: If kids are overly materialistic, it is because the rest of us are.

Blaming Advertisers

Beyond blaming kids themselves, advertising is an easy target to blame for our culture of consumption. According to a 2006 poll, 92 percent of parents agreed that there is too much advertising to children.[30] Advertising might seem like a good explanation for young people's consumer desires. After all, advertisers speak directly to kids, sometimes working against parents' attempts to curb their material desires.

Advertising represents a challenge to parental boundaries. Advertisers don't ask parents' permission to speak with their children; they bypass parents and tell kids about things parents sometimes don't want them to know about, like candy and sugary cereals. The fact that children are a viable target market upsets many adults; it reminds us that children's influences have expanded beyond their parents alone, and that popular culture is a major part of childhood.

There is no shortage of people who believe advertisers have an unfair advantage over children, as a variety of news reports reveal. A spring 2000 *USA Today* article reported that psychologists have considered sanctioning colleagues who consult with advertisers.[31] A *Boston Herald* story described an advocacy group called "Stop Commercial Exploitation of Children," which calls for the federal government to create new regulations like those in Norway and Sweden, which ban advertisements targeted at children under twelve.[32] The group describes advertising as "A $12.8 billion-a-year industry that targets society's most vulnerable minds and deliberately excludes parents."[33] Articles in *The Nation* and *The American Prospect* describe children as "exploited" by marketers and in need of government protection because they are vulnerable to "being programmed" and are "too young to understand . . . that advertising may be harmful."[34]

Critics frequently describe advertising as "emotionally harmful" to children, created by "corporate exploiters of children."[35] During her first campaign for the Senate, Hillary Rodham Clinton called for limits on "advertising that is harmful to children," which begs the question: When is advertising harmful?[36] Are we living in "a toxic cultural environment," as author Jean Kilbourne says, created by advertising?[37] And how exactly should we define "harm"? For some, the fact that teenagers can easily identify brands of beer from advertisements is cause for alarm.[38]

The concept of danger is difficult to empirically demonstrate but is instead described anecdotally to support demands that advertising is a clear hazard to children. Children are threatened, the logic goes, and therefore some adults ask the government (or have anointed themselves) to protect children from allegedly all-powerful advertisers. Kids are often targets of aggressive marketing campaigns, and this creates worry and anger. Children are presumed helpless in the face of advertising, described as "sacrificed for corporate profit" by manipulative, greedy Madison Avenue executives.[39] Parents are encouraged to "combat the effects of advertisements" and protect their children.[40]

There's a problem with this line of thinking, and it stems from the sentimentalized caricature of children and childhood. These advertising fears feed on this stunted, oversimplified view of children's knowledge and abilities. It's also a way to demonize advertisers as the sole source of our society's materialism without taking responsibility ourselves. Of course young people—and adults—can be influenced by advertising campaigns and enjoy partaking in consumer culture. But before we assume children are always naïve consumers, it would be wise to find out what children already know, what capabilities and limitations they possess.

So how effective are advertisers' techniques on children? Adults tend to view themselves as seasoned enough not to be vulnerable to advertising, which communication scholars call the "third-person" effect; we rarely think that we are influenced by advertising, but are certain others are, especially people we consider less competent than us.

A great deal of research suggests that children are more capable than many of us may realize. It shouldn't be a big surprise that people raised in a media-saturated society would have the ability to think beyond simply see-want-buy. Research indicates that children under six may be critical of ads and by the age of eight nearly all children are skeptical of advertisers' claims.[41] Preschool children may be less critical, but they are also far less likely to recall advertisements later.[42] One psychologist concludes that "children younger than age eight do not understand that the intent of commercials is to persuade them to buy." This makes it seem as though young children are uniformly incapable of any critical thinking. But the actual study that this claim is based on found that while children under eight are less likely than their older counterparts to get the intent of advertisers, *half* of the first-graders in the study did know that ads are about persuasion.[43]

Marketing scholar Deborah Roedder John's review of twenty-five years of advertising research suggests that preadolescents' (ten- to twelve-year-olds) knowledge about advertising tactics and skepticism level is similar to that of young adults.[44] This finding reflects psychologist Jean Piaget's theory of cognitive development, which argues that critical thinking skills appear around the age of eleven, and thereafter kids are capable of analytical reasoning. Yes, both children and adults can become more critical consumers, but we have to keep in mind that adult competencies are not dramatically better than adolescents' or even many preadolescents'.

Yet media fears continue to insist that we view children's minds as blank slates that advertisers can easily manipulate. This reinforces adult power, since critics claim to defend the allegedly weak from harm. Protection can be used to restrict, to censor, and to attempt to deny children's desires. But according to a 1998 study, teens who watch more television tend to be *more* skeptical of advertising and have greater marketplace knowledge.[45] It is too simple to view kids as helpless victims instead of as decision makers with varying levels of critical ability—like adults.

Kids also know how to influence the adults around them, which drives a lot of parents' anger at advertisers. Apparently many parents find their children's powers of persuasion irresistible, or at least annoying. As Juliet B. Schor describes in *The Overspent American: Why We Want What We Don't Need,* parents are more likely to buy items for their children when they believe that not doing so would impair their chances for success or popularity.[46] Perhaps parents are the ones that are often easily persuaded by their kids, or have trouble saying no. While it might be easier for parents if advertising for kids disappeared, helping children negotiate desires and delay gratification is an important part of parenting. As long as children and teens continue to spend billions of their own money (estimates suggest that teens spent $159 billion in 2005) they will be a sought-out market.[47] Rather than simply demand that advertising stop, we would be better off helping children become more critical of advertising and consumption more generally. But we have to start by finding out what kids already do know, rather than presuming that they are incapable of learning more.

The reality of advertising is that selling to kids is not nearly as simple as many of its detractors would have us believe. Advertisers know this and work to understand children on their terms—something the rest of us might try to do more often. While many adults jump to conclusions about children's supposed lack of critical thinking ability, advertisers' use of research enables them to have a better understanding of central issues important to young people. In fact, advertisers describe marketing to children as a bigger challenge than selling to adults.

By talking with kids for market research purposes, advertisers learn about the power struggles many children feel between themselves and their parents and reflect this back in their ad campaigns. Marketers see young people of all ages trying to create separate identities from their parents, and thus food, toys, and fashion are all marketed as ways to be distinct from adults, yet similar to their friends. Public discussions describing young people as incapable of making informed decisions enhance the tensions they feel towards adults. Of course, advertisers are certainly not child advocates, and are only interested in what kids think in order to sell them things. The imbalance of power, as well as the desire to feel grown up, to be independent yet part of the crowd, are real elements of children's lives that many adults overlook when focusing only on children's shortcomings as consumers. But advertisers don't.

Behind the Advertising Curtain

Advertising is a multibillion dollar industry, and it is easy to presume that companies wouldn't spend so much money on something that doesn't work. That's partly correct; if advertising had no impact whatsoever it probably wouldn't exist. But it also isn't a slam-dunk. Just as politicians pay political consultants millions of dollars to get elected, but sometimes lose badly, advertising—to kids especially—is not as easy as it might seem.

About a century ago, advertising became big business for several reasons unrelated to its effectiveness. First, as brands nationalized, mass advertising made more sense. With distribution channels making delivery of products easier, national brands helped consumers develop a sense of trust about the quality of the products they purchased during a time when food quality was sometimes questionable. And perhaps most importantly, a corporate excess profit tax levied after World War I meant that when businesses increased their advertising budgets they could avoid paying more taxes. Even if advertising was only mildly successful in promoting sales, it was a valued tax write-off.[48]

In order to make best use of their resources today, advertisers make a significant effort to study their target markets and learn about their values, beliefs, and lifestyles. Unlike critics who tend to make sweeping generalizations about both popular culture and young people, marketers actually talk with kids to learn about their interests and beliefs before making generalizations about them. Of course marketers are mercenaries; they are not trying to learn about people because they care, but because they want to know how best to sell to them. I am certainly not suggesting we celebrate market research departments because they listen to children; their main interest lies in co-opting youth culture and transforming it into a commodity, and the information they gather is not used to improve children's lives in a serious sort of way. Nonetheless, advertisers cannot afford to make assumptions about children's incompetence like many of the rest of us do; there is simply too much money at stake.

So how do advertisers know what they know? They rely on research in the form of surveys with older groups, but more often than not researchers become anthropologists of "kid culture."[49] They do this by conducting focus groups, where marketers select about a dozen kids from the targeted age range while a facilitator guides them in a discussion about products, what's hot and what's not. A good facilitator puts aside the role of omniscient adult long enough to let the young participants become the experts and inform the researchers about specific trends and their opinions about a product or other more general issues.

As a 2002 episode of PBS's *Frontline* titled "The Merchants of Cool" detailed, marketers struggle to pin down what is currently cool, something constantly shifting.[50] To discover the mystery of cool, researchers rely on "cool consultants," or a panel of fashion-forward young people who report on trends within their peer groups for a fee. Very young (or young-looking) marketing staffers sometimes go out in the field themselves to mingle with teens to spy on them and co-opt any new trends. Of course the preeminent goal is selling a product, but marketing research is one of the few instances where adults treat kids as the experts of their own culture, and offer a chance for them to be heard—and paid.

Companies also target fashion-forward young people who they think will influence their peers, giving them free stuff in hopes that the popular style leaders will lend their cool to new products. Marketers encourage the kids to have parties where they show their friends new products and give them samples. While critics rightly question marketers' involvement in kids' lives and the ethics of acting as if they are their friends, it is also important to consider young people's perspective in this arrangement. Not only do they get things for free (who doesn't love free stuff?), this is one of the few opportunities for young people's ideas to be valued by adults. Perhaps if their ideas were taken more seriously by their elders and they had other meaningful ways to earn money, marketers would not be so appealing to kids.[51]

Based on this research, advertisers create ads that they think will reflect central concerns that resonate with their audience, be they children, teens, or adults. Marketing executives make a priority of finding out what kids in their target demographic are most concerned with. Sociologist Michael Schudson explains that "advertisements pick up and represent values already in the culture . . . [and] pick up some of the things that people hold dear and re-present them . . . assuring them that the sponsor is the patron of common ideals."[52] Advertisements for children thus appear to be sympathetic to kids and at times critical of adults. They mirror back whatever the target market wants to hear, and this message is clearly threatening to adults.

Here's some of what market researchers have found: Not surprisingly, children often long for freedom and independence and feel constrained by adult authority while still wanting to know that they will be loved and cared for. Jane Hobson, associate director of Research International, notes, "The trick is to aim a product just high enough so that older kids pick up on it and then it can filter down."[53] Jane Mathews, a British advertising specialist, similarly reports, "Children want to seem older and in control in an adult world . . . and they want to be accepted by their friends."[54] In fact, peers are more important sources of information for young people than advertising and influence their purchases more directly. Teens are also less likely to watch television than adults, particularly if they are from affluent families.[55]

But simply understanding a target group's central concerns won't guarantee sales.[56] In fact, advertisers consider an ad campaign successful not simply based on sales but on whether ads increase brand awareness and market share. Advertising has been relatively unsuccessful in changing the size of a market and is instead most effective in obtaining a larger market share of those already consuming a product. If we consumers have an image to associate with a product, it may make us more likely to choose one particular brand over another, yet research demonstrates that brand awareness does not necessarily lead to acceptance of a product or a purchase.[57]

This does not mean that advertising is unimportant or inconsequential. On the contrary, the content of ads reveals a great deal about central issues of concern within American society. But advertising doesn't work the way many of us think it does. Commercials don't necessarily make anyone—child or otherwise—immediately think "I have to have that." Instead, advertising often works to remind us of a brand name and to link a particular image with their product. That's why most of us would feel more comfortable brushing our teeth with Crest toothpaste than a generic tube. We think we know something abut Crest, based on experience and from advertising.

Even liking an ad doesn't mean a child will want a product. For instance, an article in *Marketing*, a British trade magazine, described a ten-year-old boy who loves a yogurt commercial yet says he dislikes yogurt and does not plan on eating any.[58] The report went on to note that children often find ads entertaining, but this does not mean they are interested in the product. So children, like adults, are not necessarily tricked into buying things by slick ads that they may enjoy. Consumer behavior is more complex than cause-effect; persuasion is multifaceted and advertising is merely part of this process.

And advertisers know this. "They may be young, but they're not dumb," wrote Kristina Feliciano in *Mediaweek*, an American trade magazine.[59] "Kids don't want to be spoken down to, and they know from 'lame,'" she warned advertisers.[60] "There is no question in my mind that [teens] are more savvy shoppers," said Kristen Harmeling of research firm Yankelovich Partners Inc.[61] This information shouldn't come as a big surprise, but it is indicative of advertisers' attempts to understand children from their own perspective, rather than consider children as simply less competent than adults. Jane Mathews, the British advertising specialist, reminds her colleagues that ads that seem patronizing to children do not work. A marketing textbook offers similar "timeless rules" of advertising to the youth market: Never talk down to youth, be totally straightforward, and treat youth as if they are rational, thinking people.[62] When adults complain about children's incompetence we almost never follow these timeless rules.

Unlike most adults, advertisers do not consider their young targets particularly gullible. "If there were a magic formula, we'd all be rich," an ad executive reports.[63] Instead, trade publications often speak of children as especially skeptical and difficult to address. *Marketing* writer Patrick Barrett notes that children are not necessarily "a gullible soft target, but in fact are hard to hit and quick to switch off . . . ad messages."[64]

Advertisers are fully aware of the knowledge they possess that other adults, particularly parents, do not when it comes to understanding children. Marketing executive Andrew Marsden finds kids skeptical and knowledgeable about the communications world, and noted that children are often more independent than their parents are willing to admit.[65] "There is an element of naïveté from parents. The world they grew up in no longer exists," he remarked in *Campaign,* a marketing trade magazine.[66] He also finds teenagers to be particularly good at manipulating parents. In spite of the popular belief that advertising must be highly effective since so much money is spent doing it, advertisers are not overly confident about their ability to reach young target markets. In fact, because children are seen as a challenge, some companies such as Burger King have hired specialized agencies to handle their children's campaign. It seems it may be easier to influence their parents.

What advertisers know is not earth-shattering. It is not surprising to learn that young people are interested in connecting with peers, and that popular culture is important, as is the chance to feel heard in an adult-centered world. These ideas surface throughout advertisements created for young people. Recurring themes in children's advertising include the triumph of children over adults, freedom and adventure, and the desire to appear older. Part of what may upset adults about advertising for children is that it tends to reflect the hostility that children sometimes feel towards them. A "good" child is obedient, conforming, and accepts adult authority. Parents' central struggles with their children are about kids' resisting parental authority, which parents fight to maintain. Advertisers are well aware of the centrality of these battles, and the fantasy of outwitting adults and subverting limits prevails in many ads aimed at young people. Advertising offers the possibility of getting around adult-placed limits, addressing the desire for kids to make their own decisions and challenge parental restrictions. Several ads go beyond children merely outwitting adults and feature direct attacks on authority figures. Commercials for kids often highlight the victory of youth over authority, a reverse of the typical social order. In these worlds, it is adults who are foolish and kids who have taken over. The desire for freedom, independence, and adventure away from parents is also a theme that advertisers use in marketing products to children. Part of children's fantasy is to live in their own world, free from adult regulation and restriction, while at the same time they take comfort in knowing parents are there for them. Ads often reflect the desire to be a grown-up, or at least older. Advertisements commonly use older actors than the actual target audience. As market researcher Jane Hobson noted, advertisers presume that if older kids appear interested in a product it will seem cooler to younger kids.[67] Actors in commercials also are older than the would-be consumers because children want to appear more grown-up. A product for young children can be associated with older kids to make it seem like a product is something that even big kids think is cool. After all, older kids have more freedom, and children are frequently told to wait until they are older for certain privileges or even answers to their questions. It is no wonder that children want to be more like those who hold power, freedom, and independence.

Those who fear the power of advertising often underestimate children's abilities. Marketers, however, try to appear to be on the kids' side, acknowledging their central struggles in commercials with a wink and a nod. Adults may complain that these are the wrong messages for advertisers to send to children. But advertisers are not the originators of this message; they are instead projecting what they have learned from their research. Advertisers also know that children derive both a sense of individual identity and group membership through consumption, which adults all too often dismiss when criticizing advertising and consumption. Advertising executives do not invent the antiauthority themes that often show up in ads—they learn them through research with young consumers and mirror them back. Adults may not like to hear this message, but they are blaming the wrong messenger. If we don't like that advertisers use antiadult themes to sell products, adults may want to give them less ammunition and stop publicly condemning kids.

We seldom listen to what young people themselves say about their relationship with advertising and consumption. Writing in the *Fresno Bee* in 2003, teen Haley Minick challenged that "I do not believe my generation is an army of brainless zombies who buy whatever they come across."[68] A 2007 article in *The Charlotte Observer* allowed North Carolina teens to share their perspectives on materialism. Several comments reflected a disdain for materialism not just in their peers, but the rest of society as well.[69] Blaming either kids or advertising for our culture of consumption masks both the complex way in which it is embedded within our economy, as well as the serious social problems hyperconsumption can create—or reflect.

Consumption and Social Problems

Concerns about children's consumption can sometimes mask more serious social problems. Take public education for example. Many school districts have allowed advertising in their hallways and on their buses, and sell sugary snacks in cafeterias and vending machines in order to raise sagging revenues. In her *Toronto Star* column, writer Rachel Geise charged that "Advertising has invaded all of children's 'safe spaces' like schools and playgrounds."[70]

Advertising did enter schools as never before during the 1990s. In 1993, a Colorado Springs school district became the first in the country to court advertisers; this district had been unable to pass a school levy for nearly twenty years at that point.[71] This occurred four years after Channel One was introduced in classrooms across the country, a newslike program containing advertisements that students in host schools had no choice but to watch. In exchange a school could receive up to $50,000 in audiovisual equipment.[72] Other examples of corporate America's entrance into public schools abound:

- Coca-Cola and Pepsi each provide six-figure signing bonuses and cash advances to schools signing exclusive contracts;
- A company called ZapMe! once offered thousands of dollars worth of computer equipment and high-speed Internet access in exchange for constant ad streams and tracking students' browsing habits;[73]
- Corporations like Exxon, Kellogg's, and Domino's Pizza mail free "educational" materials like videos, posters, booklets, book covers, and software directly to teachers.

Advertisers have stepped in to fill the void left behind by a society that has steadily divested from public education. California, for example, changed property tax laws in 1978, which led to a sharp drop-off in the state's overall rank of expenditures per student.[74] A San Diego area calculus teacher dealt with cuts in his photocopying budget by selling ad space on his exams, rather than cut back on the number of practice tests for his students.[75] In some communities the local tax base has been decimated by tax breaks to lure corporations to relocate there. So as distasteful as corporate-sponsored schools, beverage contracts, and in-class market research may be, many communities have created a situation where schools are faced with few other options.

Money, lesson plans, computers, books, and audiovisual equipment are all things that schools need that we all too often fail to provide. In response to this trend, many schools currently ban sales of soda and junk food in schools, and in August 2007 a bill proposed in Massachusetts would bar any advertising and materials with logos in its schools.[76] On a smaller scale, groups such as the Center for Commercial-Free Public Schools have convinced some school board members to reconsider accepting corporate funding. But until school districts receive adequate public funding, school boards will feel pressure to take corporate money. The sad fact is advertisers often value children as consumers more than our society values them as students, and advertisers are fronting the money to prove it.

And yet young people can use the advertising in their schools to begin thinking critically about advertising. Some teachers report using the ads from Channel One or the corporate-sponsored curriculum materials to teach about propaganda and bias. Ironically, the omnipresence of ads may itself serve to drain the influence out of advertising. "They just fade into the background," a high school student remarked about the ads in his school, which are so widespread he barely noticed them anymore.[77] This is what advertisers call "clutter," turning ads into white noise that we become so accustomed to that we cease to see them after a while. Schools are beginning to look like the rest of American society, where public space is branded space.[78]

Ironically, while many people complain about corporations' influence in school, public education policy has increasingly mirrored a business model, trying to foster competition between schools via standardized tests and using funding as a reward rather than a right. This model of education makes students themselves a product. It seems that many adults have a hard time understanding success outside of the logic of consumption . . . yet we think children are especially vulnerable to corporate influence?

Advertising in schools make visible our failures in providing enough resources, yet our culture of consumption also has serious hidden costs to the environment. Buying new stuff means that the old stuff has to go somewhere, and old electronics are particularly toxic in landfills. The Environmental Protection Agency (EPA) estimates that in 2007 Americans dumped 1.84 million tons of electronic items.[79] Think about all of the devices that seem to become obsolete after just a year or two, such as cell phones, which service plans encourage us to turn over quickly. Every new phone requires assembly, and the components often create toxic gases that affect those working on assembly lines and generate pollution in the area.[80] The EPA estimates that in 2007, 126 million cell phones ended up in landfills. Some old electronics get dumped in developing countries, where workers pull apart computers and televisions with their bare hands, causing not just injury but exposure to dangerous gases.[81]

This is one area where young people are often on the forefront. As *Business Week* reported in April 2007, many college campuses are sites of environmental activism and passion.[82] For those concerned about materialism, focusing on its effects on the environment rather than condemning young people as ignorant and incapable of critical thinking is a much more powerful approach. Instead of seeing consumption as only children's problem, in reality it impacts everything from our wallets to the air we breathe.

Critical Consumerism

Consumerism is deeply intertwined with the American economy, and linked with economic growth. It is likely not going away. Instead of simply trying to eliminate children's relationship with consumer culture and suspend the inevitable, I advocate critical consumerism, which acknowledges that we are part of a consumption-based society. This means admitting that the experience of consumption can be fun and enjoyable but can also be empty, expensive, negatively impact the environment, and ultimately cannot fill every emotional need, as it often promises. Advertising is just a piece of a big puzzle and consumerism is built into the fabric of American economic and cultural life.

Parents and teachers ought to focus on preparing children to be members of a consumer-driven culture, or, if truly concerned about our consumption-based society, attempt to change the nature of the culture itself, starting with their own consumer habits. This, of course, is a much more difficult task, since many adults have no intention of changing their own behavior. So rather than continually attempting to shield children from the pervasive culture of consumption, which eventually fails, we can work to create more critical consumers, starting with ourselves.

To do so we must first acknowledge the pleasurable aspects of our own consumption and recognize that children experience the same feelings. This process must be reflective rather than authoritative; people don't want to be told they have bad taste, including children. Adults should move beyond only controlling what children purchase and seek to learn what meaning children give to products. Simply using the word "no" is not a lesson in critical consumption; teaching about the value of earning and saving through offering children the chance to earn and spend their own money is more effective than buying or not buying something for a child.

And both adults and children would benefit from challenging the belief that consumption and happiness go hand in hand. This first requires that adults think critically about why they buy what they do, and incorporating a dialogue into consumer purchases with children. As researchers Lan Nguyen Chaplin and Deborah Roedder John reported in a 2007 study, when children's self-esteem is lower they tend to seek material items for a boost. In their study, even small positive comments were effective.[83] I would predict if they replicated this study with adults their findings would likely be similar.

The fear of advertising stems from adult ambivalence about the nature of our consumer-based culture, but also from children's power to influence adults. Additionally, children use consumption to create cultural experiences separate from their parents, by aligning their tastes with peers. All of these things represent a loss of adults' control over children's worlds and thus a perceived reduction in adult authority. A child with independent tastes and desires represents a step away from conventional adult power. But rather than recognize the autonomy children may express, we are quick to blame advertisers for imposing "false" needs on children. To deny any influence of marketing and media culture would be naïve, but so too is any view of children that negates the complex process of peer culture and identity in negotiating desire.

Until we deal with the tension created by the imbalance of power between adults and children, advertisers will be able to continue to utilize this tactic to gain the trust and attention of young people. Uniformly condemning children as ignorant consumers easily swayed by advertising deepens the rift between generations. Adults cannot legislate taste or identity, nor can we ensure that kids grow up to be exactly who we hope they will become. Both children and adults can be empowered by learning to become more critical and knowledgeable about consumption, but this can't happen by only focusing on kids.

Notes

1. Mike Strobel, "College Student Hires Himself Out as a Living Billboard to Raise Money For His Tuition, Discount Jeans and Pasta Dinners," *Toronto Sun,* March 4, 2006, p. 6.

2. Kate Zernike, "And Now a Word from Their Cool College Sponsor," *New York Times,* July 19, 2001.

3. For examples, see Commercialism in Education Research Unit (CERU)'s Web site, http://epicpolicy.org/ceru-home.

4. Martha Irvine, "Youthful Dreams of Wealth," *Associated Press,* January 23, 2007.

5. Harris Interactive Press Release, "Teaching Appreciation Diminishes the Impact of Materialism," January 8, 2007, http://www.harrisinteractive.com/news/allnewsbydate.asp?NewsID=1141.

6. Julie Deardorff, "Boost Children's Self-Esteem, Curb 'Gimme' Attitude," *Chicago Tribune,* December 27, 2007.

7. Ylan Q. Mui, "At School, Labels a Runway Hit," *Washington Post,* November 29, 2004, p. A1.

8. Nancy Gibbs, et al., "Who's In Charge Here?" *Time,* August 6, 2001, p. 40.

9. Marci McDonald and Marianne Lavelle, "Call it 'Kid-fluence,'" *U.S. News & World Report,* July 30, 2001, p. 32.

10. Ibid.

11. Stephanie Schorow, "Sales Pitches Strike Out: Advocacy Group Protests Marketing to Children," *Boston Herald,* September 10, 2001, p. 31.

12. "Grandparents in U.S. Spend $27.5 Billion Annually on Their Grandchildren," *Senior Journal,* September 4, 2007, http://seniorjournal.com/NEWS/Grandparents/2007/7-09-04-GrandparentsInUS.htm.

13. Linda Bortell, "Antidote to Ad Blitz: Spending Time," *Los Angeles Times,* December 9, 2000, p. B11.

14. Daniel Bell, *The Coming of Post-Industrial Society: A Venture in Social Forecasting* (New York: Basic Books, 1976).

15. Kim Campbell, "Deprived of Parent Time? Not Most Kids," *Christian Science Monitor,* April 5, 2000, p. 1.

16. Ibid.

17. Betsy Hart, "Kids Need Parents Who Know How to Say No," *Chicago Sun-Times,* August 5, 2001, p. 28.

18. "94% of Parents Polled Say Today's Kids are Spoiled, But 55% Say Their Own Kids Are Part of Problem," *Reuters,* December 12, 2007, http://www.reuters.com/article/pressRelease/idUS165984+12-Dec-2007+PRN20071212.

19. Ann Perry, "Don't Give Your Kids Too Much, Experts Say," *San Diego Union-Tribune,* January 20, 2002, p. H1.

20. Gibbs, et al., "Who's In Charge Here?" p. 40.

21. John De Graaf, David Wann, and Thomas H. Naylor, *Affluenza: The All-Consuming Epidemic* (San Francisco: Berrett-Koehler Publishers, 2001).

22. Don Oldenburg, "Ads Aimed at Kids," *Washington Post,* May 3, 2001, p. C4.

23. Hart, "Kids Need Parents."

24. Low income is defined as families earning two times the federal poverty level or less, middle income as two to four times the poverty threshold, and high income is at least four times the poverty level. Based on U.S. Census Bureau, *Current Population Survey, 1981 to 2007 Annual Social and Economic Supplements,* http://www.childstats.gov/americaschildren/tables/econ1b.asp?popup=true and http://www.childstats.gov/americaschildren/econ_fig.asp#econfigure1b.

25. Viviana A. Zelizer, "Kids and Commerce," *Childhood* 9 (2002): 375–396.

26. Cindy Dell Clark, *Flights of Fancy, Leaps of Faith: Children's Myths in Contemporary America* (Chicago: University of Chicago Press, 1995).

27. Ellen Seiter, *Television and New Media Audiences* (Oxford: Oxford University Press, 1999).

28. Kimberly Amadeo, "July Credit Card Debt Holding Steady at $8,200 per Household," *About.Com:US Economy*, August 7, 2008, http://useconomy.about.com/b/2008/08/07/july-credit-card-debt-holding-steady-at-8200-per-household.htm.

29. Valli Herman-Cohen, "The Key to Life? It's in a Handbag," *Los Angeles Times*, February 1, 2002, p. E1.

30. Marty McGough, "Parents Eyeing Youth Marketing," *PR Week*, February 27, 2006, p. 8.

31. Marilyn Elias, "Selling to Kids Blurs Ethical Picture," *USA Today*, March 20, 2000, p. D7.

32. Schorow, "Sales Pitches Strike Out"; Ira Teinowitz, "FTC Opinion Stirs Advertiser Fears; Hands-Off Stance on Violence in Marketing May Invite Legislation," *Advertising Age*, November 27, 2000, p. 4.

33. Schorow, "Sales Pitches Strike Out."

34. Steven Manning, "Branding Kids for Life," *The Nation*, November 20, 2000, p. 7; Susan Linn, "Sellouts," *The American Prospect*, October 23, 2000, p. 17.

35. Manning, "Branding Kids for Life."

36. Ibid.

37. Lisa Prue, "Author: Advertisers Harmful to Children," *Omaha World-Herald*, April 20, 2001, p. 39.

38. Ronald Brownstein, "As Youths are Bombarded With Ads, A Pro-Family Group Counterattacks," *Los Angeles Times*, April 30, 2001, p. A5.

39. Prue, "Author."

40. Linda Bortell, "Antidote to Ad Blitz: Spending Time," *Los Angeles Times*, December 9, 2000, p. B11.

41. Michael Schudson, *Advertising, the Uneasy Persuasion: Its Dubious Impact on American Society* (New York: Basic Books, 1984), p. 233.

42. Donna R. Powlowski, Diane M. Badzinski, and Nancy Mitchell, "Effects of Metaphors on Children's Comprehension of Print Advertisements," *Journal of Advertising* 27 (1998): 83–97.

43. Sandra L. Calvert, "Children as Consumers: Advertising and Marketing," *The Future of Children* 18 (2008): 216–219.

44. Deborah Roedder John, "Consumer Socialization of Children: A Retrospective Look at Twenty-Five Years of Research," *Journal of Consumer Research* 26 (1999): 204. Also see David M. Borish, Marian Friestad, and Gregory M. Rose, "Adolescent Skepticism Toward TV Advertising and Knowledge of Advertiser Tactics," *Journal of Consumer Research* 21 (1994): 166.

45. Tamara F. Mangleberg and Terry Bristol, "Socialization and Adolescents' Skepticism Toward Advertising," *Journal of Advertising* 27 (1998): 11–20.

46. Juliet B. Schor, *The Overspent American: Why We Want What We Don't Need* (New York: HarperPerennial, 1998).

47. Teenage Research Unlimited Press Release, "TRU Projects Teens Will Spend $159 Billion in 2005," December 15, 2005, http://www.teenresearch.com/PRview.cfm?edit_id=378.

48. For discussion of the excess profits tax, see Martha Olney, *Buy Now, Pay Later: Advertising, Credit, and Consumer Durables in the 1920s* (Chapel Hill: University of North Carolina Press, 1991), p. 4.

49. Tom McGee, "Getting Inside Kids' Heads," *American Demographics* 19 (1997): 53–59.

50. "The Merchants of Cool," *Frontline,* Public Broadcasting System, February 27, 2001.

51. Alissa Quart, *Branded: The Buying and Selling of Teenagers* (New York: Basic Books, 2003); Susan Linn, *Consuming Kids: The Hostile Takeover of Childhood* (New York: The New Press, 2004).

52. Schudson, *Advertising, the Uneasy Persuasion*, p. 233.

53. Andy Fry, "Just Who are You Kidding? Techniques for Marketing to Children," *Marketing,* October 9, 1997, p. 26.

54. Patrick Barrett, "Are Ads a Danger to Kids?" *Marketing,* September 4, 1997, p. 15.

55. David L. Louden and Albert Della Bitta, *Consumer Behavior: Concepts and Applications,* 4th ed. (New York: McGraw-Hill, 1993), p. 153.

56. Reinhold Bergler, director of the Institute of Psychology at the University of Bonn, critiques what he calls "naïve everyday psychology" as employed to explain advertising's alleged effects on children. "There are no mono-causal links between advertising and the effect it has on behavior," he stated in response to the belief that young people are easily manipulated by informed advertisers. Reinhold Bergler, "The Effects of Commercial Advertising," *International Journal of Advertising* 18 (1999): 412.

57. Lucy Henke, "Young Children's Perceptions of Cigarette Brand Advertising Symbols: Awareness, Affect, and Target Market Identification," *Journal of Advertising* 24 (1995): 13–28.

58. Barrett, "Are Ads a Danger."

59. Kristina Feliciano, "Just Kidding," *Mediaweek,* May 1, 2000, p. 58.

60. Ibid.

61. Becky Sisco, "Sweet Buy and By," *Telegraph Herald,* January 9, 2005, p. B1.

62. Louden and Della Bitta, *Consumer Behavior*, p. 154.

63. Fry, "Just Who," p. 26.

64. Barrett, "Are Ads a Danger," p. 15.

65. Jade Garrett, "Are Children an Advertiser's Perfect Audience?" *Campaign,* August 25, 2000.

66. Garrett, ibid.

67. Barrett, "Are Ads a Danger."

68. Haley Minick, "Expensive Habits," *Fresno Bee,* June 8, 2003, p. H8.

69. Young Voices, "Materialistic Youth?" *The Charlotte Observer,* January 30, 2007.

70. Rachel Giese, "Those Gap Kids Ads are Not Alright!," *Toronto Star,* August 17, 2000.

71. Steven Manning, "Students for Sale," *The Nation,* September 27, 1999, p. 11.

72. See Roy Fox, *Harvesting Young Minds: How TV Commercials Control Kids* (Westport, CT: Praeger, 2000).

73. ZapMe! has since changed names and is no longer involved in educational marketing.

74. Mike A. Males, *Framing Youth: Ten Myths about the Next Generation* (Monroe, ME: Common Courage Press, 1999), chapter 9.

75. Greg Toppo and Janet Kornblum, "Ads on Tests Add up for Teacher," *USA Today*, December 2, 2008, p. 1A.

76. "Massachusetts Could Ban Advertising in Schools," Radio broadcast by KPFK Los Angeles, August 3, 2007, http://uprisingradio.org/home/?p=1755.

77. Manning, "Branding Kids for Life."

78. See Naomi Klein, *No Logo: Taking Aim at the Brand Bullies* (New York: Picador USA, 1999).

79. U.S. Environmental Protection Agency, "Statistics on the Management of Used and End-of-Life Electronics" (Washington, DC: Government Printing Office, 2007), http://www.epa.gov/osw/conserve/materials/ecycling/manage.htm, accessed December 1, 2008.

80. Sierra Club, "The World Trade Organization: Trading Away Environmental Health and Safety," http://www.sierraclub.org/trade/summit/factsa.asp.

81. Jennifer Alsever, "The 'Green' Way to Dump Electronic Junk," *msnbc.com*, April 22, 2008, http://www.msnbc.msn.com/id/24163506/.

82. Heather Green, "The Greening of America's Campuses," *Business Week*, April 9, 2007, p. 62.

83. Lan Nguyen Chaplin and Deborah Roedder John, "Growing up in a Material World: Age Differences in Materialism in Children and Adolescents," *Journal of Consumer Research* 34 (2007): 480–493. See also http://www.sciencedaily.com/releases/2007/11/071112133809.htm.

Popular Culture May Be Hazardous to Your Health

Can popular culture make kids both obese and anorexic? This seems like a contradiction, but critics charge that both are effects of our mediated culture. In particular, television, food advertisements, and video games are often blamed for contributing to child obesity (but rarely adult obesity). A *Boston Globe* article cites two prime causes, inactivity and overeating, and notes that "TV watching is linked to both of them."[1] "The simplest way to reduce obesity risk is to cut TV time," an expert quoted in the article explains. Does television really make kids fat? The American Academy of Pediatrics thinks so, which is why in 1999 they suggested that doctors ask about children's media use during check-ups.[2] One observer blames ads for junk food and watching television for creating "an obesity machine."[3]

Yet at the same time, many people blame images on television for encouraging young girls to diet. "Look at Beyoncé and Hilary Duff and all the stars you see on TV and in magazines. They're thin and they have flat stomachs and perfect everything," a seventh-grade student told a Toronto newspaper, also noting that she had two classmates with anorexia.[4] Fashion models and the magazines that feature them are also charged with contributing to body dissatisfaction. Additionally, online communities of people with anorexia and bulimia sometimes encourage and support each other in their quest to get even thinner. Is popular culture ruining our health?

In this chapter we will critically examine these claims, looking at both the complaints and the research to better understand the relationship between eating, health, and popular culture. More centrally, we will consider why popular culture once again finds itself in the center of focus, and what other causes we overlook in the meantime. Poverty, the continued objectification of women, and lack of access to quality health care seem less important when the more exciting explanations of television, advertising, video games, and fashion command our attention and interest.

Obesity

By now you have likely heard about the trend in weight gain for children and adolescents. Between 1980 and 2000, the number of children classified as overweight doubled for those aged two through eleven, and tripled for adolescents twelve to nineteen.[5] To some the reason is clear and the solution simple: Turn off the TV. Whether ads for sugary, fattening foods, or just the act of watching itself is blamed, many public health advocates, such as the Kaiser Family Foundation, believe that popular culture is the key to the problem. Here's the crux of their argument: The long-term increase in weight gain comes from the intensified marketing of low-nutrient, high-calorie foods to children, which encourages snacking while watching television.

"Our children are spending more time than ever in front of the television," writes Steven Gortmaker of the Harvard School of Public Health. He adds that because today children's programming is on around the clock, "devoted to entertaining them all day," that "kids are being taught to lead unhealthy lives from a very young age."[6] This sounds very reasonable on first glance. After all, sitting and eating in front of the television for long periods of time *is* a good way to gain weight. Spending a lot of time watching television means you are likely not doing something physically active like exercising. Problem solved?

Not so fast. Let's consider some other factors in play here. First, those who blame television advertising presume that there are more ads today for kids than in the past. But a Federal Trade Commission (FTC) study from 2005 found that kids see *fewer* ads today than they did in the 1970s, when children weighed considerably less.[7] I was a kid then, and remember ads for cereals like Super Sugar Crisp and Sugar Smacks featuring fun cartoon characters. Once upon a time, advertising that cereal had sugar wasn't just a plus for kids but for parents too. After World War II, cereal makers developed the technology to make sure added sugar stayed on cereal so parents wouldn't have to take the time to add sugar themselves. It stayed on the flakes better and most of it didn't sink to the bottom of the bowl. At a time when parents were less concerned about obesity, a sweetened cereal meant their child would likely finish their breakfast.

Second, *adults* are actually more likely to be overweight and obese than children or teens, and their rates rose even faster. Four times as many men over sixty were considered overweight in 2000 than in 1960, and three times as many women twenty to thirty-four have become overweight in this same time period.[8] In a 2005–2006 study, over one third of American adults were classified as obese (defined as having a body mass index of thirty or higher)—and nearly 40 percent of adults in their forties and fifties are obese.[9] By contrast, just over 16 percent of two- to nineteen-year-olds were deemed obese (weight above the 95th percentile for their age), with older teens more likely to be obese than young children.[10]

And yet critics only use the television explanation for children and adolescents, implying that young children are the most vulnerable to advertising. These explanations ignore the more serious problem of adults who are overweight and obese, the population more vulnerable to serious and immediate health risks of cardiovascular disease,

Type II diabetes, and many forms of cancer. Certainly public heath officials are paying serious attention to overweight adults, but the television explanation is curiously only applied to children. While adults who sit and eat in front of the TV for long stretches aren't doing themselves any favors, the existing research linking childhood obesity and television is actually much weaker than we are often told.

As with other reports that locate popular culture as a source of significant problems, the *New York Times* and other major newspapers tell us that advertising is a major culprit. A 2005 *Times* article describes "compelling evidence linking food advertising on television and the increase in obesity" based on a study by a federally appointed advisory group. The author of the study describes their research as "the nail in the coffin" in spite of the fact that we cannot definitely make a cause-effect connection between advertising and children's weight. Tom Harkin, the senator who requested the study, told the *Times* that advertising must be effective in getting kids to buy their products, otherwise they wouldn't spend the billions that they do.[11]

This claim that advertising must work because industries do it is based on circular logic: In effect, it is saying that something must be because it is. Industries do spend a great deal of money on advertising, but as I discussed in the last chapter, this doesn't mean it necessarily has the outcome advertisers intend. A 2007 *Times* article, "Study Says Junk Food Still Dominates Youth TV," also focuses on food ads as a central contributor to child obesity, after a Kaiser Family Foundation study observed that 50 percent of the advertising during children's programming are for food ads, mostly snacks and fast food.[12] "TV Helped Create the Child Obesity Problem," a *Washington Post* headline asserts.[13] Stories like these make it seem as though television is a major cause of child obesity.

A closer examination of the research reveals that the connection is not so simple. Researchers have been studying the possible link between television and obesity since at least 1985, when a large study found a correlation between television viewing and obesity.[14] A correlation indicates an association, but not causation. Some studies found similar connections, but yet others did not. A study published in 2004 found that television was not related to weight, but that video game playing had a complex relationship with children's weight: Those whose weights were higher played moderate levels of video games, while thinner kids played both low *and* high amounts. The authors found an equally complicated relationship with computer usage—those who were heavy used the computer very little or a lot, with lower weight associated with moderate levels of use.[15] Both short-term and long-term studies have been mixed in their findings. This doesn't mean that watching television for long periods of time with lots of snacking and little exercise is a good idea, just that the causes of obesity are more complex than media use. Nonetheless, experimental interventions, where one group is encouraged to watch less or no television and/or video games, have found declines in weight in the group that is supposed to watch less television.[16]

But these studies ignore one major question: What factors *lead* to more television watching and other sedentary activities in the first place? Rather than just a bad choice, watching more television and staying indoors have causes themselves. For one, children in low-income urban areas often have few safe places to play outdoors. Parents' work schedules often require these kids to have many hours with little supervision, and while watching television or playing video games inside may not be good for their waistlines, they keep them safe from potential harm on dangerous city streets. Steven Gortmaker, of Harvard's School of Public Health, barely acknowledges the significance of these issues in his *Boston Globe* op-ed. "Parents of various socio-economic backgrounds and ethnicities are reluctant to acknowledge the problem because they often feel that their parenting skills are being called into question," Gortmaker notes, suggesting that an attitude adjustment is all that these parents really need.[17]

This is about more than stubborn, prideful parents, but rather large-scale structural patterns. The Centers for Disease Control and Prevention's data on Americans and weight has found that African American and Mexican American children and adolescents are more likely to be overweight than their white counterparts. In data collected from 2005–2006, six- to eleven-year-old African American and Mexican American children were nearly twice as likely to be in the 97th weight percentile as white children in this age group. For twelve- to nineteen-year-olds, the difference is most pronounced among girls, as African Americans are more than twice as likely to be in the 97th percentile than white girls are, while the differences for boys are less dramatic, paralleling adult patterns, where significant ethnic disparities are only found in women.[18]

African Americans and Latinos are also significantly more likely to be poor than whites. According to 2007 U.S. Census data, nearly one in four African Americans lives in poverty, compared with 22 percent of Latinos and just over 8 percent of whites.[19] Poor people of color are more likely to live in urban areas with fewer playgrounds and safe spaces. These neighborhoods also have fewer grocery chains and little affordable high-quality fresh produce, but instead have an abundance of low-cost fast-food restaurants. When public health officials ignore the very real challenges parents in lower-income communities face they fail to fully address the causes of obesity.

Beyond socio-economic status, obesity itself may be a causal factor for watching more television. Low self-esteem and social rejection, which many overweight children experience, may keep them inside and perpetuate the weight-gain cycle. And where are adults in this equation? Parents who lead sedentary lives are likely to be a major determinant here. As anyone who has tried to lose weight knows, changes that may seem simple to others might not be as easy for people for whom weight it a deep-seated issue. If it were as simple as watching less television, eating healthier and exercising more, there would be no need for the weight loss industry. From the unregulated products hawked on infomercials to mainstream pharmaceuticals and bariatric surgery, obesity is, excuse the pun, a growth industry. While turning off the TV seems like an easy solution, it fails to take into account the complex realities of today's health care needs and the economic realities of many families dependent on cheap, high-fat food living in neighborhoods with few safe spaces for children to play. While poverty ironically now is a predictor of obesity, when starvation happens in the U.S. and other industrialized nations it is often the result of an eating disorder.

Anorexia and Bulimia

Just as critics blame television and other forms of popular culture for weight gain, they also blame celebrities, magazines, Web sites, and the fashion industry for contributing to eating disorders. How can watching images of mostly underweight people on television both make viewers want to eat more and less at the same time? We might carry this contradiction out by suggesting that some people respond differently to the same images, or that popular culture both makes people heavier and hate their bodies more, but no research supports this idea. Nonetheless, stories about "thinspiration" Web sites with pictures of participants and celebrities seemingly starving to death next to advice about how to continue eating disorders are unnerving. It is very compelling to think that seeing super skinny models and other celebrities in magazines, movies, and fashion show runways cause people—especially young girls—to develop eating disorders.

If this is the case, it is the extreme minority of people who are impacted in this way. It's hard to know for certain, but estimates of the number of Americans with anorexia and/or bulimia range from 7 to 9 million.[20] Focusing only on females, the National Institute of Mental Health (NIMH) notes that 0.5 percent to 3.7 percent of females will develop anorexia, and 1.1 percent to 4.2 percent will suffer from bulimia at some point in their lives.[21] While rare, these are serious disorders that can lead to major health complications and death. While the conventional wisdom has been that this is a female problem, a 2007 Harvard University study found that a quarter of their sample with eating disorders were male.[22]

Even if very few people develop eating disorders, the fashion industry seems to employ many of them. Researchers who interviewed young women found that many used modeling and other activities like gymnastics as a cover for anorexia, which suggests that rather than creating eating disorders, the fashion industry may draw some who are already anorexic and validate their behavior.[23] In 2006, two young models in Brazil and Uruguay died, apparently due to the effects of starvation. This led to calls for change within the fashion industry. That same year, Spain declared that all runway models must have a Body Mass Index (BMI) of at least 18; for instance, a five foot ten inch model needs to weigh at least 126 pounds to meet this threshold.[24] Rather than change models' body size, critics argue that this is likely to simply decrease the amount of runway work in Spain. Italy's Milan-based Chamber of Fashion proposed that models hold a license, obtainable after a panel of health experts evaluate their mental health status and verify that they have a BMI of at least 18.5 to be certified healthy.[25] The Australian Medical Association called for a similar restriction for models in Australia.[26] Going a step further, Buenos Aires province in Argentina passed a "law of sizes," which requires that clothing shops carry larger sizes or face a fine or even be forced to close.[27]

In 2008, France's National Assembly passed a bill making it illegal to publicly "incite extreme thinness." This means that creators of Web sites like the pro-anorexia and pro-bulimia sites as well as magazines could be fined up to the equivalent of $47,000 and even jailed if they appear to be providing advice and encouragement for people to become dangerously underweight.[28] Specifically, any attempt to "provoke a person to seek excessive weight loss by encouraging nutritional deprivation that would have the effect of exposing them to risk of death or endangering health" would become illegal, although perhaps difficult to prove.[29] As of this writing the bill is pending in the French senate.

Similar restrictions would violate the First Amendment in the United States, but the fashion industry here has faced pressure to make changes nonetheless. In 2007, the Council of Fashion Designers of America created a list of recommendations, including scheduling fittings for younger models earlier in the day to ensure proper sleep patterns, asking designers to "identify models with eating disorders" and to provide "more nutritious backstage catering."[30] But to paraphrase the cliché, you can bring a model to food, but you cannot make her eat, and the American industry has made it clear that they will not impose a minimum BMI for models. Clearly many of the young women—and teen girls—who walk the runways and whose images appear in fashion magazines are extremely thin and perhaps have an eating disorder. Likewise, gossip magazines are quick to point out when celebrities lose (and gain) a great deal of weight and producers are notorious for suggesting that stars lose weight. Working in the entertainment industry and living in the limelight can certainly promote unhealthy weight loss. But what about everybody else?

It may seem like a logical extension that people—especially young girls—who see these teens and young women glorified may themselves develop eating disorders. But the connection is not so simple. Psychologists who research eating disorders in all their complexity are typically reluctant to site popular culture as a key causal factor. Michael Levine, a professor of psychology at Kenyon College who studies eating disorders, told the *New York Times* in response to the proposed French law that "you're going to be hard pressed to demonstrate in a very clear way that [Web] sites have a direct negative effect" in causing eating disorders.[31] Michael Strober, director of UCLA's Eating Disorders Program told the *Los Angeles Times* that changes in the fashion industry would not necessarily reduce the incidence of eating disorders. "I don't think you can assume that there will be a dramatic protective effect if the fashion industry alters its standard of body aesthetic," he told the *Times,* but added that the attention to the problem of eating disorders was in itself positive despite the lack of any proven causal link between popular culture and eating disorders.[32] Ian Frampton, a psychologist at Exeter University, told the *Times* of London, "We need to move away from this idea that supermodels are to blame. It is probably not good for them to look as they do. But for anorexics, the desire not to eat and to be thin seems to be already in them and not something they can pick up by looking at a magazine. There were, after all, anorexics before super-thin models."[33]

Rather than a "virus" spread through media images, anorexia and bulimia's roots are much more tangled. While several studies have demonstrated a relationship between reading fashion magazines and symptoms of eating disorders (but not necessarily the actual development of a diagnosable disorder), it is very likely that those highly focused on their appearance would be drawn to such magazines.[34] So we cannot conclude from these studies that magazine reading *causes* eating disorders. Several studies have found little relationship between television and symptoms of eating disorders.[35] Respondents who report wanting to look like celebrities are more likely to increase their physical activity level, which is not necessarily a negative thing, but they are also more likely to use diet supplements.[36] Other research has pointed to family and peers as a more central influence in body image and symptoms of eating disorders. A study published in the *Journal of Marriage and Family* found that a critical family environment and having domineering parents is a key factor in adolescents with eating disorders.[37] Another study of girls aged eight to eleven found that peer body dissatisfaction is the strongest predictor of a girl's own dissatisfaction with her body (the study found that the more children's television programming the girl watched, the *less* dieting awareness she had). Watching more music videos and reading teen magazines was positively correlated with more dieting awareness, but these relationships are not as strong as peer influence. [38]

While glamorizing super-thin models and celebrities is problematic on a number of levels, body dissatisfaction and eating disorders have social and environmental roots beyond the media. Yes, popular culture has a meaningful impact on what we think of as beautiful. But because the fashion and celebrity industries provide us with so many examples of extremely thin people, we often overlook other important social factors.

As I discussed earlier in this chapter, race and poverty create important disparities in rates of obesity. But rather than just genetic or cultural differences, these differences have sociological roots as well. Sociologist Becky Wangsgaard Thompson interviewed women of varied racial, ethnic, and socioeconomic backgrounds and argues that we need to look beyond the "culture of thinness" explanation to understand what she terms "eating problems." Traditionally the culture of thinness approach focused only on young, middle-class, white, heterosexual girls and women, and ignores most others. Through her interviews, Thompson found that many of the women who are compulsive eaters or dieters had been sexually and/or physically abused; eating, dieting, or over-exercising became a coping mechanism. Likewise, some of the women noted that the stress of poverty, or dealing with racism or homophobia also led to their behavior. While the culture of thinness explanation characterizes women as simply vain and appearance obsessed, Thompson reminds us that eating problems are often not really about looks at all.[39]

Sociologists Penelope A. McLorg and Diane E. Taub also spoke with women with anorexia and bulimia, as well as observing them in university self-help group meetings. They describe how people with eating disorders often have parents who are very focused on diet and exercise, so they receive high praise for their thin appearance from both families and friends.[40] To understand the social factors that influence body dissatisfaction, we have to go beyond just looking at images in popular culture.

There are many contradictions to consider here as well. African American girls report that they are more satisfied with their bodies and focus less on trying to lose weight, a good thing if we are looking through the eating disorder lens, but not if we focus on obesity.[41] Public health officials also ironically encourage body dissatisfaction, particularly in those who are overweight and possibly at risk for weight-related ailments. So while research suggests that those who read a lot of beauty magazines might feel less satisfied with their bodies, at least in the short term, this does not mean that most of these people will develop eating disorders, particularly since most research is done with a non–eating disordered population.[42] Do media images contribute to a sense of body dissatisfaction? Quite possibly. But contributing is not the same as causing the problem in the first place, as those who are troubled about their bodies are likely to seek out information on weight loss and unfavorable comparisons that justify their negative sense of self.[43]

Still, when super-thin models represent images of beauty that are not only unrealistic but unhealthy, it is worth asking why extreme thinness became equated with beauty. Americans have been ambivalent about weight for a long time. As a nation of both plenty and poverty, we have roots in the Puritan ethic of self-restraint but also celebrate conspicuous consumption. It makes sense that we would be profoundly confused about weight and the question of how much is enough. As Hillel Schwartz, author of *Never Satisfied* writes, "On the one hand we seem to want more of everything; on the other hand we are suspicious of surplus."[44]

To understand the contemporary American focus on thinness, we have to go back much further than we might think. Further back than Twiggy, the boyishly thin supermodel of the late 1960s, and well before the current crop of stars accused of making anorexia a chic fashion statement. Many people look back to the 1950s, during Marilyn

Monroe's heyday, and mistakenly conclude that in history being full-figured was considered beautiful, and the body ideal just gets thinner and thinner over time. This might be true for a short period of time, but we need to go much further back to really understand the context of bodies and beauty.

"Fasting girls," who claimed to abstain from eating for weeks, months, or even years, have gained notoriety throughout history, from the Middle Ages through to the nineteenth century. Rather than being seen as vain or mentally ill, these girls were thought to embody spiritual purity and holiness. Some claimed to eat nothing but the holy Eucharist wafer, and thus be filled by the body of Christ alone. Many at the time thought that their lack of consumption was a bona fide miracle. Most of these claims were later debunked and found to be fraudulent, but nonetheless their existence reveals the historical connection between declining food and sanctity.[45]

As religious doctrine began to lose influence and science became more predominant, the meaning of thinness also shifted. As the medical profession gained status, doctors gradually took over as experts in matters of the body and health. But more importantly, another American institution would hold perhaps the biggest influence on body size and normality: the insurance industry. Starting in the 1830s, life insurance rates privileged thinner clients. Based on mortality rates of mainly white, middle-class people seeking policies, the definition of healthy weight fell consistently below national averages. And the industry frequently redefined healthy weight downward in order to increase premiums on a large number of customers, even as average heights increased.[46]

So an emphasis on thinness is not new. But because emaciated celebrities often parade before us, it is easy to see them as the central impetus for young girls to hate their bodies. American girls have been monitoring their body size and comparing themselves unfavorably to others for at least a century.[47] Ironically, the rise of feminism coincided with increased attention to weight. The women's movement of the late nineteenth century challenged the restrictive corsets that dominated middle-class female fashion at the time. Made with bone or metal stays, these undergarments were not just uncomfortable but impeded women's movement, breathing, and digestion at a time when doctors encouraged more exercise and focused on gastric health.[48] Obesity transitioned from being perceived as sinful—a sign of gluttony—to an illness that physicians frequently warned the public to prevent. Women learned to create internal control and take over the function that the corset once served. In the later decades of the nineteenth century, ready-made clothes became available at department stores and mail-order catalogs, further demanding conformity. Scales became more widely available at nearly any grocery or druggist's shop in an attempt to attract customers, encouraging everyone to monitor their weight.[49]

This brings us to a central point about bodies deemed too thin and too fat: Body dissatisfaction is big business. Beyond cultural shifts, genetic inheritance, and media images lies capitalism. If we all suddenly decided our bodies are just fine, we would no longer channel billions of dollars into the appearance industry. Gym memberships, cosmetic surgery, diet centers, drug and supplement manufacturers are just a few of the industries that benefit from helping to nurture body dissatisfaction. As Maggie Wykes and Barrie Gunter describe in their book *The Media and Body Image: If Looks Could Kill*, beauty holds "cultural currency," a commodity that needs to be virtually unattainable in order to maintain its value. So body dissatisfaction is not just an unfortunate side effect of beauty magazines, but in some ways a central facet of the way we do business.

Health Hazards

While we are busy worrying about what's advertised on television or how thin models and celebrities are, America's health care system is in a state of emergency. The biggest threat to American children's health is not the fashion or advertising industries, but the failure of the health care industry. In 2000, the World Health Organization listed the U.S. health care system as 37th in the world—well below other industrialized nations in the top ten and a notch below Costa Rica's.[50]

A growing number of people considered middle income have no health insurance; 53 percent of low-income families, 41 percent of moderate income households and 18 percent of middle-income families went without health insurance for part or all of 2005.[51] Between 2000 and 2006, the number of uninsured Americans grew by 8.6 million, many of them children with working parents who cannot afford the extra costs of health care coverage.[52] As a 2008 *60 Minutes* story detailed, many struggling families have forgone regular medical care and waited in line for hours to be seen at a volunteer center staffed by doctors, dentists, and nurses who normally donate their services in developing nations.[53] This problem is likely to continue, as fewer employers offer health insurance—down from 70 percent of employers in 2000 to 60 percent in 2007. For jobs that do offer insurance, premiums have also skyrocketed from an average of just over $7,000 a year in 2001 to over $12,000 in 2007, making health insurance increasingly unaffordable to many working families who earn too much for state or federal aid. The increase in health care costs also increases expenses for businesses, which must either raise prices for consumers and/or freeze wages for employees in order to afford to provide insurance.[54] According to the authors of *The Fragile Middle Class,* over half of bankruptcies in the U.S. are caused by the costs associated with a serious health problem.

The Children's Defense Fund (CDF) published a report in 2006 that found that the interplay between environmental factors, economic disparities, and the lack of quality health care has led to a growing gap in life expectancy.[55] According to the CDF report, in

2002 about 10 percent of African American children and 21 percent of Latino children had no health insurance. By comparison, nearly 7 percent of white children had no health insurance and 3 percent had no usual place of health care. Nearly 6 percent of African American and 12 percent of Latino kids had no regular health care source.[56]

These racial/ethnic disparities carry over into other arenas of life too: Lower income children of color are more likely to attend schools in cities without playgrounds and with large (if any) physical education classes.[57] The CDF report recommends a community based approach to dealing with obesity, recognizing the need to address infrastructure issues like transportation and group programs rather than individual-based suggestions like just turning off the television set. CDF also suggests creating culturally-based activities, such as using hip-hop or Latin music and dance, and incorporating Native American traditions of running into community activities.[58] Rather than pronouncements from mostly white upper-middle class researchers, real change comes from partnering with communities and recognizing the realities of their circumstances in order to create opportunities for leading healthier lifestyles.

Rather than focusing primarily on television viewing, public health officials need to take full consideration of children's lives into account. A study published in the *New England Journal of Medicine* in 2007 found that when children do see a doctor, the quality of care is often lacking (the authors note that care for adults is similar). Researchers observed that children received appropriate care from physicians less than half of the time. Children with acute medical problems got the proper care the most, nearly 68 percent of the time according to the study, but just over half of the time (53 percent) for chronic conditions, and just under 41 percent of the time for preventative measures.[59] Further, the study found that just 31 percent of children aged three to six were weighed and measured, while only 15 percent of adolescents stepped on a scale.[60] With this in mind, it seems unrealistic to encourage pediatricians to ask extended questions about children's media habits when the basics are often left out of routine check-ups for those that can afford them.

Yes, it's a good idea for those who are on the heavy side to watch less television and get more exercise, and we ought to critically question why models and celebrities are encouraged by their employers to maintain an unhealthy weight. We should think about why we often narrowly define beauty, and the health risks models and celebrities take in order to achieve this impossible ideal. In asking these questions, however, we need to keep the big picture in mind, that popular culture is not the biggest threat to our health as fewer and fewer Americans have access to any health care at all.

Notes

1. Cathryn M. Delude, "Your Health: Time to Take a Vacation from Television as School Ends, Keep Kids Healthy by Limiting TV Time," *Boston Globe,* June 10, 2003, p. C14.

2. Marilyn Elias, "Pediatricians Defend Media Exam; They Cite TV's Effects on Health," *USA Today,* August 3, 1999, p. 10D.

3. Nat Ives, "As National Geographic Explores Obesity, Critics Question Food Ads in its Magazine," *The New York Times,* July 21, 2004, p. C1.

4. André Picard, "Dieting Commonplace Among Preteen Girls," *Globe and Mail* (Canada), May 11, 2004, p. A21.

5. Cynthia L. Ogden, et al., "Prevalence and Trends in Overweight Among US Children and Adolescents, 1999–2000," *Journal of the American Medical Association* 288 (2002): 1728–1732, table 4.

6. Steven Gortmaker, "Twin Scourges for Kids: Obesity and Television," *Boston Globe,* October 19, 2004, p. A23.

7. Caroline E. Mayer, "Fewer Food Ads in Kids' TV Diet, New Study Finds," *Los Angeles Times,* July 16, 2005, p. E15.

8. Katherine M. Flegal, et al., "Prevalence and Trends in Obesity Among US Adults, 1999–2000," *Journal of the American Medical Association* 288 (2002): 1723–1727, table 4.

9. Cynthia L. Ogden, et al., "Obesity Among Adults in the United States: No Change Since 2003–2004," NCHS data brief no 1 (Hyattsville, MD: National Center for Health Statistics, 2007), http://www.cdc.gov/nchs/data/databriefs/db01.pdf, accessed December 3, 2008.

10. Cynthia L. Ogden, Margaret D. Carroll, and Katherine M. Flegal, "High Body Mass Index for Age Among US Children and Adolescents, 2003–2006,"

Journal of the American Medical Association 299 no. 20 (2008): 2401–2405, http://jama.ama-assn.org/cgi/content/short/299/20/2401.

11. Marian Burros, "Federal Advisory Group Calls for Change in Food Marketing to Children," *New York Times,* December 7, 2005, p. C4.

12. Elizabeth Olson, "Study Says Junk Food Still Dominates Youth TV," *New York Times,* March 29, 2007, p. C10.

13. Cecilia Capuzzi Simon, "Move it, Kid; TV Helped Create the Child Obesity Problem. Can It Help Solve it?" *Washington Post,* February 25, 2003, p. F1.

14. William Dietz and Steven Gortmaker, "Do We Fatten our Children at the TV Set? Obesity at Television Viewing in Children and Adolescents," *Pediatrics* 75 (1985): 807–812.

15. Elizabeth A. Vandewater, Mi-suk Shim, and Allison G. Caplovitz, "Linking Obesity and Activity Level with Children's Television and Video Game Use," *Journal of Adolescence* 27, no. 1 (2004): 71–85. See also T. Robinson, et al., "Does Television Viewing Increase Obesity and Reduce Physical Activity: Cross-Sectional and Longitudinal Analyses among Adolescent Girls," *Pediatrics* 81 (1993): 273–280; R. Durant and T. Baranowski, "The Relationship among Television Watching, Physical Activity, and Body Composition of Young Children," *Pediatrics* 94 (1994): 449–455.

16. Henry J. Kaiser Family Foundation, "The Role of Media in Childhood Obesity" (Washington, DC: Henry J. Kaiser Family Foundation, 2004).

17. Gortmaker, "Twin Scourges."

18. Ogden, Carroll, and Flegal, "High Body Mass"; Ogden, et al., "Obesity Among Adults."

19. U.S. Census Bureau, *Income, Poverty,* and *Health Insurance Coverage in the United States: 2007* (Washington, DC: Government Printing Office, 2008).

20. For examples of estimates, see www.anred.com.

21. National Institute of Mental Health, "The Numbers Count: Mental Disorders in America" (Washington, DC: National Institutes of Health, 2008), http://www.nimh.nih.gov/health/publications/the-numbers-count-mental-disorders-in-america.shtml#Eating.

22. Sandra G. Boodman, "Eating Disorders: Not Just for Women," *Washington Post,* March 13, 2007, p. HE1.

23. Penelope A. McLorg and Diane E. Taub, "Anorexia Nervosa and Bulimia: The Development of Deviant Identities," *Deviant Behavior* 8 (1987): 177–189.

24. Siri Agrell, "Are Thinness Laws Too Heavy-Handed?" *Globe and Mail* (Canada), April 19, 2008, p. A14.

25. Eric Wilson, "Health Guidelines Suggested for Models," *New York Times,* January 6, 2007, p. C3.

26. AAP General News Wire, "NSW: Fashion Week Moves to Ban Skinny Models," *AAP News* (Australia), March 4, 2007, p. 1.

27. Annie Kelly, "A Tiny Step for Womankind," *New Statesman,* March 27, 2006, http://www.newstatesman.com/200603270013.

28. Devorah Lauter, "France may make it illegal to promote extreme thinness," *ABC News,* April 15, 2008, http://abcnews.go.com/Health/Diet/wireStory?id=4655366.

29. Doreen Carvajal, "French Bill Takes Chic Out of Being Too Thin," *New York Times,* April 16, 2008, p. A6.

30. Eric Wilson, "Health Guidelines Suggested for Models," *New York Times,* January 6, 2007, p. C3.

31. Carvajal, "French Bill."

32. Valli Herman, "Is Skinny Going Out of Style?" *Los Angeles Times,* December 16, 2006, p. E1.

33. Fran Yeoman, "Anorexia 'Cannot be Picked up by Looking at Photographs of Super-Thin Models,'" *The Times* (London), December 17, 2007, http://www.timesonline.co.uk/tol/life_and_style/health/article3060191.ece.

34. For examples, see Kimberley K. Vaughan and Gregory T. Fouts, "Changes in Television and Magazine Exposure and Eating Disorder Symptomatology," *Sex Roles* 49 (2003): 313–320; Renee A. Botta, "For Your Health? The Relationship Between Magazine Reading and Adolescents' Body Image and Eating Disturbances," *Sex Roles* (2003): 389–400.

35. See Vaughan and Fauts, "Changes in Television"; Alison E. Field, et al., "Exposure to the Mass Media, Body Shape Concerns, and Use of Supplements to Improve Weight and Shape among Male and Female Adolescents," *Pediatrics* 116 (2005): 484.

36. Field, et al., "Exposure."

37. Susan Haworth-Hoeppner, "The Critical Shapes of Body Image: The Role of Culture and Family in the Production of Eating Disorders," *Journal of Marriage and Family* (2000): 212.

38. Hayley K. Dohnt and Marika Tiggemann, "Body Image Concerns in Young Girls: The Role of Peers and Media Prior to Adolescence," *Journal of Youth and Adolescence* 35 (2006): 141–152.

39. Becky Wangsgaard Thompson, "'A Way Outa No Way': Eating Problems Among African American, Latina, and White Women," *Gender and Society* 6 (1992): 546–561.

40. McLorg and Taub, "Anorexia Nervosa."

41. See Renée A. Botta, "The Mirror of Television: A Comparison of Black and White Adolescents' Body Image," *Journal of Communication* 49 (2000): 144–159.

42. Maggie Wykes and Barrie Gunter, *Media and Body Image: If Looks Could Kill* (London: Sage, 2005), pp. 189, 191.

43. Ibid., p. 175.

44. Hillel Schwartz, *Never Satisfied: A Cultural History of Diets, Fantasies and Fat* (New York: The Free Press, 1986), p. 5.

45. See Joan Jacobs Brumberg, *Fasting Girls: The History of Anorexia Nervosa* (New York: Vintage Books, 2000), chapter 2.

46. Schwartz, *Never Satisfied*, pp. 27, 157.

47. Brumberg, *Fasting Girls*, p. 162.

48. Schwartz, *Never Satisfied*, pp. 56, 65.

49. Ibid., p. 160.

50. World Health Organization, "Health System Attainment and Performance in all Member States, Ranked by Eight Measures, Estimates for 1997," *The World Health Report 2000* (Geneva, 2000), Annex Table 1, p. 152.

51. The Commonwealth Fund Biennial Health Insurance Survey, nationally representative telephone survey of 4,350 American adults nineteen and over, conducted August 18, 2005–January 5, 2006. Low income is defined as earning less than $20,000, moderate is more than $20,000 but less than $35,000, and middle income is between $35,000 and $59,999.

52. National Conference of State Legislatures, "Number of Uninsured" (Washington, DC: National Conference of State Legislatures, 2008), http://www.ncsl .org/programs/health/forum/chap/access.htm.

53. "U.S. Healthcare Gets Boost from Charity," *CBS News*, February 28, 2008, http://www.cbsnews.com/stories/2008/02/28/60minutes/main3889496.shtml.

54. National Coalition on Healthcare, "Facts on Health Insurance Coverage," (Washington, DC: National Coalition on Healthcare, 2008), http://www.nchc .org/facts/coverage.shtml.

55. Children's Defense Fund, "Improving Children's Health: Understanding Children's Health Disparities and Promising Approaches to Address Them" (Washington, DC: Children's Defense Fund, 2006), p. 9, http://www.childrensdefense.org/ site/DocServer/CDF_Improving_Children_s_Health_FINAL.pdf?docID=1781.

56. Ibid., p. 13.

57. Karen Sternheimer, *Kids These Days: Facts and Fictions About Today's Youth* (Lanham, MD: Rowman and Littlefield, 2006), pp. 44–47.

58. Children's Defense Fund, "Improving Children's Health," pp. 36–37.

59. Rita Mangione-Smith, et al., "The Quality of Ambulatory Care Delivered to Children in the United States," *New England Journal of Medicine* 357 (2007): 1515–1523, http://content.nejm.org/cgi/content/full/357/15/1515.

60. RAND Corporation Press Release, "New Study Finds Serious Gaps In Health Care Quality for America's Children," October 10, 2007, http://www.rand.org/ news/press/2007/10/10/index1.html.

Popular Culture Promotes Substance Abuse

I f we can be sure about anything, it is that alcohol and drug abuse contribute mightily to a variety of societal problems. Family disruption, domestic violence, general violence, and property crimes often share roots in substance abuse. Estimates from the Substance Abuse and Mental Health Services Administration (SAMHSA) suggest that about 5 million alcohol abusers have children under eighteen living with them. These parents were also very likely to smoke cigarettes and use other drugs, both legal and illegal, and their homes were more turbulent than those without substance abusing parents.[1] It is highly likely that these families also tax local social service agencies, the foster care system, and occasionally the criminal justice system. Smoking and drug and alcohol abuse also contribute substantially to health care costs; drinking and drug abuse led to approximately 1.5 million emergency room visits in 2005.[2] In 1998 the National Institute on Drug Abuse (NIDA) estimated the costs of alcohol and drug abuse to be $246 billion a year, including the costs of health care, criminal justice, and lost productivity.[3]

Understanding the causes of substance abuse is obviously in our national interest. Yet typically when we hear about smoking, drinking, and drug use, we focus only on teens, and primarily on popular culture. For instance, in 2008, hip-hop mogul Sean "Diddy" Combs appeared in ads for Ciroc vodka, adding his brand of cool to portray Ciroc as the drink of the high-end club scene. Does Combs's endorsement encourage young fans to drink alcohol? What about the CW show *Gossip Girl*, which frequently features teen drinking in a manner that *Newsday* calls a "fairly accurate depiction of teen partying across the country"?[4] Likewise, do celebrities who smoke in their movie roles promote teen smoking? Can music provide the impetus for drug use? There is no question that smoking contributes to a number of serious illnesses, including America's number one killer, cardiovascular disease. As noted above, alcohol and drug abuse lead to thousands of emergency room visits, violence, and family instability. What role does popular culture play in these problems?

As we will see in this chapter, we tend to associate substance use with teens, despite the fact that *adults* are actually more likely to smoke, drink, and take drugs. Built on the faulty assumption that kids are a key to the problems of substance abuse, many people presume that popular culture is the central culprit in creating use and abuse. Both of these assumptions help us overlook the most important reasons for abuse, and the role that parents and other adults often play in the addiction process. There are also significant economic, ethnic, and gender differences that tend to get lost when we focus so much on the media. Not only do we shift the blame onto popular culture, we also use concerns about smoking, alcohol, and drugs to demonize young people more generally.

Smoking

If there is anything to celebrate about young people today, it is the tremendous decline in the number that smoke cigarettes. According to Monitoring the Future, a nationally representative study of high school students conducted by the University of Michigan each year since 1975, about 45 percent of high school seniors reported that they had ever tried smoking in 2008. By contrast, in the 1970s nearly three-fourths of high school seniors had smoked a cigarette.[5] The number reporting smoking a half a pack or more each day also declined to less than 6 percent in 2007, down from nearly 20 percent in the late 1970s.[6] Reasons for this positive shift include an increase in public information about the dangers of smoking, taxes making cigarettes more expensive, and unique public service campaigns created by teens for teens that avoid condescension, to name just a few. Perhaps the most important explanation is the simplest: that their parents are less likely to smoke. Between 1965, when the CDC first gathered data, and 2006, the percentage of American adults who smoke was cut in half from 42 percent to 21 percent.[7]

Nonetheless, it is still important to understand what factors make someone more likely to smoke, since smoking is a major risk factor for a wide range of serious health problems. During the 1990s private tobacco industry memoranda became public and confirmed what many antismoking groups had long suspected: cigarette makers knew that the nicotine in cigarettes was addictive. This revelation led to a landmark settlement with many states to reimburse public health costs. At one point, the Food and Drug Administration (FDA) even pondered regulating tobacco products as drugs, a move that would have seriously threatened the industry's profitability. But the FDA backed off this threat; some tobacco makers reorganized, changed their names, and have largely continued unfettered. The focus gradually shifted away from the cigarette manufacturers and onto other industries that were alleged to be key sources of smoking in teens: movies and advertising.

As Mike A. Males discusses in his book *Framing Youth: Ten Myths About the Next Generation,* teens became an easy target. First, because most smokers are actually adults, the tobacco industry would lose little business (and gain some good PR) by coming out against teen smoking. Second, smoking became defined as a problem caused by reckless youth who are allegedly easily swayed by peers and popular culture. And finally, there is little political downside to focusing on teens. Adult smokers tend to resent politicians' attempts to restrict where and when they can smoke, and unlike teens, they can vote. Even nonsmokers sometimes see regulations like no smoking in public areas, as some local ordinances now require, as examples of the government overstepping individual freedoms. In their study "Blowing Smoke: Status Politics and the Shasta County Smoking Ban," published in the journal *Deviant Behavior*, sociologists Justin L. Tuggle and Malcolm D. Holmes found that a smoking ban in restaurants and bars in a northern California town was met with a great deal of resistance from its working-class residents, who saw the ban as a government intrusion.[8]

The popular culture argument enables us to overlook the biggest influence on teen smoking—family members who smoke—and blame Hollywood. I'm not suggesting that images of smoking have no impact and don't merit our critical scrutiny, only that we often get sidetracked by what is at best one of many factors in the process of deciding to smoke. And focusing on popular culture itself seems to implicate teens, who we presume are more vulnerable than the rest of us to media influences. Adult smokers get redefined as victims of their teenage selves, and get left out of the equation.

Of course we get a lot of help by the press. Other epidemiological research about smoking can be dry and perhaps too complex for a cool feature story, so the pop culture explanation grabs the spotlight. "Critics Want Smoking in Movies Doused No Ifs Ands or Butts" said a clever headline in a September 2007 issue of the *Toronto Star*. The *Christian Science Monitor* asks if there is "A Link Between Teen Smoking and Movies?" and the *Washington Times* states that "Study Links Teen Smoking to Movies." These stories appear in a variety of sections, most notably the entertainment and features sections; when other studies about smoking get published they are likely small and buried in papers' front sections—and less likely to be lead stories on the publications' Web sites. The movie angle by its very nature commands our attention.

A 2005 *Christian Science Monitor* article asked the question many people have been encouraged to wonder: Is there a link between teen smoking and movies? Quoting Stanton Glantz, director of the Center for Tobacco Control Research at the University of California at San Francisco, the article suggests that movies "[deliver] 400,000 kids a year to the tobacco industry," an ominous figure to be sure.[9]

But what does this really mean? The story cites a study published in the journal *Pediatrics* titled "Effect of Parental R-Rated Movie Restriction on Adolescent Smoking Initiation: A Prospective Study." The *Monitor* reported that "The teens who watched the most movies that featured smoking were 2.6 times more likely to try smoking than other adolescents," making it appear as though the movies were the central cause of their decision to smoke.[10]

But a closer look at the study itself reveals that the answer is not so simple. First, 90 percent of the kids they studied never smoked, regardless of whether they watched R-rated movies or not. The study mentions other important factors associated with smoking, including rebelliousness, low self-esteem, high sensation-seeking, and of course having parents who smoke. Yet the complexity of how these issues are connected does not make it into the *Monitor* story, leaving us to focus on the movies. Lastly, this study tells us about an association, not necessarily a causal connection. It could well be that lenient parents who allow young teens to see more R-rated movies provide limited monitoring overall, a factor associated with more adultlike behavior. Teens who go out a lot, regardless of where they are going, have more opportunities to smoke the less time they are committed to other nonsmoking activities. The study found that the relationship between trying a cigarette and R-rated movies is strongest for those whose parents do not smoke, an interesting finding. In all likelihood, a host of factors contributes to deciding to smoke, and yes, popular culture might be among them.

As the authors of the *Pediatrics* article acknowledge, having parents who smoke means that kids have access to cigarettes without buying them and the detailed knowledge of how to smoke. They also concede that trying a cigarette is not the same thing as becoming a regular smoker (although of course it may lead to becoming one).

A *Toronto Star* article about another study claims that it can predict who "will become lifelong smokers."[11] But the study, "Exposure to Smoking Depictions in Movies," published in the *Archives of Pediatrics and Adolescent Medicine,* only followed their subjects for two years, way too short a time for us to conclude who is a "lifelong" smoker. The authors note that at the end of their study, 125 of the 4,575 participants who remained in the follow-up group were "established smokers," a term not clearly defined, but still at less than 3 percent of their sample, far too few to conclude that "Pediatricians should . . . encourage parents to limit viewing to no more than two movies per week."[12] Like other similar studies, this one found a correlation between teen smoking and movie viewing, and as with others, the authors highlight the movie connection while downplaying other factors, such as age, race, smoking by parents and peers, lower parental education, poor school performance, and less participation in extracurricular activities. By dropping these factors from their discussion, movies do seem like a problem. But why penalize all youth when most *do not* take up the habit?

While it is important to consider the messages that popular culture communicates about smoking, we must not overlook other, arguably more central, reasons people smoke. Kids sometimes get cigarettes directly from parents, either by sneaking them or worse yet, bumming one directly off of mom or dad. Peers who smoke are also a strong predictor, as is poor school performance. Another strong predictor of trying a cigarette may seem obvious: age. The older one gets, the more likely they are to experiment with adult behaviors that are off-limits to kids.

Among adults, there are several factors that are associated with greater likelihood of smoking. According to the CDC's data, men have been and remain more likely to smoke than women. Whites and African Americans are more likely to smoke than Latinos and Asian Americans, but less likely than Native Americans are. Smoking stays relatively constant throughout the life course, diminishing only after age sixty-five. Patterns of cigarette smoking indicate that the percentage of people who have ever smoked is highest for older people, with the exception of those over sixty-five (possibly because those who never smoked have a greater likelihood of reaching sixty-five). But those who have had at least one cigarette in the past month do tend to be young adults: More than 40 percent of those between nineteen and twenty-nine report smoking at least once in the past month. By contrast, older teens sixteen through eighteen have rates of smoking in the past month similar to adults thirty-five to sixty-four. And adults over sixty-five are more likely to have smoked in the past month than their twelve- and thirteen-year-old grandchildren.[13]

Differences in education and socioeconomic status are very important determinants of who smokes. In 2006, 33 percent of adults with less than a high school diploma smoked, compared with 26 percent of high school graduates, 23 percent of those who attended college, and just 9 percent of those who completed a bachelor's degree or more. About 31 percent of people living below the poverty level smoke, compared with 20 percent at or above.[14] A 1998 Surgeon General's Report, "Tobacco Use Amongst U.S. Racial/Ethnic Minority Groups" found that much of the racial/ethnic differences found disappear when income is taken into account. The report also concludes, as we might suspect, that no single factor explains tobacco use.[15] If movies were really a central determinant of who smokes and who doesn't, it would be unlikely that we would see these huge gaps in terms of gender, race, and income.

While movies may not make us smokers, they do provide an interesting cultural backdrop to examine. When most movies were shot in black and white, smoke provided an additional visual layer in an otherwise gray backdrop. Smoking is also a storytelling shortcut that can connote attitude, relationships, desperation, anger, and a multitude of other emotions. Frankly, it is often used as a crutch by filmmakers. While smoking in movies may have reflected a common pastime midcentury, smoking is no longer a regular part of most American adults'—or teens'—lives, so it is worth questioning its inclusion, especially when it seems gratuitous. Cigarettes have all but left American television, especially compared with smoking newscasters, television hosts, and entire programs sponsored by tobacco makers in television's early years. Celebrities who smoke are subject to "gotcha" paparazzi shots in tabloids, creating potential embarrassment for those who try to maintain clean smoke-free images.

If anything, it seems that Hollywood is not keeping up with the changes in actual Americans' movement towards being non-smokers. A study conducted by researchers from Massachusetts Public Interest Research Group (MASSPIRG) found that smoking in PG-13 movies increased by 50 percent in the two years following the 1998 tobacco settlement, when the industry agreed to pay several states $245 billion over twenty-five years.[16] As fewer people smoke, it becomes harder to make the case that movies with characters who smoke are merely reflecting reality. Should directors think twice about whether a character smokes when it may be gratuitous or even a cliché? Sure. Movie smoking may be a last-ditch effort of the tobacco industry to advertise through product placement, but that has not been as effective as we might presume, even when kids are watching. Most of them just aren't lighting up.

If not the movies, what about the cartoon character Joe Camel? Did he convert any unsuspecting kids through his ads, T-shirts, and other products? Critics blamed him for being cute and enticing to a generation of would-be smokers. But the data tell us otherwise. If we look at smoking trends for high-school seniors after Joe's 1988 debut, we might be surprised. In 1988 about 66 percent of high school seniors reported that they had ever smoked a cigarette; that percentage would never be as high again. After dropping for several years, the number briefly rose to 65 percent in 1997, but then continued its decline to a low of 45 percent of high school seniors who ever tried a cigarette in 2008.[17] So while critics feared Joe Camel would seduce a new generation to smoke, the numbers don't bear that out.

Sociologist Michael Schudson analyzed the history of advertising and smoking in his book *Advertising: The Uneasy Persuasion,* and concludes that "major consumer changes are rarely wrought by advertising."[18] In the early twentieth century, female smoking posed a threat to the gender order, and women were the target of concern. Cigarette manufacturing made smoking more convenient—no longer would users need to roll their own—and the new blends made the taste milder, thus attracting more smokers. At the same time, soldiers received cigarette rations during wartime, in part because they helped with alertness and curbed appetites. Rather than the result of advertising, Schudson argues that "change in consumption patterns . . . has roots deep in cultural change and political conflict that advertising often responds to but rarely creates."[19]

I know you might be thinking, okay, that might have been true in the early decades of the twentieth century, when advertising was in its infancy, but what about its more sophisticated turn at the *end* of the century?

First, as noted earlier, regardless of the amount of money spent on ads, particularly during the Joe Camel years, use declined. Second, a 1995 study published in the *Journal of Marketing* found that a majority of very young kids (three to six years old) recognized Joe Camel and the Marlboro Man when prompted by researchers. However, the older the children were, the more likely their attitude about cigarettes was negative—it was the promotional products that the kids liked.[20] Yes, it is in bad taste to have cartoon characters promoting cigarettes, and the bad PR Camel received led to Joe's demise. But a 1997 study tells us a little more about the relationship between kids and cigarette ads. Psychologist Robin Maria Turco found that kids who have *already tried* smoking tend to have a more positive association with the ads than the fifth-, seventh-, and ninth-grade kids in her study who had never smoked. Her subjects tended to view non-smokers more positively than smokers, especially if they had never smoked themselves. This tells us that advertising itself doesn't necessarily cause kids to start smoking, and that those who do are primed by their own behavior to recognize the ads. So the ads do have an impact, particularly among those who have already smoked.[21]

Alcohol

Okay, but what about all the ads for beer during just about any sporting event? Remember those Budweiser frogs and other funny ads (although to be honest, I still don't get why people found the "Whatsuppppp?" ads so funny)—can they make drinking seem essential to having fun? In contrast to smoking, which is gradually being phased out of many forms of social life, alcohol is not. Oprah Winfrey frequently includes recipes for her favorite cocktails on her show. Our biggest celebrations, fancy meetings, and casual gatherings often involve alcohol as a normal part of adult life. It's more than popular culture that encourages young people to think that drinking is normal.

The vast majority of adults over twenty-one have had alcohol at least once, but having a drink in the past month is highest for people in their twenties and thirties. Young teens are the least likely to have had an alcoholic beverage in the past month: less than 2 percent of twelve-year-olds, and under 6 percent of thirteen-year-olds. The percentage rises with age, but fifteen- to seventeen-year-olds are still less likely to have had a drink in the past month than anyone their senior. Not surprisingly, the biggest jump in recent consumption happens when young people turn twenty-one and drinking alcohol is legal.[22]

But there is one surprise, one we seldom hear about: according to the National Survey on Drug Use and Health (NSDUH), in 2006 fifty- to fifty-four-year-olds were equally likely to binge drink (five or more drinks in the same occasion) as seventeen-year-olds. The percentage of sixty- to sixty-four-year-olds who binge drink was slightly *higher* than that of fifteen-year-olds (13 versus 12 percent), and those sixty-five and over are more likely to binge drink than young teens twelve to fourteen. In 2006, the peak for binge drinking was twenty-one, and it only gradually leveled off for people in their thirties and forties. Put another way, adults have to reach the age of *fifty-five* before they are less likely to binge than teens seventeen and younger.[23] Heavy drinking—binging more than five times within one month—also peaks at twenty-one and tapers off by thirty. But fifty-year-olds are equally likely to be classified as heavy drinkers as seventeen-year-olds (just under 7 percent of both age groups); the fifty-five to fifty-nine group is on par with sixteen-year-olds in heavy drinking, and adults sixty-five and over have heavy drinking rates similar to fifteen-year-olds (at just under 2 percent of each group). Teens twelve to fourteen are the least likely to be heavy drinkers of any age group.[24] A study released in June 2007 by the National Institute on Alcohol Abuse and Alcoholism (NIAAA) found that adults thirty to sixty-four are most likely to have alcohol abuse problems, with the average age of onset at age twenty-two and a half years old. White men earning over $70,000 are particularly likely to abuse alcohol, according to this report.[25] Also, teens with parents who binge drink are more likely to binge themselves.[26]

Yes, alcohol and cigarettes are legal for adults, and therefore adults over twenty-one and eighteen respectively have the right to drink and smoke as much as they like. While legal, these behaviors contribute substantially to public health costs, accidents, and family instability. The problem is that our typical focus only on teens takes the spotlight off of the vast majority of substance abusers: their older siblings, parents, and grandparents. The popular culture explanation that teens are uniquely vulnerable to media images due to their age doesn't even attempt to explain the persistence of substance use among adults throughout their lives, or why teens are among the *least* likely to use both legal and illegal substances.

Yet still we have a tendency to want to blame various forms of the media for enticing kids to drink. A 1998 study found that 40 percent of television shows show people consuming alcohol, including teens, although the authors found that drinking teens tend to be portrayed negatively.[27] That same year, a study published in the journal *Pediatrics* claimed that increased music video viewing contributed to the onset of drinking alcohol. The authors followed ninth graders in the San Jose, California, area for two years. While television viewing itself was not associated with drinking, nor was video game playing or computer use, the authors argue that watching music videos was a strong predictor.

Yet like most studies claiming media effects, this one only measured a correlation between the two, which the authors acknowledge does not allow them to assess causation directly. They also acknowledge that they only assessed the amount of music videos watched without regard to the content; additionally, the kids who dropped out of the study were more likely to be drinkers, further diminishing the predictive value of their findings. In spite of these shortcomings, they claim a strong association exists, measured by the odds ratio of 1:3, meaning that kids who have had a drink watch about a third more music videos than nondrinkers.[28]

Perhaps the best predictor of drinking that may be associated with greater interest in music and music videos is age. It is likely that both increase as people get older. But studies like these get news coverage, as this one did on CNN, *USA Today*, and the *Washington Post* because the media explanation is itself a hook to get our attention. Headlines like *USA Today*'s "Teen Drinking Linked to Music Videos, TV" make it appear as though the results are conclusive and clear.[29]

The rationale that music videos, laden with alcohol advertising, promote drinking might feel compelling when these and other headlines emerge. Likewise, attempts to hold advertising responsible have led to many other studies. For example, in 2006 a study published in the *Archives of Pediatrics and Adolescent Medicine* purported to find evidence that watching more television and ads for alcohol leads young people to drink more over time. "Adverts Do Make Teens Drink More," London's *Daily Mail* reported upon the study's release.[30] Their study asked respondents between the ages of fifteen and twenty-six a number of questions, including how often they drink alcohol and how much they drink, as well as how many times they had seen ads for alcohol. In addition, they found out how much money had been spent on alcohol advertising in their area, and claimed that both of these factors are positively associated with more drinking.[31] But this study has several major shortcomings, enough that other researchers publicly critiqued this study's claims within the same issue of the journal in which it was published.

The critics challenge that the majority of the sample dropped out during the study, leaving doubt to the claim that the study is really a long-term analysis of young peoples' drinking patterns. Only 31 percent of the original participants remained, in part because young adults are likely to move or change phone numbers, making it difficult to keep track of them. Second, one critic contended that the data even show the opposite of the researchers' claims: that more advertising was linked with *less* drinking.[32]

In my review of this study, two other issues stand out. While the authors suggest that people do not selectively pay attention to alcohol ads if they drink more, it is likely that people are more likely to *recall* seeing ads for alcohol if drinking is more of a regular part of their lives. And while it is interesting to assess how much money is spent on alcohol advertising within each market, the dollar amount itself does not necessarily translate into more ads shown. For instance, the authors note that during 1999–2000, alcohol advertisements cost $88,750,000 in Los Angeles, and $78,000 in Tulsa, Oklahoma, and teens in L.A. drank more. Not only are advertising costs higher in L.A., there are many more media outlets than in Tulsa (especially if we factor in ads during sporting events, with major league baseball, basketball, and other events held there). But besides the amount of advertising, we need to consider other regional factors. Compared with L.A., Tulsa is a much more religiously conservative area, and it is likely harder for young people to obtain alcohol there. These factors get left out of the study, which simply presumes strong media effects without looking at the broader context.

A similar study from 2001 found that the most important factor associated with teen drinking was positive beliefs about drinking, despite the paper's provocative title, "Frogs Sell Beer."[33] There are other important disparities not explained by media exposure; males typically drink more than females and are about twice as likely to drive after drinking. Whites and Native Americans are also more likely than other racial/ethnic groups to drink heavily, particularly in comparison with African Americans.[34] The advertising explanation can't explain these differences very well.

Does the cultural backdrop help shape ideas about drinking alcohol? Sure. But is it the most important when it comes to predicting dangerous, risky behaviors? Not exactly. According to 2004 data from the NSDUH, drinking among teens twelve to eighteen is lower than any other age group, and increases until peaking in the early twenties.[35] While teens get the lion's share of focus, drinking among minors is not nearly as big an issue as it is for young adults, who are more likely to binge drink than any other age group. One of the best predictors of alcohol consumption is getting closer to adulthood. This suggests that our ideal of quasi-prohibition has a dangerous side effect: Once young adults are away from parental supervision, lots of young people then take advantage of their newfound freedom. Young adults enrolled in college generally out-drink their peers. Nearly 19 percent of eighteen- to twenty-two-year-olds enrolled in college had a drink in the previous month, compared with just under 14 percent of those not enrolled.[36]

Drinking and driving also increases dramatically after eighteen, from 10 percent of sixteen- and seventeen-year-olds to 20 percent of eighteen- to twenty-year-olds. If you think those percentages are high, 28 percent of twenty-one- to twenty-five-year-olds have driven after drinking. Yes, 10 percent of the most inexperienced drivers getting behind the wheel after drinking is cause for concern, but so is the fact that it is only after age fifty-five that drivers are less likely to have been drinking than the teens we so often fear.[37]

Often left out of the story is the fact that although most teens will have had a drink before high school graduation, they are much less likely to than their predecessors were. According to Monitoring the Future (MTF), the annual University of Michigan survey of high school students conducted since 1975, the percentage of high school seniors who ever had a drink hovered between 90 and 93 percent throughout the 1970s and 80s, then began dropping. In the 2000s, the percentage fell below 80 for the first time and in 2008 was at 72 percent.[38]

But let's be honest about alcohol—having tasted it is not necessarily the first step on the path towards crime and depravity. In many families, including my own, we were given tastes of wine as children during religious rituals. My grandmother also had a taste for fine liqueurs, and thought that giving me little sips of brandy would refine my palate. This might seem shocking today, but by the time I was thirteen I had sampled many kinds of alcohol, all supervised by family members who themselves rarely drank and whom I *never* saw drunk. I understand that this was illegal, but in many families and in other countries this is a common practice. Alcohol never took on the forbidden fruit mystique for me, in part because I had role models of how to drink responsibly and only on special occasions.

I am not suggesting my experience be the model for other families, but our current approach to thinking about any alcohol consumption by teens as irresponsible clearly isn't working. A 1994 study in the *Journal of Health Policy* found that only about 5 out of 100,000 occasions of underage drinking draw the attention of an agency of control.[39] While the authors of this study suggest increasing enforcement, the reality is it will be extremely costly and difficult to enforce formal laws. For most adults, drinking is a widely accepted practice, and adults often convince themselves that they can handle their alcohol better than teens. Yet we don't have many opportunities for young people to learn responsible drinking behavior with older adults, but instead encourage secret drinking only among peers.

Perhaps, as Norman Constantin, director of the Public Health Institute's Center for Research on Adolescent Health and Development suggests, we try a different approach. He notes that we miss the opportunity for adults to teach young people how to drink in moderation before they leave home, which has led to the unsafe drinking practices that we so often fear.[40] This isn't easy for parents to do—as Michael Winerip writes in the *New York Times,* concerns about teen smoking and drinking has "been turned into a war of good versus evil," making adults who do drink even in moderation seem hypocritical. Teens can see that people who drink alcohol are not necessarily harming themselves, so this message ultimately fails. But as he details, parents often have no clear guidelines for teaching young people how to drink in moderation. Some parents think this means buying alcohol and allowing drinking in their homes, figuring this is safer than being someplace else. But this is not teaching moderation. Winerip decided that any evidence that his teen sons had been drinking means they had too much and would be punished. Perhaps this is why teens who live with their parents are less likely to drink as much and, more importantly, are less likely to drink and drive than teens at college are. Fear of their parents' reactions often serves as the most powerful form of control. And drinking without intoxication or other impairment is the definition of moderation. Some university presidents questioned American drinking laws in 2008, calling for a national dialogue on how to most realistically address young adults' alcohol use and abuse.[41]

There is a big difference between tasting and abusing alcohol. In 1991, MTF began asking kids if they had ever been drunk, a more important measure then ever having a drink. In 1991, 65 percent of seniors reported that they had been drunk at least once. This number has declined to 55 percent in 2008; still higher than one might prefer, but directionally the change is positive. Despite ads, MTV, movies, and other media we so often blame for promoting drinking, kids are doing it less. Maybe this is what we should be focusing on more: What has made teens *less* likely to drink alcohol in recent years?

Legal and Illegal Drugs

Teens' use of illegal drugs has also declined recently. Just under half of high school seniors had tried marijuana, the most common illegal drug, in the late 1990s, and that number declined to just under 42 percent in 2008. While it had been under 40 percent in the early 1990s, between 1978 and 1982 it hovered close to 60 percent, and stayed above 50 percent until 1988. Lifetime use for most other drugs remains low: less than 10 percent had ever tried cocaine or ecstasy, less than 3 percent had tried crystal meth, and less than 2 percent had tried heroin.[42]

Despite these and other improvements, teens remain the central target group of concern, particularly in the news media. A *Washington Post* article cites "Magazines, reality television, and movies" for their portrayal of "young, female celebrities as successful, thin—and drug users."[43] A 2005 *USA Today* story called "More Television Characters are Going to Pot" notes fears that "the glamorization of pot could boost its use among youths." Citing shows like HBO's *Entourage*, FX's *Over There*, and Showtime's *Weeds* (not exactly teen-oriented programs), the article quotes a representative for the Partnership for a Drug-Free America, who says that "These are trend-setting shows. They affect behavior and attitudes, particularly teens. When glamorization of drugs has climbed, changes in teen attitudes followed."[44] In the two years of data available since this article ran, the number of teens who ever used marijuana *fell* 3 percent. The article also addresses an important and frequently debated issue: Should popular culture portray real-life situations, which sometimes include drugs, or idealized behavior, and sacrifice a sense of reality?

Pop culture references to drugs are certainly not new; there are plenty of examples from the 1960s and even from earlier times. Songs like Cole Porter's "I Get a Kick out of You" from 1936 originally included a line about cocaine. Fats Waller's 1934 song "Viper's Drag" is about a man dreaming of "a reefer." Just as drug references have been around for decades, so have drugs. Starting with peddlers selling "health tonics" in the nineteenth century, Americans regularly dosed themselves with concoctions containing alcohol, cocaine, marijuana, morphine, and heroin, mostly without knowing that dangerous addiction could follow. In a time when the temperance movement was strong, alcohol-free tonics gained popularity, like Coca-Cola, which originally contained cocaine. At the same time, the rise of the medical profession brought with it the belief that medicines could cure everyday ailments as well as diseases. It is very likely that the period in American history that produced the most drug addicts was the Victorian era, not contemporary times. The difference is that no drugs were illegal then. The ones that became illegal were made so not just because of the danger they posed, but the allegedly dangerous *people* who took them. From fears of African Americans in the Deep South to Mexican Americans in the southwest and the youth counterculture movement, drugs associated with these groups became illegal in response to the feared threat posed by these groups.[45] While much of our angst now focuses on teens, they are only a small part of the drug-taking population.

According to the Substance Abuse and Mental Health Services Administration, in 2006, 45 percent of Americans twelve and over had ever used an illegal drug (marijuana, cocaine, heroin, hallucinogens, inhalants, or nonmedical use of pharmaceuticals). When we break down the percentage by age, we see an interesting picture, one of generational drug use jump-started by the baby boom generation. Nearly 62 percent of adults forty-five to forty-nine had used an illegal drug in their lifetime, compared with 12 percent of twelve-year-olds.[46] This percentage increases with age, up to 50 percent by age eighteen and approaching their parents' experience by the early twenties. The generational divide is clear: My age group of thirty to thirty-nine has a *lower* percentage of trying illegal drugs than those older and younger, as do those of my parents' generation over sixty, where less than 30 percent reported ever using an illegal drug. The group with the highest reported illegal drug use in the past year are eighteen- to twenty-one-years-old, with 20 to 24 percent reporting use in the past year. But illegal drug use continues through the twenties and thirties at double-digit percentages, dropping below 10 percent over age thirty-five, around the same rate as fourteen-year-olds. The recent drug use of twelve- to thirteen-year-olds is lower than all age groups except those fifty-five and older.

A significant portion of the population begins taking drugs as adults, contrary to conventional wisdom. According to the 2004

National Survey on Drug Use and Health, 42 percent of people who tried an illegal drug for the first time were over eighteen. Adults are also more likely to end up in the emergency room due to their drug use than teens; only the over-fifty-five age group is less likely than twelve- to seventeen-year-olds to go to the ER because of an illegal drug. For instance, in 2005 adults thirty-five to forty-four were almost ten times more likely than teens twelve to seventeen to visit the emergency room for cocaine use, and more than twenty times more likely to end up in the emergency room for heroin use.[47]

Recently we have heard a lot about prescription drug abuse, particularly as the Internet makes it easy to buy drugs illegally without a doctor's prescription. A *USA Today* story warns parents that teens not only use the Internet to buy drugs but talk about using them online too.[48] But using pharmaceuticals (pain relievers, tranquilizers, stimulants, or sedatives) without a prescription is also widespread among adults. The percentage peaks in the mid-twenties, with about a third having used drugs without a doctor's order, but remains relatively stable until age fifty-five. By contrast, twelve- to fourteen-year-olds' use of pharmaceuticals without a prescription is about the same as their grandparents over sixty, as young teens' use is about 6 to 10 percent, compared with about 12 percent of adults sixty to sixty-four and 4 percent for those sixty-five and older.[49]

Age is not the only factor that is associated with drug use: Males are more likely to have used any illegal drug, as are Native Americans.[50] Among those eighteen to twenty-five, the age group most likely to currently use drugs, less education is associated with drug use in the past thirty days, although not with lifetime use. Latinos and Asian Americans are less likely to use illegal drugs than other racial ethnic groups.[51] Just as with other substance use, it is likely that these factors are among the most important in understanding why people use and misuse drugs, alcohol, and tobacco. Using substances may be a coping mechanism to deal with the stress or the lack of opportunity many Native Americans feel living on reservations, with very high unemployment rates.

At the same time, we live in a society that encourages better living through chemistry. The endless ads to enhance male sexual functioning, to take away our aches and pains, to counter our poor eating habits, and just about anything else that affects a large enough group to mass produce a drug for them reminds us that drugs can make our lives better. Yes, most of these in theory require a prescription, but as CNN reported in 2008, many sites only include an online checklist instead of an in-person medical exam, meaning all anyone needs to buy drugs is an Internet connection and a valid credit card.[52] While this remains mostly unregulated, pharmaceutical companies profit from what may seem like a safe—and less demonized—way to take drugs.

Beyond the Youth-Media Diversion

By associating substance use and the problems they bring with teens and popular culture, we allow ourselves to ignore several important factors. First among them is the significant number of adults who both use and abuse alcohol, tobacco, and other drugs. While popular culture should be critically examined, sometimes it helps us to ignore the role that alcohol, tobacco, and pharmaceutical manufacturers play in selling their products to the entire population, not just youth. Most importantly, we overlook the problems that adult users cause their children and others around them on the road, at work, and elsewhere. A 2001 study found that sons of alcoholics who also exhibit antisocial behaviors perform worse in school and thus become more likely to fail academically and perpetuate the cycle of substance abuse.[53] And lastly, use is not the same as abuse; as much as it might pain our Puritan-rooted culture to acknowledge, many young people try a cigarette, drink alcohol, or even take drugs without becoming addicted or engaging in problematic behaviors. I am certainly not condoning substance use, especially in minors, but this is our reality. Use is not abuse.

Valid concerns about substance abuse enable us to engage in another favorite pastime: youth-bashing. Groups with the least social power are the easiest to blame for problems they are certainly not alone in causing. Historically, fears of youth have risen in times of demographic or economic flux, much like we are experiencing in the new millennium. As noted in Chapter 2, for the past seventy-five years young people have had increasingly less contact with adults, by virtue of institutionalized age segregation in schools and often in the workforce. This has led to the creation of a segmented youth culture that is often unknown, misunderstood, and dismissed by older adults.

Fearing youth and media culture may be a popular pastime, but it is a dangerous one. First, we consistently underestimate young people. Second, we create a hostile environment in which control and punishment replace patience and support. The popular culture so many adults decry resonates with young people in ways that adults often cannot. When adults treat teens as an enemy, even well-intended messages about smoking, drinking, and drugs can be dismissed more easily, particularly when young people see adults engaging in the same behaviors. Do as I say, not as I do will never be an effective solution. Insisting that young people are uniquely gullible to images in popular culture also creates hostility towards adults, whom teens often feel underestimate them and do not take them seriously. Instead, curbing youth substance abuse is best done in partnership with young people, who have been able to help create campaigns that do more than preach what can be seen as hypocritical messages. Treating teens as reasonable, thinking individuals has been effective in reducing smoking. By speaking to youth cynicism, rather than creating it, messages will be more effective. But first we have to refrain from the urge to demean both young people and popular culture.

Notes

1. National Survey on Drug Use and Health, "Alcohol Dependence or Abuse among Parents with Children Living in the Home," *The NSDUH Report* (Rockville, MD: Substance Abuse and Mental Health Services Administration, 2004), http://www.oas.samhsa.gov/2k4/ACOA/ACOA.htm.

2. Substance Abuse and Mental Health Services Administration, Office of Applied Studies, *Drug Abuse Warning Network, 2005: National Estimates of Drug-Related Emergency Department Visits,* DAWN Series D-29, DHHS Publication No. (SMA) 07-4256 (Rockville, MD: 2007), http://dawninfo.samhsa.gov/files/DAWN2k5ED.htm#Alced3.

3. National Institute on Alcohol Abuse and Alcoholism Press Release, "Economic Costs of Alcohol and Drug Abuse Estimated at $246 Billion in the United States," May 13, 1998 (Bethesda, MD: National Institute on Alcohol Abuse and Alcoholism), http://www.niaaa.nih.gov/NewsEvents/NewsReleases/economic.htm.

4. "An Epidemic of Teen Drinking," *Newsday,* October 23, 2007, p. B12.

5. University of Michigan, Monitoring the Future Study, "Long-Term Trends in Thirty Day Prevalence of Use of Various Drugs For Twelfth Graders," Survey Research Center, Institute for Social Research, 2008, table 15.

6. Ibid., table 17.

7. Centers for Disease Control and Prevention, "Percentage of Adults who were Current, Former, or Never Smokers, Overall and by Sex, Race, Hispanic Origin, Age, Education, and Poverty Status," National Health Interview Surveys, Selected Years—United States, 1965–2006 (Atlanta: Centers for Disease Control and Prevention, 2007), http://www.cdc.gov/tobacco/data_statistics/tables/adult/table_2.htm.

8. Justin L. Tuggle and Malcolm D. Holmes, "Blowing Smoke: Status Politics and the Shasta County Smoking Ban," *Deviant Behavior* 18 (1997): 77–94.

9. Randy Dotinga, "A Link Between Smoking and Movies?" *Christian Science Monitor,* November 22, 2005, p. 2.

10. James D. Sargent, et al., "Effect of Parental R-Rated Movie Restriction on Adolescent Smoking Initiation: A Prospective Study," *Pediatrics* 114 (2004): 149–156.

11. Brooks Bolick, "Critics Want Smoking Doused No Ifs Ands or Butts," *Toronto Star,* September 7, 2007, p. E9.

12. James Sargeant, et al., "Exposure to Smoking Depictions in Movies," *Archives of Pediatric and Adolescent Medicine* 161 (2007): 849–856.

13. National Survey on Drug Use and Health, "Tobacco Product Use in Lifetime, Past Year, and Past Month, by Detailed Age Category: Percentages, 2005 and 2006," 2006 National Survey on Drug Use & Health (Rockville, MD: Substance Abuse and Mental Health Services Administration, 2008), http://oas.samhsa.gov/NSDUH/2k6NSDUH/tabs/Sect2peTabs1t042.htm#Tab2.11B.

14. Centers for Disease Control and Prevention, "Percentage of Adults."

15. U.S. Department of Health and Human Services, *Tobacco Use Among U.S. Racial/Ethnic Minority Groups—African Americans, American Indians and Alaska Natives, Asian Americans and Pacific Islanders, and Hispanics: A Report of the Surgeon*

General (Atlanta: U.S. Department of Health and Human Services, Centers for Disease Control and Prevention, National Center for Chronic Disease Prevention and Health Promotion, Office on Smoking, 1998), http://www.cdc.gov/tobacco/data_statistics/sgr/sgr_1998/sgr-min-sgr2.htm.

16. Crystal Ng and Bradley Dakake, "Tobacco at the Movies: Tobacco Use in PG-13 Films" (Boston: Massachusetts Public Interest Research Group, 2002).

17. University of Michigan, Monitoring the Future Study, Table 15.

18. Michael Schudson, *Advertising: The Uneasy Persuasion* (New York: Basic Books, 1984), p. 179.

19. Ibid., p. 197.

20. Richard Mizerski, "The Relationship Between Cartoon Trade Character Recognition and Attitude Toward Product Category in Young Children," *Journal of Marketing* 59 (1995): 58–70.

21. Robin Maria Turco, "Effects of Exposure to Cigarette Advertisements on Adolescents' Attitudes Towards Smoking," *Journal of Applied Social Psychology* 27 (1997): 1115–1130.

22. National Survey on Drug Use and Health, "Alcohol Use in Lifetime, Past Year, and Past Month, by Detailed Age Category: Percentages, 2005 and 2006," 2006 National Survey on Drug Use & Health (Rockville, MD: Substance Abuse and Mental Health Services Administration, 2008), http://oas.samhsa.gov/NSDUH/2k6NSDUH/tabs/Sect2peTabs1t042.htm#Tab2.15B.

23. National Survey on Drug Use and Health, "Alcohol Use, Binge Alcohol Use, and Heavy Alcohol Use in the Past Month, by Detailed Age Category: Percentages, 2005 and 2006," 2006 National Survey on Drug Use & Health (Rockville, MD: Substance Abuse and Mental Health Services Administration, 2008), http://oas.samhsa.gov/NSDUH/2k6NSDUH/tabs/Sect2peTabs1t042.htm#Tab2.16B.

24. Ibid.

25. National Institute on Alcohol Abuse and Alcoholism Press Release, "Alcohol Survey Reveals 'Lost Decade' Between Ages of Disorder Onset and Treatment," July 2, 2007 (Bethesda, MD: National Institute on Alcohol Abuse and Alcoholism), http://www.niaaa.nih.gov/NewsEvents/NewsReleases/disorder_onset.htm. Also see Karen Sternheimer, "Drinks Anyone?" *Everyday Sociology Blog* (New York: W.W. Norton and Company, 2007), http://nortonbooks.typepad.com/everydaysociology/2007/07/drinks-anyone.html.

26. Substance Abuse and Mental Health Services Administration Press Release, "New Nationwide Report Estimates that 40 Percent of Underage Drinkers Received Free Alcohol from Adults Over 21," June 26, 2008 (Rockville, MD: Substance Abuse and Mental Health Services Administration), http://www.samhsa.gov/newsroom/advisories/0806250013.aspx.

27. Susan Lang, "Teen Alcohol Use is a Prime-Time TV Staple, Study Finds," *Cornell Chronicle*, November 5, 1998, http://www.news.cornell.edu/Chronicle/98/11.5.98/TValcohol.html.

28. Thomas N. Robinson, Helen L. Chen, and Joel D. Killen, "Television and Music Video Exposure and Risk of Adolescent Alcohol Use," *Pediatrics* (1998): 102–107.

29. "Music Videos Linked to Teen Drinking," *CNN.COM,* November 2, 1998; Marilyn Elias, "Teen Drinking Linked to Music Videos, TV," *USA Today,* November 3, 1998, p. 1D; Mary Jo Kochakian, "When Message is Drinking, Teens Listen," *Washington Post,* November 21, 1998, p. V4.

30. Julie Wheldon, "Adverts Do Make Teens Drink More," *Daily Mail* (London), January 3, 2006, p. 18.

31. Leslie B. Snyder, et al., "Effects of Alcohol Advertising Exposure on Drinking Among Youth," *Archives of Pediatric and Adolescent Medicine* 160 (2006): 18–24.

32. Don E. Schultz, "Challenges to Study on Alcohol Advertising Effects on Youth Drinking," *Archives of Pediatric and Adolescent Medicine* 160 (2006): 857. Reginald Smart, "Limitations of Study on Alcohol Advertising Effects on Youth Drinking," *Archives of Pediatric and Adolescent Medicine* 160 (2006): 857–858.

33. Douglas A. Gentile, et al., "Frogs Sell Beer: The Effects of Beer Advertisements on Adolescent Drinking Knowledge, Attitudes, and Behavior," Paper Presented at the Biennial Conference of the Society for Research in Child Development, Minneapolis, MN, April 2001.

34. National Survey on Drug Use and Health, "Results from the 2004 National Survey on Drug Use and Health: National Findings," 2004 National Survey on Drug Use and Health (Rockville, MD: Substance Abuse and Mental Health Services Administration, 2005), http://www.oas.samhsa.gov/NSDUH/2k4NSDUH/2k4results/2k4results.htm#3.1.

35. Ibid.

36. Ibid.

37. Ibid, see table 3.6.

38. University of Michigan, Monitoring the Future Study.

39. Alexander C. Wagenaar and Mark Wolfson, "Enforcement of the Legal Minimum Drinking Age in the United States," *Journal of Public Health Policy* 15 (1994): 37–53.

40. Quoted in "An Epidemic of Teen Drinking," *Newsday,* October 23, 2007, p. B12.

41. Justin Pope, "College Drinking Debate: 18 or 21?" *Chicago Tribune,* August 19, 2008, http://archives.chicagotribune.com/2008/aug/19/health/chi-college-drinkingaug19.

42. University of Michigan, Monitoring the Future Study.

43. Ceci Connolly, "Teen Girls Using Pills, Smoking More Than Boys," *Washington Post,* February 9, 2006, p. A3.

44. Gary Strauss, "More Television Characters are Going to Pot," *USA Today,* August 1, 2005, p. 1D.

45. Eric Schlosser, *Reefer Madness: Sex, Drugs, and Cheap Labor in the American Black Market* (New York: Houghton Mifflin, 2003).

46. National Survey on Drug Use and Health, "Illicit Drug Use in Lifetime, Past Year, and Past Month, by Detailed Age Category: Percentages, 2005 and 2006," *2006 National Survey on Drug Use & Health* (Rockville, MD: Substance Abuse and

Mental Health Services Administration, 2008), http://oas.samhsa.gov/NSDUH/2k6NSDUH/tabs/Sect1peTabs1t046.htm#Tab1.1B.

47. Substance Abuse and Mental Health Services Administration, Office of Applied Studies, *Drug Abuse Warning Network, 2005: National Estimates of Drug-Related Emergency Department Visits*, DAWN Series D-29, DHHS Publication No. (SMA) 07-4256 (Rockville, MD: 2007), http://dawninfo.samhsa.gov/files/DAWN 2k5ED.htm#Tab3; see figure two, table 3.

48. Donna Leinwand, "Drug Chat Pervasive Online," *USA Today*, June 19, 2007, p. 4A.

49. National Survey on Drug Use and Health, "Illicit Drug Use," Table 1.17B.

50. National Survey on Drug Use and Health, "Illicit Drug Use in Lifetime, Past Year, and Past Month among Persons Aged 12 or Older, by Demographic Characteristics: Percentages, 2005 and 2006," *2006 National Survey on Drug Use & Health* (Rockville, MD: Substance Abuse and Mental Health Services Administration, 2008), http://oas.samhsa.gov/NSDUH/2k6NSDUH/tabs/Sect1peTabs1t046.htm#Tab1.17B.

51. National Survey on Drug Use and Health, "Illicit Drug Use in Lifetime, Past Year, and Past Month among Persons Aged 18 to 25, by Demographic Characteristics: Percentages, 2005 and 2006," *2006 National Survey on Drug Use & Health* (Rockville, MD: Substance Abuse and Mental Health Services Administration, 2008).

52. Drew Griffin and David Fitzpatrick, "Widow: My Husband Died from Online Drugs," *CNN.COM*, May 22, 2008, http://www.cnn.com/2008/HEALTH/05/21/online.drugs/index.html?iref=newssearch.

53. Andrew K. Whitacre, "Alcoholic Traits: Like Father, Like Son," *PsycPort*, March 15, 2001, http://www.psycport.com/news/2001/03/15/eng-millenniumhealth/eng-millenniumhealth_181153_76_9414797378704.html.

Rap Music Promotes Misogyny, Homophobia, and Racism

In 2007, radio talk show host Don Imus created a national uproar by calling the women of Rutgers University's basketball team "nappy-headed hos" after their second place finish in the National Collegiate Athletic Association (NCAA) finals. Imus managed to load issues of race, gender, and sexuality into one insult. The misogyny in the comment was clear: These mostly African American women excelled in a male-dominated sport, challenging traditional conceptions of femininity. For this, Imus chided them on their appearance in a uniquely racialized way; "nappy" hair is a way of denigrating African Americans' hair that does not conform to traditional European standards of beauty. And by referring to the women as "hos," Imus drew upon an old stereotype of African American women as oversexed in contrast to the pedestal of purity that white women (particularly in the South) have been hoisted upon.

Imus eventually apologized, briefly lost his syndication job (although another network hired him months later), and even met with the women in a closed-door discussion. While it may be tempting to view this comment as an isolated incident, the radio host has a long history of making racially insensitive remarks. After African American journalist Gwen Ifill, now with PBS, then a White House correspondent for the *New York Times*, declined an invitation to appear on his show in 1993, Imus allegedly said that the *Times* "lets the cleaning lady cover the White House."[1]

Yet after he was fired in 2007, supporters viewed Imus as a scapegoat. The *New York Post* chided "all those politically correct types who piled on" the radio host after his return to radio later that year. Another supporter and radio guest, private detective Bo Dietl, criticized regular guests like Al Roker for "abandoning [Imus] in his hour of need," and even said that in the end the Rutgers basketball team "really benefited" from the derogatory remarks because they brought national attention to the team.[2]

This comment did create a unique opportunity for Americans to examine their deep-seated beliefs about race, gender, and sexuality. And while many commentators were quick to denounce Imus, almost immediately Imus and others deflected our attention off of him and onto rap music. Aren't the lyrics of many songs basically the same as—or worse than—the phrase that got Imus fired? Imus himself claimed that the comment was meant to be a joke and an imitation of rap lyrics. As Imus slipped out of the public eye, hip-hop culture once again found itself on trial.

While public outcry over rock and roll, heavy metal, and so-called "shock rock" has sporadically erupted during the last few decades, rap music has sustained steady criticism since its introduction to mass audiences in the 1980s. Critics decry it as "the worst kinds of images emanating from a postmodern society" and believe that rap is "sugar-coated poison."[3] After New York *Daily News* columnist Stanley Crouch wrote an editorial criticizing gangsta rap in 2005, readers flooded the paper with supportive comments. One self-described white suburban mom called rap "disgustingly pornographic, hateful, women-bashing, violence and drug-loving crap." "Hip hop is not only dead but the stench from its rotting corpse is deplorable," wrote a New York City high school teacher.[4]

It is true that rap lyrics are occasionally shocking, brutal, and sometimes rife with misogyny and obscenities. I admit that I am not a fan of rap music. I don't like aggressive-sounding lyrics and music and am appalled by some of the language, particularly when it degrades women. But at the same time I realize this music is largely misunderstood and underestimated by my fellow non-fans. It's very easy to criticize music we find offensive to the ear as noise and still recognize that one person's noise is another's melody.

Rap music specifically and hip-hop more generally details a large variety of experiences, but most critics focus on lyrics depicting sex, drugs, and violence.[5] Taste is not only what is at issue here. Adults may not like the sexualized teen pop of the early 2000s, but rarely do politicians speak out as vociferously against it. On the surface, explicit lyrics may appear to be hip-hop's biggest violation, but underneath concerns about sex or violence in music lie fears of politically explicit language that challenges not only adult sensibilities, but the current power structure as well. Note how the entire genre, not just specific acts or songs come under fire. Why is this the case?

As writer Terry McDermott described in the *Los Angeles Times*, country music has historically been peppered with stories of violence and misogyny, yet no political movement has tried to censor and prevent its performance with the same vehemence as with rap.[6] Race and politics make this musical genre more than just offensive to "polite" society; rap music poses a threat to the social order as well. This is the fear that motivates the public and political outcry over foul language.

Rap music started in a decidedly populist fashion in the 1980s, not courted by traditional record labels but popularized through local clubs.[7] With no radio or video play, its popularity grew through word of mouth. Public concern seemed to erupt when rap made it to white suburban audiences, who are now estimated to be rap's largest audience.[8] In fact, the first rap album to go platinum was *License to Ill* by the white suburban-raised Beastie Boys. This was the turning point.

It was one thing for African American youth in urban New York and Los Angeles to rap about their anger towards police. But it was entirely another thing for white kids to hear such strong antiauthority messages, to learn about the violence and drugs in urban areas that resulted from economic divestment from central cities in the 1980s, and to co-opt the music themselves. Fears of rap draw on anxieties similar to those in the early 1950s when white parents feared what influence "black" rock and roll would have on their kids; fear of rap is a way to displace anxieties about race without having to talk about race directly.

The threat to polite society involves more than using the F-word and other profanities, though use of language to shock is one tactic used to disrupt mainstream norms.[9] In fact, as authorities worked harder to silence the seminal rap group NWA (Niggas with Attitude) in the late 1980s—via an FBI letter and arrests after concerts—their record sales skyrocketed. Writer Terry McDermott explains:

> The content of youth culture today is, to a significant extent, hip-hop. . . . Just as rock music was a vehicle for counter-cultural attitudes that provoked social upheaval among the middle classes in the 1960s, hip-hop in general and gangsta rap in particular have carried urban underclass sensibilities to the wider society—which has reacted with equal parts enchantment, imitation, and outrage.[10]

Complaints about lyrics periodically enter public and political discourse because it is easier to target youth culture than to examine problems within the adult-created social structure. If we are truly so disturbed by the lyrics and imagery in some musical genres, we ought to examine where these themes are rooted, rather than simply demand they go away. Targeting popular culture enables us to restrict and condemn young people—often young people of color—without appearing to discriminate.

That said, I'm not attempting to excuse the bad language some music contains or to change anyone's musical preference, but instead to look critically at the worry that music actually causes misogyny, homophobia, or racism. We rarely consider the positive role that hip-hop may play in people's lives—the way some of it reflects the experience of being black in America, of dealing with racism, and sometimes challenging the structure of power itself. While these messages are not necessarily what draws all listeners, the entire genre is often condemned for the lyrics of a few.

Music speaks to people in many different ways, and certainly preferences vary by generation. We will see that beyond the four-letter words often lie antiauthority themes (as has been the case for decades) that do more than simply offend sensibilities, but challenge the nature of power and authority. In particular, a great deal of hip-hop culture directly questions the traditional social order, while other genres that may contain equally violent and sexist imagery escape the same level of public outcry. But rather than seek to understand why antiauthority themes or images of violence and misogyny resonate so well with some young people, we tend to focus only on the alleged danger of the music and what it might "do" to them.

Questions continue about the responsibility of musicians: Aren't pop stars role models for millions of young people? Do recording artists justify and reinforce antisocial beliefs in their listeners? Typically we listen to music because it strikes an emotional chord with us on some level. But music alone certainly does not create homophobia or misogyny, and focusing only on music enables us to ignore other places they exist.

That said, just like video games, the content of music is occasionally pretty shocking. I have sometimes asked students to bring in lyrics to songs about relationships to analyze messages in music. I have to admit that some of the lyrics were so obscene I felt completely embarrassed when students read them aloud. So I am not claiming that lyrics people find objectionable are all okay or people should just lighten up, but instead suggest that we dig deeper to uncover the roots of sexism, homophobia, and racism in American life, beyond the music.

Does Music Create Misogyny?

There is no shortage of examples of rap lyrics and videos that are demeaning to women, casting them as sex objects, deriding them as gold diggers and other more colorful derogatory terms. In 2007, political scientists Michael D. Cobb and William A. Boettcher III published a study based on their experiments with college students, predicting that listening to ràp music would increase sexist attitudes. They conclude that, "Priming latent sexism is not the same thing as causing it. At worst, we would conclude that rap music might exacerbate pre-existing tendencies, particularly among males." In other words, sexism in rap music or other forms of popular culture exists in a context of a society still mired in gender inequality. "It makes more sense to view rap music as arising from larger society and cultural norms that encourage and foster misogyny and other antisocial behaviors, rather than as a root cause of these behaviors," conclude Cobb and Boettcher.[11]

Rap is certainly not the first musical genre to contain overtly sexist lyrics. Country western, heavy metal, and even mainstream pop all have a history of misogyny. Remember the song "If You Wanna be Happy" (which recommends finding an ugly girl to make your wife) or the Beatles' "Run for Your Life" (which threatens to kill a girlfriend if she is unfaithful), the Rolling Stones' "Under My Thumb" or the song from *My Fair Lady* when Henry Higgins wonders aloud "Why can't a woman be more like a man?" Yet in September 2007, in the wake of the Imus scandal, Congress held hearings about the impact rap has on sexism in America, without exploring other important reasons that gender discrimination persists.

We should criticize lyrics to raise awareness of the prevalence of sexism in our culture, and challenge the ease with which some young men (and women) adopt very misogynist views. Yet we seldom hear public outcry about any other form of music, and these discussions usually stop at music's "effects" without exploring the persistence of sexism in society itself. As Todd Boyd, professor in the School of Cinematic Arts at the University of Southern California told the *Christian Science Monitor,* "It's one thing to challenge cultural representations in society at large . . . but to single out hip-hop is another example of people criticizing hip-hop without knowing much about it."[12]

You might be thinking that there is a big difference between lyrics that allude to male supremacy and some of the more direct, aggressive rhymes in rap, some of which are so explicit that I choose not to repeat them here. Rather than only examine what the lyrics might do to listeners, it is also useful to explore the context in which they are written and why they might appeal to many listeners. To do so, it is helpful to begin with the concept of hegemonic masculinity, where men are encouraged to strive to be dominant and powerful over not just women, but other men as well.[13] Not all men seek this ideal, nor do many accomplish it; instead hegemonic masculinity is held out as what makes a man a "real man." In addition to subordinating women, hegemonic masculinity demands that men show physical strength and aggressiveness, hyper-heterosexuality and emotional detachment, and economic as well as physical domination over others.

Many rap lyrics directly reflect this heightened form of masculinity. And as Richard Major and Janet Mancini Billson, authors of *Cool Pose: The Dilemmas of Black Manhood in America* point out, "Presenting to the world an emotionless, fearless, and aloof front counters the low sense of inner control, lack of inner strength, absence of stability, damaged pride, shattered confidence and fragile social competence that come from living on the edge of society."[14] To Major and Billson, the "cool pose" is a response to African American disempowerment, a defense mechanism for managing emotions in a highly racialized society.

And it is this cool pose that adds an edge of urban authenticity to rap, speaking not only to those who experience the same marginalization that Major and Billson write of, but to suburban white kids, who purchase between 70 and 75 percent of rap CDs, according to Mediamark Research Incorporated.[15] Perhaps not coincidentally, in recent years the press has focused on white rapper Eminem's lyrics, which supposedly inspired actual violence against women.

Eminem told *Rolling Stone* in a profanity-laced August 2000 phone interview that he is tired of responding to critics of his lyrics. He uses his song "Stan" as an example of his criticism of those who take his lyrics too seriously. "'Stan' is about a sick f—ing kid who took everything I said literally—and he crashes his f—ing car, kills his bitch and dies," the performer explained.[16] "The kids listening to my music get the joke. They can tell when I'm serious and when I'm not. They can tell the entertainment of it."

I have to confess, I am not a fan of his music nor do I agree that we should write off his prolific use of the words "fag" or "bitch" as a joke. These words draw on existing feelings of homophobia and misogyny that both Eminem and his fans apparently find compelling. But while I am not a fan, Eminem has received much critical acclaim. "He is a genuinely brilliant rapper," said British music critic James Delingpole, citing his clever rhymes, rife with complex metaphors and humor.[17] Robert Hilburn, former music critic for the *Los Angeles Times*, noted that Eminem's albums have "a power and complexity almost unrivaled on the contemporary pop scene."[18] Others note that the characters he creates within his lyrics do not necessarily reflect beliefs he is promoting, but rather criticizing.

Despite the plaudits of music critics, two domestic assault cases in 2001 brought attention to Eminem's "Stan," a song about a troubled fan who drives off a bridge with his girlfriend tied up in the trunk. A British man who was apparently a big fan of the rapper and this particular song attacked his ex-girlfriend with a padlock and chain while she was working at a hair salon.[19] The eighteen-year-old woman had stopped seeing the nineteen-year-old man months earlier because "he was becoming too obsessive and possessive" and he had assaulted her before the attack in the salon. The brutal beating took place in front of terrified co-workers, who tried to pull him away from her.

For those who work with victims of domestic violence, the story sounds familiar: A possessive boyfriend lashes out when a woman attempts to end the relationship and free herself from control. The Eminem angle probably explains why the case made the news; in that sense it may even help raise awareness about the danger some women face when trying to escape abusive relationships. But the news report focuses more on Eminem than the ongoing problem of domestic violence. *The Times* of London report begins with a shocking opening line: "A teenager who believed he was the rap star Eminem brutally assaulted his former girlfriend."[20] Referring to a nineteen-year-old (a legal adult) as a teenager draws on the well of fears that surround kids and popular culture. The article reported that his home was "crammed with Eminem posters, albums and merchandise," which seemed to imply that the man was obsessed. Further, there is no evidence that the man actually believed he was Eminem (which would be a serious psychiatric condition). It appears that the man who bleached his hair like the rapper was instead a big fan, drawn to angry lyrics against women.

A similar case made headlines in Canada in the spring of 2001, when a thirty-five-year-old man was accused of assaulting his common-law wife. A judge asked to hear the lyrics to Eminem's song "Kim," about a man abusing his wife, which was alleged to have sparked the domestic assault.[21] Apparently the assault occurred one evening after the man played "Kim" for the couple's guests, who included friends and their children. The beating allegedly happened after the woman begged him not to play the song, which she said contained "abusing lyrics." In this case, the music may have been used to humiliate the woman in front of their friends, as part of what was clearly a violent relationship. According to reports, it was a relationship "she was afraid to be in but also afraid to end."[22]

Clearly, these two men were troubled and found a sense of connection with songs containing lyrics that tell of violence against women. They were likely drawn to misogynist imagery because it validated their angry worldview. The problem with focusing so much on the music is that we avoid asking why violence against women persists and why themes of misogyny resonate with so many people of all ages. Eminem's lyrics, as offensive as people may find them, are a good starting point to begin exploring why violence against women has been and remains so widespread. But the music is the symptom, not the disease. Music alone cannot create violence: Violence against women is often a way for people who feel powerless in some regard to assert their power over someone they feel entitled to control.

While these stories grab the headlines because of the alleged connection with Eminem's songs, millions of domestic assaults do not; critics of music's negative "effects" get far more national and international attention than advocates against domestic violence do. We should not ignore music containing troubling lyrics, but they can instead be an introduction to discussing sexism, misogyny, and violence against women. Many presume that music is responsible for creating hatred and resentment in youth and fail to take a look in our societal mirror to see how sexism is built into other social institutions. We have a long and deep history of ambivalence towards both women and sexuality in American society. So while discussions of misogyny are often started via rap lyrics, rap itself remains virtually the only topic of discussion. We rarely talk about how cultural values of women still focus on appearance and sexuality, but easily criticize music videos for being overtly sexual. Without rap music very little would be different in regards to the overall status of women—we need to stop pretending that music is the cause, rather than the symptom.

While disturbing lyrics get our attention, sociologists Terri M. Adams and Douglas B. Fuller argue that rap is just a continuation of a long history of demonizing women, particularly black women. The "Jezebel" myth (the modern-day "ho") of the hypersexual woman who uses her wiles to manipulate men dates back to slavery, and served as an excuse for white men to violate African American women. Similarly, the "Mammy" myth (today's "bitch") also has roots in slavery as the bossy woman who orders men around while serving her white masters. In more contemporary times, politicians have used these characterizations to blame women for black urban poverty: Ronald Reagan's 1980s era "welfare queen" who allegedly can't stop having babies, and Senator Daniel Patrick Moynihan's emasculating matriarch of the 1960s, supposedly destroying the African American family with her strength.[23] While politicians may use more genteel language, the outcome of reduced funding for children in poverty carries far more potential destructiveness than the prolific use of profanity in rap. In fact, part of the insidiousness of sexism lies in the use of language to cover and obfuscate its continued importance in American life. The realities of discrimination and violence against women are less sensational than rap's in-your-face lyrics, but they are still with us.

For example, according to the National Crime Victimization Survey, a nationally representative survey conducted by the Department of Justice each year, in 2005, 176,540 American women and girls over twelve reported being raped or sexually assaulted, a rate of about 1.4 per thousand.[24] Intimate partner violence accounted for 22 percent of nonfatal violence against women, and 30 percent of homicides against females in 2005 (in contrast to just 5 percent of male victims of homicide), according the Bureau of Justice Statistics.[25] This is partly because females are generally less likely to be victims of violence than males are, but also highlights the dangers women often face from those closest to them. Women still earn less than men—even in the same occupational categories and after earning the same levels of education. According to the U.S. Census, in 2004 the median salary for men in managerial positions was nearly $62,000, compared with just over $42,000 for women. Men with professional degrees earned a median salary of just under $72,000, compared with women's earnings of just over $47,000.[26] While rap lyrics merit our attention, they should not crowd out other issues in our discussion about gender inequality in the United States. Yes, degrading lyrics and images in popular culture can reinforce beliefs about sexism in both male and female consumers. But even if the music went away, we would still have to deal with the persistence of misogyny, even as women have made tremendous strides in American life during the past decades.

Hip-Hop and Homophobia

After the fallout from the Don Imus comments had spread to hip-hop, mogul Russell Simmons suggested that rap exclude the use of the words "bitch," "ho," and the N-word from its lexicon. Yet as Sarah Rodman of the *Boston Globe* noted, neither Simmons nor any involved in the national discussion about hip-hop after the Imus scandal questioned the prolific use of another slur, the F-word that is derogatory slang for homosexual.[27] In addition to the multitude of sexist lyrics within rap, blatant homophobia is also central to many songs, as cataloged on the Web site "Da Dis List" at http://www.phatfamily.org/dadislist.html.

In 2006, the FBI reported over 1,400 hate crimes against bisexuals, lesbians, and gays in the United States, the vast majority of victims being assaulted or threatened.[28] While it is tempting to look to hate-filled rap lyrics, the roots of homophobia run much deeper than rap and it would be a mistake to criticize only the lyrics without looking deeper. Homophobia is a central part of the concept of hegemonic masculinity, that narrowly constructed idea of what it means to be a "real man." As I discussed in the previous section, rigid definitions of manhood demand heterosexuality, thus antigay slurs are a prime way that men degrade one another. In fact, homophobia affects men regardless of their sexual orientation, since it is used as both a putdown and a way to enforce strict adherence to hegemonic masculinity. For example, in a 2005 MTV interview, performer Kanye West spoke out against homophobia within hip-hop, noting that a cousin of his is gay and that "everyone in hip-hop discriminates against gay people."[29] When this comment led to taunts that West himself must be gay, he told the *New Musical Express,* a British music magazine, "I'm still homophobic myself to a certain extent . . . You know, I wouldn't go to a gay parade and feel comfortable. I wouldn't ever go to a gay club."[30] Even speaking out against homophobia becomes dangerous, and West backtracked from his previous message of tolerance.

Being openly homophobic has little public downside. In a 2004 interview, Rapper 50 Cent told *Playboy* that "I don't like gay people around me," and that "It's OK to write that I'm prejudiced . . . We refer to gay people as faggots, as homos. It could be disrespectful, but that's the facts."[31] What's particularly interesting is that his late mother was apparently bisexual, and these comments came following questions about her. Perhaps he felt the need to reassert his heterosexuality in order to ward off the possibility of being linked with homosexuality in any way.

Homophobia is also deeply connected with misogyny. As anything connected with femininity becomes devalued, men who appear to relinquish their superior position in the gender order are also subject to ridicule. Reaffirming heterosexuality and renouncing homosexuality is one way to reclaim status, status that is often limited for men of color in particular. As a marginalized group, African American men have historically had serious economic constraints, reducing their ability to achieve the economic domination associated with hegemonic masculinity. In our capitalist consumer-oriented society, this creates a major sense of emasculation. The civil rights struggles of the 1950s and 1960s were not only about rights as citizens, but rights as *men;* many marchers carried placards reading "I Am a Man," emphasizing the struggle that African American men have faced in claiming the privileges of manhood. According to a 2008 report from the Bureau of Labor Statistics, black men working full time earned less than 74 percent of white men's weekly earnings (by contrast, black women earned about 85 percent of white women's wages).[32]

Homophobia is not limited to the world of rap, and is often used to promote the idea of manhood. One controversy erupted in Dallas in 2007, when the deputy mayor's campaign for young males to pull up sagging pants led to a hip-hop artist's song linking sagging pants to gay sex. The lyrics implied that boys who wear their pants low do so because they are "on the down low," or secretly having sex with other men.[33] J. L. King's 2004 book, *On the Down Low: A Journey into the Lives of "Straight" Black Men* raised many questions about African American men who identified as heterosexual but had homosexual sex.

The author told *Advocate* magazine, "Gay is white. It's a culture I do not want to be part of. In Chicago you can't be black and gay on the south side. You can't live in your community. You can't go to church. You can't join a fraternity. You can be black, or you can move out."[34] For African American men, promoting a strong sense of masculinity has been part of the struggle for equality with white men. As King's comment reveals, the pain for gay African Americans can be even more acute, as they face the possibility of not just racism but rejection from others in their community.

African Americans hold no monopoly on homophobia, though. According to a 2003 Pew Research Poll, 55 percent of Americans believed that homosexual behavior is a sin, and half held unfavorable opinions about gay men (48 percent held unfavorable opinions about lesbians).[35] About 20 percent reported feeling uncomfortable around homosexuals; the number is double for evangelical respondents. Federal policies such as "Don't Ask, Don't Tell," which prohibits openly lesbian and gay Americans from serving in the military, efforts in states around the country to outlaw gay marriage (and a proposed constitutional amendment), as well as battles over openly gay clergy in several denominations underscore the rejection gays and lesbians face in a multitude of settings. Yes, we should be critical of homophobia in rap lyrics, but this should be the beginning, rather than the end of the discussion.

Rap and Racism

To understand many rap lyrics as well as much of rap's criticism, we also have to explore its connection with racism. Sociologist Bethany Bryson analyzed data from the General Social Survey, a nationally representative random household survey, and found strong associations between musical intolerance and racial intolerance. She notes that "people use cultural taste to reinforce symbolic boundaries between themselves and categories of people they dislike. Thus, music is used as a symbolic dividing line that aligns people with some and apart from others." Bryson also observed a correlation between dislike of certain groups and the music associated with that group.[36] So for many people, rap becomes a polite proxy for criticizing African Americans without appearing overtly racist.

It is certainly a mistake to insist that *any* critique of rap lyrics constitutes racism. But with the exception of feminist or gay rights advocates, mainstream concerns about homophobia or misogyny seldom address other forms of popular culture, or more importantly the broader social structure itself. For instance, in the 1990s, antilaw enforcement lyrics in songs like Ice-T's "Cop Killer" drew outrage from the general public (in contrast to Eric Clapton's cover of "I Shot the Sheriff" in the 1970s). These and other lyrics reflect the long history of police brutality African American men have experienced at the hands of law enforcement across the country. Cases like the 2006 police shooting of Sean Bell, a twenty-three-year-old African American man leaving his bachelor party, who allegedly got into a car accident with plainclothes officers driving in an unmarked van, contribute to African Americans' sense of outrage. Officers fired more than fifty shots, killing him and severely injuring two of his friends.[37] A judge found the three officers involved not guilty due to lack of sufficient evidence against them, although as of this writing the New York City Police Department is conducting an investigation into the incident.[38]

Unfortunately, incidents like this have echoed throughout history; while they may seem like unfortunate mistakes to others, for African Americans who live in fear of the police—not because they have committed crimes, but because of their skin color—this event feels all too common. Officer-involved shootings of African Americans have sparked most of the major urban upheavals of the last half century, most recently the 1991 beating of Rodney King in Los Angeles and the 1992 acquittal of the officers involved.

For whites that never experience racial profiling and see being pulled over as a nuisance rather than potentially life-threatening, the simmering rage might be hard to comprehend. Sociologist Elijah Anderson's ethnography of African Americans' experiences within a northeastern city highlights the disparity. "Scrutiny and harassment by local police makes black youths see them as a problem to get beyond," Anderson notes, and describes the actions of the "downtown police" as "looking for 'trouble.' They are known to swoop down arbitrarily on gatherings of black youths standing on a street corner. They might punch them around, call them names, and administer other kinds of abuse, apparently for sport."[39] Yet Anderson observes that the white members of the community are less aware, or less concerned about such treatment. He quotes a middle-aged white woman and long-time resident as saying, "When I call the police, they respond. I've got no complaints. They are fine for me. I know they sometimes mistreat black males. But let's face it, most of the crime is committed by them, and so they can simply tolerate more scrutiny."[40] For this woman, and likely many others who do not fear for their own safety or the safety of their children, police harassment is not a problem. Yet what she and others overlook is the number of law-abiding African Americans for whom it is a problem. Rap lyrics can be the starting point towards better understanding the historical and continuing animosity between some police and African American communities.

The troubled relationship with law enforcement is only one disconnect between African Americans and the broader society. For people who feel they harbor no racist beliefs, racism itself might be difficult to observe. Much of the anger rap lyrics contain draws on the experiences of being marginalized and disrespected by the wider society, marginalization that many white people never see. For instance, immediately after Don Imus's racially charged comment, an *ABC News/Washington Post* poll found that 73 percent of African Americans thought he should be fired; just 47 percent of whites agreed.[41] In January 2008, a CNN/ORC poll asked American adults how serious a problem they believed racial discrimination against blacks is in the United States today. Fifty-six percent of African Americans said "very serious," while just 12 percent of whites agreed.[42]

Yet one of the biggest concerns critics of rap lyrics have is the prolific use of the N-word in many songs. Does the repeated use of the word by African American male rappers in effect neutralize its power to dehumanize? This question has led to a great deal of debate and often reveals a generational divide. When the politically oriented cartoon *Boondocks* was set to debut as an animated series on Comedy Central in 2005, creator Aaron McGruder caused a stir by saying that, "At a certain point, we all have to realize that sometimes we use bad language. And the N-word is used so commonly, by not only myself, but by a lot of people I know, that it feels fake to write around it and to avoid using it."[43] By contrast, many older adults from the Civil Rights Era recoil at the use of the word by anyone, casually or otherwise. In an NAACP (National Association for the Advancement of Colored People) "funeral" for the N-word in 2007, Michigan Governor Jennifer M. Granholm announced, "Good riddance to this vestige of slavery and racism and say hello to a new country that invests in all its people."[44] This controversy has led to many recent books on the subject. Jabari Asim, author of *The N Word: Who Can Say It, Who Shouldn't, and Why*, contends that hip-hop artists who use the word do little to challenge the long-standing socioeconomic impact that the word has had. Only the shrewdest social critics, he argues, should use it.

Some hip-hop artists have made a decision to stop using the word, particularly after hearing white people use it. Rapper Master P told the New York *Daily News* in 2007 that, "I am a businessman trying to prove that clean music sells. . . . You can keep it real and keep it clean without the cussin'."[45] Of course the challenge has been economic; record companies have much to gain by rough language. In April of 2007, the month of Don Imus's comments, the Billboard Top 10 rap singles featured songs with lyrics that made ample use of the N-word and other derogatory terms. "It's like black on black crime," Vanderbilt University professor T. Denean Sharpley-Whiting told the New York *Daily News*.[46] Rapper Chamillionaire, born Hakeem Seriki, decided that his second album, released in 2007, would not include the N-word, to mend the generational divide the use of the word frequently creates.[47] He was also troubled to see white concert goers singing along with him at his shows when he used the word.

The N-word takes on a different meaning and context when used by whites, as rapper Eminem found when an old recording of his surfaced in 2003. Recorded in 1993 before his mega-success, Eminem used the N-word in his song and was deeply apologetic when news of its existence came out, and went as far as getting a court order to prevent its release.[48]

Beyond the rap world, some whites complain that if African Americans can use the N-word, then they can too. This very different context overlooks the violent history of the word's connotation when used by whites to address blacks. Not only has the N-word been used to degrade African Americans, but it often signaled very serious threats of violence. Claims that "I was just imitating rap music," as Imus claimed, are an attempt to deny the hostility of the word's user. For example, on Halloween in 2006, a seventeen-year-old used the N-word to address a police officer in Queens, New York. "That's just the way I talk," the teen said, adding that he "meant it in a friendly way."[49] While in court the teen held up a rap CD, as a claim that he is not racist. Ultimately he denied ever using the N-word. In a prior incident in the Howard Beach section of Queens, an area with a long history of violence against African Americans, another man made the same claim that the N-word was a friendly greeting—one he used before beating an African American man, for which he is serving a fifteen-year sentence.

Beyond words lies the very real conditions of racism that still persist, despite many gains of the past decades. As Donna Bailey Nurse wrote in the *Toronto Star*, when whites have called her the N-word it might have hurt, but to her it is not nearly as painful as being treated as a second-class citizen. She describes an experience that many middle-class African Americans have had during a job interview. Upon her arrival to discuss the position of a literary reporter, she was told the position was no longer vacant, and that she probably didn't have the experience they needed anyway. Nurse concludes that beyond the use of the word is its *application*—much more powerful, and ultimately more damaging.[50]

So to call for a ban on the use of the word, which many city councils have symbolically done, only combats one small, visible, part of the problem. As Maryland member of Congress Justin D. Ross wrote in the *Washington Post*, rap might have one serious side effect: desensitizing white listeners to the violence and continued racism African Americans face. Listening to rap might be a way of claiming that we are beyond racism. To paraphrase a cliché, "some of my favorite performers are black" might allow people to believe that they are immune from racist thoughts or action. Ross observes that often whites "are insensitive to crime against black people, drugs being sold, [and] black people being killed." He goes on to note that "you'll seldom hear politicians talking about . . . [the fact that] African Americans are five times more likely than whites to be victims of homicide."[51] But you will hear them talk about rap. From the halls of Congress to state legislative bodies, calls to condemn rap music are purely symbolic but nonetheless politicians seem to believe it is important to speak out against rap.

In 2008, a Kansas state representative proposed a resolution condemning rap in order to "send a message that this is not something that Kansas approves of or welcomes."[52] For the record, the state of Connecticut also condemns rap music. Passing resolutions, holding hearings, and the like have little impact on the music industry and even less effect on the actual conditions that rap often addresses. Michael Eric Dyson, professor of sociology at Georgetown University, described rap music this way to the Senate during a 2000 Senate Committee hearing: "they tell truths about their situations that are avoided in textbooks and schools, and dare we say, in the United States Senate at some points. . . ." He went on to describe the damage done by domestic policy itself. "If we're really concerned about the lives of kids, then we've got to not shred the safety net in terms of welfare reform, [because it] targets poor black and Latino and poor white kids in very specific ways. Because if there's diminished capacity for providing health care, and providing child care, for your children, that is much more destructive than a rap lyric."[53]

Despite the continued political focus on rap's alleged threat, listening to rap can be transformative. Todd Boyd, professor of race and popular culture, suggests in his book *The New H.N.I.C: The Death of Civil Rights and the Reign of Hip-Hop* that the popularity of hip-hop culture among whites may promote broader understanding of African Americans' experiences and encourage greater racial acceptance.[54] Sociologist Rachel E. Sullivan studied adolescents' reasons for listening to rap, and found that white teens may gain greater levels of racial awareness, but they only consciously note liking the music for the beat. In contrast, for African American teens the music often affirmed their experiences of being black in America. She argues rap offers a unique outlet, as African Americans "are less likely to have their experiences reflected in the dominant culture." The paucity of mainstream popular culture that deals with issues like discrimination, racial profiling, and the danger within central cities makes rap specifically, and hip-hop culture more generally, all the more important. In that regard, the continual focus on the purportedly negative nature of rap may feel like yet another slight in a culture that marginalizes minority youth to begin with.[55]

Author Tricia Rose writes in "'Fear of a Black Planet': Rap Music and Cultural Politics in the 1990s" that the discourse surrounding rap is a way to further construct African Americans "as a dangerous internal element in urban America—an element that if allowed to roam about freely will threaten the social order."[56] She goes on to describe how rap concerts have been portrayed as bastions of violence in order to justify greater restrictions on black youth from public spaces.[57] Likewise, sociologist Amy Binder studied news stories about gangsta rap and found that heavy metal is feared for being potentially dangerous for individual listeners, but rap's critics have focused on its alleged danger to society as a whole.[58]

Sociologist Theresa A. Martinez analyzed rap lyrics of the early 1990s, particularly gangsta rap, and argues that rap is a distinctly oppositional culture and a form of resistance. While she focuses specifically on the social criticism in lyrics of songs like "Revolutionary Generation" and "Freedom of Speech," which have overt political messages, we can even extend her analysis to argue that lyrics that disrupt the conventions of proper public language may also be a form of oppositional culture. While profanity and explicit lyrics do not necessarily carry political messages, they do disturb the cultural peace.[59] Disrupting polite society may not create social change, but it does in some way challenge the social order.

Behind the Music

Music serves as a proxy, an excuse to marginalize and condemn its fans as potential threats while obfuscating the real fear: in this case fear of critiques of the white power structure. Concerns about rap serve to further demonize poor African American youth living in urban communities and to frame them as a potential threat based on music, while ignoring the structural undercurrents of their experiences, like lack of opportunity and racism. It allows us to blame a few wealthy young African American male rap stars for deep-seated social problems like sexism and homophobia, and ironically the N-word itself. Yes, they sometimes make these issues visible—occasionally uncomfortably visible—but focusing the majority of our energy on blaming rap will not lead to real solutions. Their anger may upset conventional norms of what constitutes polite language, but changing the words will not eliminate the underlying frustration many people experience.

When this anger is co-opted by white middle-class audiences, it ironically both creates fear and loses its potency; to a large extent rap today has become more about style than about politics. Yet the fear stems from the threat that white middle-class youths will also challenge the power structure and dominant social institutions. Rap can be far more than linguistically obscene; its messages threaten business as usual. Yet white middle-class adults need not fear: rap's co-option has made mainstream media conglomerates rich and its suburban listeners feel cool without really changing a thing.

In contrast with rap, Disney cartoons are widely considered acceptable fare for children, yet contain subtle but significant messages of sexism and racism. Unlike rap, Disney-style animation tends to support the dominant view of the world. Thinking back to classic Disney films like *Snow White* (1937) and *Cinderella* (1950), we might argue that the traditional messages about gender clearly mirrored the times in which they were produced. In each, the love of a powerful, handsome (and almost always white) man saves the beautiful heroine, who is often of a lower social status than he is. Now we might look back and say, boy, we have come a long way. Women don't need to wait for men to provide them with a new life. We can look at pre–civil rights America and might conclude that the whitewashed world of the classic films reflected old ways of thinking, that we are more enlightened now, that the colonialism reflected in *The Jungle Book*, for instance, is a thing of the past.

But a closer look at contemporary Disney-style films reveals that things have not changed as much as we would like to think. These stories are still told through the lenses of Euro-whites; the presumptions about gender and nationality are more complex but still intact. In the Disney version of history, Euro-whites are presented as mostly benevolent visitors to the "exotic" lands they encounter. Explorers refine "savages," so European power appears natural and for the greater good. The use of European voices, for instance, are used to imply high status in films like *The Aristocats, Tarzan,* and *Beauty and the Beast.* *Aladdin* may be set in the Middle East and its characters similar in skin tone, but heroes speak with American accents, while villains have Middle Eastern accents and stereotypical facial features, like heavy beards and large noses.[60]

While critics of rap condemn its frequent objectification of women, in Disneyesque stories girls and women are nearly always love objects. The common message: be nice, loving, and above all beautiful (in a European sort of way), and you will be rewarded with a man and riches. One way these films explain the reactionary view of gender is that they are set in the past. In this past older women are mostly absent (as in *Beauty and the Beast, Aladdin,* and *Pocahontas*) or they serve as the nemesis to the young and beautiful (*Snow White, The Little Mermaid,* and *Cinderella*). Sure, there are men who are demeaning to women, but there are plenty of kind gentlemen and handsome princes to save women from these scoundrels. Of course the realities of women's disenfranchisement are absent: no scarlet letters, no legal beatings, rapes, or murders, as was often the case when women challenged patriarchy throughout history. In this past women knew their place and if they played their cards right could end up in the lap of luxury. Beauty is bestowed on the good, ugliness on the evil. Male dominance seems natural and without negative consequences for "good" women.

I make these points not to suggest that we start having congressional hearings about Disney films or even stop watching them, but instead to illustrate how other forms of popular culture receive far less scrutiny for their images of gender and race. Yes, there are significant differences between the language and visual imagery in Disney films and rap, but sometimes the messages are not as far apart as we might think.

In the grand scheme of things, though we might see evidence of misogyny, homophobia, and racism in popular culture, we must not divert our attention from the material realities that these forms of inequality produce in people's everyday lives, not just within entertainment. A better understanding of the violence and economic disparities all three of these forms of discrimination produce needs to come first.

And most centrally, to pull out these societal weeds we must dig to the roots to learn where they come from.

Notes

1. Editorial, "Racist Misogyny in the Morning," *Albuquerque Journal,* April 27, 1007, p. A6; Gwen Ifill, "Trash Talk Radio," *New York Times,* April 10, 2007, p. 21.

2. "Imus Bashers Face Vengeance," *New York Post,* November 29, 2007, p. 12.

3. Suzanne Fields, "Bad Raps: Music Rebels Revel in Their Thug Life," *Insight on the News,* May 21, 2001, p. 48; Val Aldridge, "A Load of Rap," *The Dominion* (Wellington), December 16, 2000, p. 19.

4. Owen Moritz, "Music to Their Ears: News Readers Embrace Writer's Attack on Rap," *Daily News,* January 23, 2005, p. 24.

5. Generally hip-hop is a broader term that includes other musical genres, styles of art, fashion, and dance. Rap is a musical genre (with several sub-genres) of hip-hop.

6. Terry McDermott, "Parental Advisory: Explicit Lyrics," *Los Angeles Times Magazine,* April 14, 2002, p. 32.

7. Ibid., p. 12.

8. Ibid., p. 14; Amy Binder, "Constructing Racial Rhetoric: Media Depictions of Harm in Heavy Metal and Rap Music," *American Sociological Review* 58 (1993): 753–767.

9. Greg Wahl, "I Fought the Law (and I Cold Won!): Hip-hop in the Mainstream," *College Literature* 26 (Winter, 1999): 101.

10. McDermott, "Parental Advisory," p. 14.

11. Michael D. Cobb and William A. Boettcher III, "Ambivalent Sexism and Misogynistic Rap Music: Does Exposure to Eminem Increase Sexism?" *Journal of Applied Social Psychology 37,* no. 12 (2007): 3025–3042.

12. Liza Weisstuch, "Sexism in Rap Sparks Black Magazine to Say 'Enough!'" *Christian Science Monitor,* January 12, 2005, p. 11.

13. R. W. Connell, *Masculinities,* 2nd ed. (Cambridge: Polity Press, 2005).

14. Richard Majors and Janet Mancini Billson, *Cool Pose: The Dilemmas of Black Manhood in America* (New York: Touchstone, 1992), p. 8.

15. Carl Bialik, "Is the Conventional Wisdom Correct In Measuring Hip-Hop Audience?" *Wall Street Journal,* May 5, 2005, accessed online at http://online.wsj.com/public/article/SB111521814339424546.html, accessed December 8, 2008.

16. A. D., "Eminem Responds," *Rolling Stone,* August 3, 2000, p. 18.

17. James Delingpole, "Your Children are Rap Victims," *The Spectator,* December 30, 2000, p. 10.

18. Robert Hilburn, "Eminem, On and On," *Los Angeles Times,* May 22, 2002, p. F1.

19. Oliver Wright, "Eminem Fanatic Turned to Violence," *The Times* (London), June 2, 2001.

20. Ibid.

21. Christopher Walker, "Judge Asks to Hear Violent Rap Song," *Ottawa Citizen*, October 23, 2001, p. B3.

22. Ibid.

23. Terri M. Adams and Douglas Fuller, "The Words have Changed but the Ideology Remains the Same: Misogynistic Lyrics in Rap Music," *Journal of Black Studies* 36, no. 6 (2006): 938–957.

24. Bureau of Justice Statistics, "Criminal Victimization in the United States, 2005," National Crime Victimization Survey (Washington, DC: U.S. Department of Justice, 2006), see table 2, p. 15, http://www.ojp.usdoj.gov/bjs/pub/pdf/cvus05.pdf.

25. Bureau of Justice Statistics, "Victim Characteristics," Intimate Partner Violence in the U.S. (Washington, DC: U.S. Department of Justice, 2007), http://www.ojp.usdoj.gov/bjs/intimate/victims.htm.

26. U.S. Census Bureau, "Income, Earnings, and Poverty," *Statistical Abstracts of the United States: 2007* (Washington, DC: Department of Commerce, 2007), p. 416.

27. Sarah Rodman, "Policing Rap Lyrics is Near-Impossible Task," *Boston Globe*, April 25, 2007, p. F1.

28. Federal Bureau of Investigation, "Victims by Bias Motivation," *Hate Crime Statistics 2006* (Washington, D.C.: U.S. Department of Justice, 2007), http://www.fbi.gov/ucr/hc2006/table7.html.

29. "Kanye West Calls for End to Gay Bashing," *USA Today*, August 18, 2005, http://www.usatoday.com/life/people/2005-08-18-kanye-west_x.htm.

30. "Kanye West Reacts to Fallout over Homophobia Comments," *New Musical Express*, August 20, 2007, http://www.nme.com/news/nme/30516.

31. Joseph Patel, "50 Cent Slams Gay Men in *Playboy* Interview, but Says Lesbians are 'Cool,'" *MTV.COM*, March 10, 2004, http://www.mtv.com/news/articles/1485657/20040310/50_cent.jhtml?headlines=true.

32. Bureau of Labor Statistics Press Release, "Usual Weekly Earnings of Wage and Salary Workers: Third Quarter 2008," October 17, 2008 (Washington, DC: U.S. Department of Labor, 2008), http://www.bls.gov/news.release/pdf/wkyeng.pdf.

33. Mike Daniel, "Gay Groups Critical of Hip-Hop Song Targeting Saggin' Pants," *Dallas Morning News*, November 1, 2007.

34. Anderson Jones, "Lowdown on the Down Low," *The Advocate*, May 25, 2004.

35. The Pew Forum on Religion and Public Life Press Release, "Religious Beliefs Underpin Opposition to Homosexuality," November 18, 2003 (Washington, DC: The Pew Forum on Religion and Public Life Press Release, 2003), http://pewforum.org/docs/?DocID=37.

36. Bethany Bryson, "'Anything But Heavy Metal': Symbolic Exclusion and Musical Dislikes," *American Sociological Review* 61 (1996): 884–899.

37. Robert D. McFadden, "Police Kill Man after a Queens Bachelor Party," *New York Times*, November 26, 2006, p. 1.

38. Michael Wilson, "Judge Acquits Detectives in 50-Shot Killing of Bell," *New York Times*, April 26, 2008, p. 1; Al Baker, "Officers Face Department Charges in Bell Killing," *New York Times*, May 21, 2008, p. 1.

39. Elijah Anderson, *Streetwise: Race, Class, and Change in an Urban Community* (Chicago: University of Chicago Press, 1990), p. 197.

40. Ibid., p. 205.

41. *ABC News/Washington Post* Poll of 1,141 Americans, conducted April 2007. Respondents were asked, "Do you think that Don Imus should have been fired for his remark about the Rutgers women's basketball players?"

42. CNN/ORC Poll of 1,393 American adults conducted January 2008. Respondents were asked, "How serious is racial discrimination against blacks *in this country.*"

43. E. R. Shipp, "Use of N-Word Demeans us All," *Daily News* (New York), November 13, 2005, p. 41.

44. Jennifer Harper, "Death Knell for 'N-Word,'" *Washington Times,* July 10, 2007, p. A1.

45. Chrisena Coleman, "Master of Rap's Lyrical Cleanup," *Daily News* (New York), September 24, 2007, p. 15.

46. Tina Moore, "Filthy, Degrading Lyrics Paying Huge Dividends," *Daily News* (New York), April 15, 2007, p. 4.

47. Steve Jones, "Chamillionaire Triumphs over Cursing on 'Ultimate Victory,'" *USA Today,* September 17, 2007, p. 3D.

48. Renee Graham, "Eminem's Old Words Aren't Hip-Hop's Biggest Problem," *Boston Globe,* December 23, 2003, p. E1.

49. Scott Shirfrel, "Teen Who Called Officer N-Word Pulls a 'Fat Nick,'" *Daily News* (New York), November 14, 2006, p. 37.

50. Donna Bailey Nurse, "The Boys Hollering at Me Didn't Shout 'N-Word,'" *Toronto Star,* February 18, 2007, p. D1.

51. Justin D. Ross, "Offended? The Rap's on Me," *Washington Post,* September 9, 2007, p. B2.

52. John Hanna, "Legislature to See Proposal that Would Condemn Gangsta Rap," Lawrence *Journal-World and News* (Kansas), January 14, 2008, http://www2 .1jworld.com/news/2008/jan/14/legislature_see_proposal_would_condemn_gangsta _rap/.

53. Michael Eric Dyson, *Debating Race with Michael Eric Dyson* (New York: Basic Books, 2007), pp. 232–233.

54. "Can Hip-Hop Be the New Driving Force behind Increased Racial Integration?" *The Journal of Blacks in Higher Education* no. 38 (Winter, 2002–2003): 64–67.

55. Rachel E. Sullivan, "Rap and Race: It's Got a Nice Beat, but What about the Message?" *Journal of Black Studies* 33, no. 5 (2003): 605–622.

56. Tricia Rose, "'Fear of a Black Planet': Rap Music and Black Cultural Politics in the 1990s," *Journal of Negro Education* 60 (1991): 279.

57. Amy Binder points out in her study of over 100 news stories on gangsta rap that in contrast to heavy metal, which is feared for being potentially dangerous for individual listeners, rap's critics have focused on its alleged threat to society as a whole (see page 754). Amy Binder, "Constructing Racial Rhetoric: Media Depictions of

Harm in Heavy Metal and Rap Music," *American Sociological Review* 58 (1993): 753–767.

58. Ibid.

59. Theresa A. Martinez, "Popular Culture as Oppositional Culture: Rap as Resistance," *Sociological Perspectives* 40, no. 2 (1997): 265–286.

60. Henry Giroux, "Are Disney Movies Good for Your Kids?" in *Kinderculture: The Corporate Construction of Childhood*, eds. Shirley R. Steinberg and Joe L. Kincheloe (Boulder: Westview Press, 1998), p. 61.

Understanding Social Problems Beyond Popular Culture: Why Inequality Matters

Popular culture may seem like the central cause of all that appears wrong with young people today based on news reports, commentary, and the publicity surrounding often questionable studies. Coupled with concerned citizens and politicians, this helps create the now taken-for-granted belief that media is a major problem. Claims makers actively work to raise awareness of what they see as the pop culture problem, which occasionally rises to the level of panic after a major incident like the Columbine High School shootings of 1999.

We have plenty of examples of media representations that portray less than ideal behaviors. While they are tempting explanations for social problems, especially for those who believe that young viewers will imitate what they see, popular culture is not the central cause of educational failure, changes in childhood, violence, sexual behavior, teen pregnancy, single parenthood, materialism, eating problems, and substance use. It is not the main reason racism, sexism, and homophobia persist. We certainly see all of these issues reflected in popular culture, and media representations can reinforce some of these things. But if we really want to improve public education, reduce violence, teen pregnancy, single parenting, and other issues of concern we need to understand what the main causes are. The media, in its many varied forms, seem like a reasonable explanation because it is by nature highly visible, clamoring for our attention. And ironically, to get our attention the news media often invokes fear of popular culture, further legitimizing the concerns of many people that the media is the main problem.

As corporate entities, media conglomerates have a lot vested in the status quo. If culture is the problem, even culture their company may take part in creating, then we stay focused on media content rather than public policies. For instance, the 1996 Telecommunications Act (which is rarely scrutinized as harshly as popular culture) enabled behemoth media conglomerates to become even bigger, to create even larger monopolies in the production of media culture. These corporations also benefit from a tax structure that minimizes their liability. They (and the politicians they lobby) benefit from our tendency to view poverty and lack of opportunity as the result of individual failings rather than a public problem. Currently, our federal budget is comprised of taxes mainly collected from individuals; only 14 percent came from corporations in 2007, compared with 17 percent in the 1980s, and 39 percent in the 1950s.[1]

Media conglomerates have a lot to gain by keeping us focused on the popular culture problem, lest we decide to close some of the corporate tax loopholes to fund more social programs. More and more, the news is just one arm of an octopus designed to feed shareholders, so the more laissez-faire our public policy remains, the better for them. It's a win-win situation for the corporations: Media phobia deflects attention away from public policy solutions and on to media culture, which the First Amendment largely protects from regulation. While we are busy clamoring for more restraint and changes in content, there is little threat of any real change in social structure or challenge to business as usual. In short, the news media promote media phobia because it doesn't threaten the bottom line. Calling for social programs to reduce inequality and poverty would.

The Problem of Poverty

Throughout this book I have discussed the widespread impact of child poverty—children comprise a majority of the nation's poor, and poverty is closely linked with many of the problems that we usually blame the media for, like violence, school failure, and teen pregnancy. While the "media made me do it" stories grab headlines, we avoid confronting the most significant problem facing American kids: The fact that nearly 13 million children live in poverty.[2]

Ads for starving children in faraway places might gain our sympathy, but poor American children are often invisible, or just seen as a threat to public safety. Traditionally, the American focus on individualism holds poor people solely responsible for their own predicament. This encourages us to ignore the plight of most of these kids. Children under six are the most likely to live in poor families, as one in five American children under six live in poverty and 43 percent of children under three live in low-income families.[3] Sixteen percent of all American households with children face food insecurity, meaning they have significant difficulty providing enough food.[4] And most of their parents work: According to the National Center for Children in Poverty at Columbia University, 51 percent of low-income families (living at double the poverty rate or less) with children have at least one parent who worked full time in 2007, and another 26 percent had at least one parent who worked full or part time for at least some of 2007.[5]

Being poor has a profound impact on children, who are less likely to have regular access to health care, less likely to see a dentist, more likely to experience chronic problems like asthma and obesity, as well as family stressors associated with poverty.[6] Their parents are less likely to be

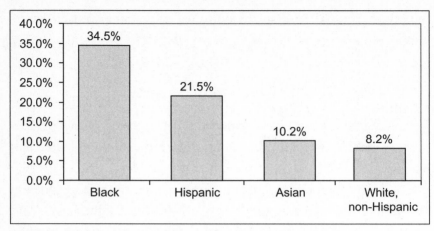

Percentage of Children Under 18 Below Poverty Line, 2007.
Source: U.S. Census.

married or remain married, and are more likely to experience depression.[7] When these children begin school, they tend to be less prepared than their more affluent peers, and attend schools that have less experienced teachers, older materials, and larger class sizes.[8] Combined with these challenges is a greater likelihood for low-income children to live in high-violence communities, particularly in urban areas that remain highly segregated, not just by race or ethnicity but by economic status.

The problem of poverty also reflects the relationship between income and race/ethnicity. Most poor children in America are white (nearly 8.4 million of the estimated 13 million people in poverty under eighteen), but a disproportionate *percentage* of children in poverty are African American or Latino, relative to their proportion in the U.S. population.[9]

African American and Latino children in poverty are also more likely to live in neighborhoods with high concentrations of poverty than poor whites. Authors of a 2008 *Health Affairs* article call this pattern "double jeopardy" or a dual disadvantage for children who are both poor and African American or Latino.[10] These segregated communities of concentrated poverty are the direct result of postwar policies such as redlining, when banks refused to lend money to white people living in neighborhoods with African Americans or Latinos, encouraging them to flee central cities. Programs like the G.I. Bill enabled many white families to buy homes with little or no money down and in some cases pay less to move into a newly constructed home than to remain in an urban area. Thus, whites who could receive mortgages in new suburban developments moved away, leaving people of color behind in communities that gradually decayed due to lack of investment. As urban communities declined, businesses and jobs moved away too, as did other basic services like hospitals and supermarkets. With an eroded tax base, schools also lost a major source of revenue and well-qualified teachers left too. As sociologists Robert Sampson and William Julius Wilson describe, social isolation resulted from decades of divestment, with white and middle-class flight leaving a high concentration of poor African Americans and Latinos behind. People in these communities confront higher rates of violence and other illegal activity, increased rates of single parenthood and teen pregnancy and higher high school drop-out rates.[11] These are the central causes of many of the problems that we tend to blame on popular culture.

Pop Culture Diversions and Economic Realities

Not only does popular culture provide its consumers a temporary escape in their own lives, it also diverts our attention from the extent to which poverty and inequality remain cancers in American society. As long as we convince ourselves that television and video games are behind disparities in academic achievement, we can stop thinking about the fact that our public schools are still very segregated racially and economically, and remain vastly unequal. High school drop-out rates for Latinos and blacks dwarf those of whites, and nearly one in four foreign-born kids does not finish high school.[12] It is easy to think of this as the failure of individuals, but it is also the failure of schools to provide students with the basic tools to succeed academically. Assigned to overcrowded classrooms in crumbling buildings, the state of many of our nation's urban schools tell young people that they aren't important and that their education does not matter.

The kids in these schools must also navigate violent communities once the school day is done. Yes, video games might seem like they play an important role in creating violence, but only if we pretend that kids are not exposed to violence anywhere besides the media. For some children, the violence starts right at home. A 2007 study of over 9,000 respondents found that those who experienced some form of child abuse were significantly more likely to perpetrate violence (including against an intimate partner) than those who did not experience a form of abuse as a child.[13] This might seem like common sense, but it is often thrown out the window when we zero in on popular culture and exclude these and other major factors.

As with violence, teen pregnancy is closely linked with poverty. Janet Rich-Edwards of the Harvard Medical School wrote in a 2002 issue of the *International Journal of Epidemiology,* "poverty, not maternal age, [is] the real threat to maternal and infant welfare. It is not just the disadvantaged, but the 'discouraged among the disadvantaged' who become teen mothers."[14] As counterintuitive as it may seem considering the high costs associated with child rearing, poor teens may feel like they have less to lose by becoming parents, coupled with often limited access to comprehensive sex education and birth control. A 2008 *New Yorker* article examined the high teen pregnancy rates of evangelical teens, the group with perhaps the strongest cultural norms against premarital sex.[15] If culture were the best predictor, we might presume that these teens would have the *lowest* teen pregnancy rates. Yet as sociologist Lisa A. Keister found in her analysis of Bureau of Labor statistics, religion is highly correlated with wealth. Members of conservative Christian denominations' net worth were approximately half the median net worth of Americans more generally.[16] Besides limited sex education, this often translates to a perception of fewer economic opportunities in the future, and therefore less of a disincentive for an early pregnancy.

Early pregnancy may also lead to early marriage, a strong predictor of divorce. While daytime talk shows might focus on a spouse's "Internet addiction" or too much time playing video games, economic instability is the biggest threat to families today. Children in single parent families also face unique challenges, including limited school readiness,[17] reduced supervision, and most centrally, an increased likelihood of living in poverty. Single parent households are often the *result* of economic inequality, rather than the cause, as federal marriage promotion programs imply. There is also a stark connection between the percentage of single parent families and race: 65 percent of African American, 49 percent of American Indian, and 37 percent of Latino children live with an unmarried parent. By contrast, 23 percent of white and 16 percent of Asian American children live in a single parent household.[18] As you can see, there is a strong relationship between these numbers and the percent of children in poverty by race, thus it is difficult to untangle the problems caused by single parent families from those of poverty.

Low-income parents may also face difficulty providing their children with healthy diets, particularly if they live in urban areas with few grocery stores and limited access to fresh produce. Couple this with little time to prepare meals and the abundance of fast food chains offering cheap food quickly in poorer neighborhoods and we see why obesity is higher for lower income children.[19] Race and ethnicity are important predictors here as well; once again, rather than simply a result of culture, we can also locate the issue of obesity as rooted in the intersection between race and socioeconomic status. The same children who have limited access to regular health care are also the most vulnerable to obesity and its related complications.

In addition to limited access to health care, low-income adults with drug or alcohol problems often have few options for rehabilitation; at the same time, the stress of struggling to get by can make substance use or overeating more appealing. While these issues are certainly not limited to the poor, the complications can become more dramatic for those without access to treatment. With increased surveillance of the drug trade in urban centers, many users are likely to find themselves incarcerated, America's largest institution for drug abusers. Parental incarceration adds to family instability and poverty: A parent in prison can't help provide for their family financially. Once released, they face even greater difficulty finding work due to a prison record.[20] According to Nell Bernstein, author of *All Alone in the World: Children of the Incarcerated,* parents who are incarcerated far from home are less likely to have frequent contact with their children and face a greater likelihood of long-term estrangement. With less family supervision and fewer parental connections, children are prone to repeat the cycle of crime and substance abuse.

When low-income people fall prey to substance abuse or otherwise struggle, their failures are often made visible. It is easy for the affluent in general, and affluent whites specifically, to see the results of inequality to further justify their prejudices. The scarcity of quality educational opportunities, jobs, and social services are not always clear to those who have not experienced the same struggles. The failure to fully comprehend the challenges faced by those at the bottom of the socioeconomic ladder is not surprising; it is built into the structure of our social system. Americans often have little interpersonal interactions with people of differing economic circumstances, and geographic segregation makes many people's day-to-day experiences a mystery.

This helps us believe that the challenges people face are largely of their own making rather than systematic inequality or discrimination. As long as we continue to focus only on individual effort and overlook social structure, we might believe that sexism and racism are just cards people "play" rather than persistent patterns, for instance. Yes, we have made gains in reducing overt discrimination, but it still lurks often beneath the surface: The job not offered because a female candidate is not seen as aggressive enough, or an African American candidate is presumed to lack motivation for no clear reason. But evidence of discrimination still exists: For example, both women and persons of color were disproportionally targeted with subprime mortgages before the 2008 collapse, even when they qualified for mortgages with lower interest rates.[21] Maintaining inequality, be it based on race, gender, or sexual orientation, serves to uphold the social order as we know it, and those at the top of the hierarchies benefit directly from their existence. Unraveling the tapestry of inequality requires us to look critically at American society, something that many people are reluctant to do. Better to blame popular culture.

But We Blame the Media Anyway

If poverty and inequality are so closely connected with the problems we claim to hope to solve, why do we focus so much on popular culture? We don't like to talk about poverty or racism in America; the persistent relationship between race and class challenges the American Dream of equal opportunity. As much as we might hope to believe that the Civil Rights Movement ended all traces of racial inequality, it was a beginning, but certainly not the end in the process of creating equality. Maybe it is easier to look to popular culture than confront the deeply entrenched nature of stratification. We might look to those with great wealth and prosperity and believe we can all get there—a more hopeful illusion than to focus on the many children with no health insurance attending deteriorating schools. When we do talk about poverty we tend to only blame the poor themselves; we tell them they aren't educated enough, are too lazy, lack ambition, and depend on welfare. Congress and former President Clinton decided in 1996 that welfare was the problem, not poverty or the untenable minimum wage, and passed "welfare reform" legislation, which limited the amount of aid families in poverty could receive.

Children are in the middle of this politically charged debate, and stand to lose the most. To face problems associated with poverty, we will have to rethink public policy choices and consider using more resources to bring more families out of poverty. But not all of our biggest challenges are related to poverty and inequality. Even well-funded schools merit a closer look to examine how well they can meet the needs of their students, how well they inspire rather than alienate the young people they are meant to serve. Schools tend to focus on conformity—both academically and socially—and need to take responsibility to support those who don't quite fit in. This, of course, can only be accomplished when the public provides better support for school systems and teachers. If we truly want to reduce violence in America, the answer will not be found in a V-chip but rather by confronting the persistence of inequality. But this is no easy task, particularly when it comes time to foot the bill for solutions. Blaming media is a cheap campaign decision—it costs relatively little to hold hearings, compared with getting at the heart of what causes violence. Blaming media takes us all off the hook: We can point our fingers at media producers and at parents we don't find restrictive enough.

Bottom line: Fear of media sells. The press is central in the development and perpetuation of fear—even of the media itself. As sociologist David Altheide writes in *Creating Fear: News and the Construction of Crisis*, things that scare us make for good drama, draw us closer, and create a sense that we need to watch or read more for our safety, and, most compellingly, for the safety of children. But too much fear tends to backfire, particularly if we feel we can't gain control of the threat. As social psychological research demonstrates, scary messages work best if the fear they create is only mild.[22] When people feel too scared, too out of control, they tend to go into denial and ignore the frightening information. So providing low doses of seemingly manageable fear draws viewers in, but presenting complex problems may make people want to avoid the news. This is why the things that we need to be concerned about, the problems without easy solutions, are not as compelling as news stories. They scare us too much.

Media fear resonates with preexisting anxieties about youth culture and new media technologies. It would be too simple to say that this fear is only the press's fault. As I have emphasized throughout this book, both youth and youth culture are symbolic of change, of a loss of adult centrality and control. Popular culture is often the bastion of the young and in many ways reflects the contemporary experience of youth, which could seem frightening to adults. We often prefer to deny both the aggression and sexual curiosity young people feel, so when we encounter these themes in popular culture we often blame media for their existence.

Lessons from Popular Culture

Media analysis is a great tool for exposing the complexities of issues like violence, gender and sexuality, racism, and homophobia. Our media culture provides a great text for both artistic and social criticism. We can ask questions, like What do shows such as *Law & Order* teach us about perceptions of the ability of the justice system to catch perpetrators, as well as how the usual victims and suspects are portrayed? We can watch *The Office* to discuss some of the banalities of corporate job experiences; or consider what *Gossip Girl* tells us about contradictions within gender and power, or how the relative absence of nonwhite professionals in a drama series reflects inequalities of race. We might look at fashion magazines and analyze *why* so many of the models are superthin, rather than just focus on possible effects of their appearance. Considering images of beauty in the context of the construction of gender is one way to use such images as a point of learning, not just condemnation.

Instead of media phobia, where we complain about what media content might do to us, we should engage in more media analysis. This means critically exploring representations of gender and race, for instance, and considering how these representations may reflect social inequality. What we ought to be discussing about media is who produces it, and for what purpose. In the United States especially, most media are produced for profit, and are often created for some audiences and consumers but not others. While green is the only real color of interest, there is more green to be found in some racial or ethnic groups than others, and these groups are more likely to have media produced with them in mind.

We can learn a lot about race, class, gender, sexuality, and age by studying media representations and linking them to systems of power. It is simply not enough to spot these patterns within media, but we also need to implicate other social and historical factors that create such conditions. Sexism, for instance, wasn't born with the advent of movies or television, but it does live and breathe there. By paying sexism a "visit" within media culture, for instance, we learn a lot more about it. Media content is a poor predictor of future behavior, but an excellent window through which we can understand social relations of power. As with any form of self-scrutiny, we tend to avoid looking at media culture in this way. Like media analysis, societal analysis doesn't mean America bashing, but rather an honest look at where we are and what we want to improve. Change is only possible when we dig below the surface, below media content, to critically explore issues of power in America.

Our media culture is a great starting point to explore our society, using references young people are already familiar with. Being media savvy alone does not necessarily lead to critical analysis, which should be a part of being educated in the twenty-first century. Media literacy education, which seeks to increase critical awareness of how texts are produced and how they represent (or fail to represent) real social issues, is essential. But adult-introduced discussions of media culture can be problematic, particularly if they are designed to create taste and promote adult value judgments, thus serving as another vehicle for media bashing. This will not engage young students, but will only alienate them further.

This is not to say that parents should ignore what their kids are watching or listening to. But parents do need to recognize that kids' taste in popular culture is not necessarily an indication that their values are different, but that their needs may be met through listening to music that parents may not approve of. To some degree, growing up happens with peers and away from parents. I think that many parents understand this, but it is sometimes difficult. Kids, especially as they become older, do need some space to enjoy popular culture on their own without having to explain themselves. Parents need to understand that teens in particular play with imagery from popular culture as they try to form their independent identities. That being said, a supportive parent who can listen without judging will understand their kids better and have a much greater impact than popular culture ever can. Informed trust and supportive monitoring will be much more productive than attempting to heavily regulate and control teens' media choices.

Kids aren't the only ones who need to work towards becoming critical media consumers. Adults often believe that kids don't know the difference between fact and fiction, but adults could stand to question whose viewpoint a news report or political pundit represents. This means questioning what we are told are facts by the news media and challenging the logic of hyperconsumption, that more is better and that fulfillment and good citizenship is accomplished by spending. Focusing on these other issues doesn't mean that popular culture doesn't merit our criticism and scrutiny. Media criticism can be the first step in beginning social analysis; it should never be the *only* focus of social analysis, however.

Media: A Sheep in Wolf's Clothing

While media may reflect and remind us of social problems, media are not the central cause of violence and the other things that truly scare us. But because media culture may not be too important in creating violence or promiscuity, it is nonetheless very powerful. Its power shapes how we schedule and fill our days and influences how we interact with others. Its content often shapes what we talk to each other about and how we think about ourselves and the world around us. Its emergence has certainly altered other institutions, such as education, government, and religion. Keeping this in mind, media merit critical analysis, as do all social institutions. If we analyze media we will better understand society, but only if our energy regarding media is not expended on maintaining illusions about childhood. The news media in particular cast a very powerful spotlight, directing our attention onto some issues and away from others. Its power is feared as harmful, but it is much more complex than that. The biggest harm media power can yield is not in creating killers, but in creating complacency.

This complacency is not due to fictional entertainment, as we so often fear; it is created from news reports based on emotion and drama rather than citizenship. We are lulled not by music or movies or video games, but by programs passing as news that only skim the surface of what we need to know about our government, our corporations, and our society. I say that media is a sheep in wolf's clothing because it gets our attention, seems scary, but underneath is much more of a follower than a real leader or creator of change. This is no accident—as I noted earlier in this chapter, media conglomerates are heavily invested in keeping things exactly as they are. That's why we continually hear reports from the news media that popular culture is the problem. Media phobia challenges nothing and fails to address the central problems that do affect millions of American children. The media sheep play follow the leader.

It doesn't have to be this way. Because media culture is so enchanting, so attention seeking, it can be used to redirect our attention to the sources of our society's problems and to provide us with a wake-up call about the persistence of inequality in the United States. While changing media culture may truly concern us at times, we need to be sure to keep our real challenges in sight. It would be a mistake to only focus on the negative in these changing times, overlooking the positive aspects of both media culture and the next generation. The problems I address in this book, education, violence, teen pregnancy, family instability, health, substance use, sexism, racism, and homophobia, all merit our attention. In order to address them directly, we can't be distracted by the lure of popular culture, which is ultimately not the problem, nor is its control the solution.

Notes

1. Executive Office of the President, *Budget of the United States Government: Fiscal Year 2009* (Washington, DC: Government Printing Office, 2008), http://www.publicagenda.org/charts/federal-budget-revenue-sources.

2. Sarah Fass and Nancy K. Cauthen, "Who are America's Poor Children? The Official Story [2006]" (New York: National Center for Children in Poverty, 2006), http://www.nccp.org/publications/pub_684.html.

3. Sarah Fass and Nancy K. Cauthen, "Who are America's Poor Children? The Official Story [2007]" (New York: National Center for Children in Poverty, 2007), http://www.nccp.org/publications/pub_787.html; Ayana Douglas-Hall and Michelle Chau, "Basic Facts About Low-Income Children: Birth to Age 18" (New York: National Center for Children in Poverty, 2008), http://www.nccp.org/publications/pub_845.html.

4. Sarah Fass and Nancy K. Cauthen, "Who are America's Poor Children? The Official Story [2008]" (New York: National Center for Children in Poverty, 2008), http://www.nccp.org/publications/pub_843.html.

5. Douglas-Hall and Chau, "Basic Facts."

6. Kay Johnson and Suzanne Theberge, "Reducing Disparities Beginning in Early Childhood" (New York: National Center for Children in Poverty, 2008), http://www.nccp.org/publications/pub_744.html; Federal Interagency Forum on Child and Family Statistics, "Health Care," *America's Children in Brief: Key National Indicators of Well-Being, 2008* (Washington, DC: U.S. Government Printing Office, 2008), http://www.childstats.gov/AMERICASCHILDREN/care.asp.

7. See marriage data in Johnson and Theberge, "Reducing Disparities."

8. See Karen Sternheimer, *Kids These Days: Facts and Fictions about Today's Youth* (Lanham, MD: Rowman and Littlefield, 2006), pp. 69–71.

9. U.S. Census Bureau, Current Population Survey, "Age and Sex of All People, Family Members and Unrelated Individuals Iterated by Income-to-Poverty Ratio and Race: 2007," *Annual Social and Economic (ASEC) Supplement* (Washington, DC: Government Printing Office, 2008), http://pubdb3.census.gov/macro/032008/pov/new01_100_03.htm.

10. Dolores Acevedo-Garcia, et al., "Toward a Policy-Relevant Analysis of Geographic and Racial/Ethnic Disparities in Child Health," *Health Affairs* 27, no. 2 (2008): 321–333.

11. Robert J. Sampson and William Julius Wilson, "Toward a Theory of Race, Crime, and Urban Inequality," in *Crime and Inequality*, eds. John Hagan and Ruth Peterson (Stanford, CA: Stanford University Press, 1995); U.S. Census Bureau, "High School Dropout Rates," October Current Population Survey, various years (Washington, DC: Government Printing Office, 2007), http://www.childtrends databank.org/indicators/1HighSchoolDropout.cfm.

12. Child Trends' calculations of U.S. Census Bureau, School Enrollment—Social and Economic Characteristics of Students: October 2005: Detailed Tables: Table 1, http://www.childtrendsdatabank.org/tables/1_Table_1.htm.

13. Xiangming Fang and Phaedra S. Corso, "Child Maltreatment, Youth Violence, and Intimate Partner Violence-Developmental Relationships," *American Journal of Preventive Medicine* 33, no. 4 (2007): 281–290.

14. Janet Rich-Edwards, "Teen Pregnancy is not a Public Health Crisis in the United States. It is Time we Made it One," *International Journal of Epidemiology* 31 (2002): 555–556, http://ije.oxfordjournals.org/cgi/content/full/31/3/555, R10.

15. Margaret Talbot, "Red Sex, Blue Sex: Why do so Many Evangelical Teen-Agers Become Pregnant?" *The New Yorker*, November 3, 2008.

16. Lisa A. Keister, "Religion and Wealth: The Role of Religious Affiliation and Participation in Early Adult Asset Accumulation," *Social Forces* 82, no. 1 (2003): 175–207.

17. Tamara Halle, et al., "Background on Community-Level Work on School Readiness," *Child Trends*, 2000.

18. "Children in Single-Parent Families, by Race: 2006" (Baltimore, MD: Annie E. Casey Foundation, 2008), http://www.kidscount.org/datacenter/compare_results.jsp?i=722.

19. For further discussion see Karen Sternheimer, *Kids These Days*, chapter 2.

20. Devah Pager, "The Mark of a Criminal Record," *American Journal of Sociology* 108, no. 5 (2003): 937–975.

21. Patrick Tucker, "Subprime Lenders Target Women Unfairly," *The Futurist* 41, no.7 (2007), http://www.wfs.org/trendmj07.htm.

22. Irving Janis and Seymour Feshback, "Effects of Fear-Arousing Communications," *Journal of Abnormal and Social Psychology* 48 (1953): 78–92.

Selected Bibliography

Adams, Terri M., and Douglas Fuller. "The Words Have Changed but the Ideology Remains the Same: Misogynistic Lyrics in Rap Music." *Journal of Black Studies* 36, no. 6 (2006): 938–957.

Adler, Patricia A., and Peter Adler. *Peer Power: Preadolescent Culture and Identity.* New Brunswick, NJ: Rutgers University Press, 1998.

Altheide, David. *Creating Fear: News and the Construction of Crisis.* New York: Aldine De Gruyter, 2002.

Ang, Ien. *Living Room Wars: Rethinking Audiences for a Postmodern World.* London: Routledge, 1996.

Arnett, Jeffrey Jensen. "Adolescents' Uses of Media for Self-Socialization." *Journal of Youth and Adolescence* 24 (1995): 519.

Bailey, Beth L. *From Front Porch to Back Seat: Courtship in Twentieth Century America.* Baltimore: Johns Hopkins University Press, 1989.

Barker, Martin, and Julian Petley, eds. *Ill Effects: The Media/Violence Debate.* London: Routledge, 1997.

Bergler, Reinhold. "The Effects of Commercial Advertising." *International Journal of Advertising* 18 (1999): 412.

Best, Joel. *Random Violence: How We Talk About New Crimes and New Victims.* Berkeley: University of California Press, 1999.

Binder, Amy. "Constructing Racial Rhetoric: Media Depictions of Harm in Heavy Metal and Rap Music." *American Sociological Review* 58 (1993): 753–767.

Borish, David M., Marian Friestad, and Gregory M. Rose. "Adolescent Skepticism Toward TV Advertising and Knowledge of Advertiser Tactics." *Journal of Consumer Research* 21 (1994): 166.

Brumberg, Joan Jacobs. *Fasting Girls: The History of Anorexia Nervosa.* New York: Vintage Books, 2000.

Bryson, Bethany. "'Anything But Heavy Metal': Symbolic Exclusion and Musical Dislikes." *American Sociological Review* 61 (1996): 884–899.

Buckingham, David. *After the Death of Childhood: Growing Up in the Age of Electronic Media.* Cambridge: Polity Press, 2000.

———. *The Making of Citizens: Young People, News and Politics.* London: Routledge, 2000.

———. "Media Education in the U.K.: Moving Beyond Protectionism." *Journal of Communication* 1 (1998): 33–43.

Buckingham, David, ed. *Reading Audiences: Young People and the Media.* Manchester: Manchester University Press, 1993.

Calvert, Karin. *Children in the House: Material Culture of Early Childhood, 1600–1900.* Boston: Northeastern University Press, 1992.

Calvert, Sandra. *Children's Journeys Through the Information Age.* Boston: McGraw-Hill, 1999.

Clark, Cindy Dell. *Flights of Fancy, Leaps of Faith: Children's Myths in Contemporary America.* Chicago: University of Chicago Press, 1995.

Cobb, Michael D., and William A. Boettcher III. "Ambivalent Sexism and Misogynistic Rap Music: Does Exposure to Eminem Increase Sexism?" *Journal of Applied Social Psychology 37*, no. 12 (2007): 3025–3042.

Cohen, Stanley. *Folk Devils and Moral Panics,* 3rd ed. New York: Routledge, 2002.

Connell, R. W. *Masculinities,* 2nd ed. Cambridge: Polity Press, 2005.

Coontz, Stephanie. *Marriage, a History: From Obedience to Intimacy, or How Love Conquered Marriage.* New York: Viking, 2005.

Cooper, Cynthia. *Violence on Television: Congressional Inquiry, Public Criticism and Industry Response—A Policy Analysis.* Lanham, MD: University Press of America, 1996.

Corsaro, William A. *The Sociology of Childhood.* Thousand Oaks, CA: Pine Forge Press, 1997.

Côté, James E., and Anton L. Allahar. *Generation on Hold: Coming of Age in the Late Twentieth Century.* New York: New York University Press, 1994.

Crawford, Garry. "The Cult of the Champ Man: The Cultural Pleasures of Championship Manager/Football Manager Games." *Information, Communication and Society* 9 (2006): 523–540.

Crawford, Garry, and Victoria Gosling. "Toys for Boys? Marginalization and Participation as Digital Gamers." *Sociological Research Online 10*, no. 1 (March 31, 2005).

Dayan, Daniel, and Elihu Katz. *Media Events: The Live Broadcasting of History.* Cambridge: Harvard University Press, 1992.

Dill, Karen E., and Jody C. Dill. "Video Game Violence: A Review of the Empirical Literature." *Aggression and Violent Behavior* 3 (1998): 407–428.

Eder, Donna, Catherine Colleen Evans, and Stephen Parker. *School Talk: Gender and Adolescent Culture.* New Brunswick, NJ: Rutgers University Press, 1995.

Felson, Richard. "Mass Media Effects on Violent Behavior." *Annual Review of Sociology* 22 (1996): 103–129.

Fiske, John. *Media Matters: Everyday Culture and Political Change.* Minneapolis: University of Minnesota Press, 1994.

Flynn, James R. *What is Intelligence?* New York: Cambridge University Press, 2007.

Fowles, Jib. *The Case for Television Violence.* Thousand Oaks, CA: Sage, 1999.

Fox, Roy F. *Harvesting Minds: How TV Commercials Control Kids.* Westport, CO: Praeger, 2000.

Freedman, Jonathan L. *Media Violence and Its Effect on Aggression.* Toronto: University of Toronto Press, 2002.

Funk, Jeanne B. "Video Games: Benign or Malignant?" *Journal of Developmental and Behavioral Pediatrics* 13 (1992): 53–54.

Gauntlett, David. *Moving Experiences: Understanding Television's Influences and Effects.* London: John Libbey, 1995.

———. "Ten Things Wrong with the Effects Model." In *Approaches to Audiences: A Reader,* edited by Roger Dickinson, Ramaswani Harindranath, and Olga Linné. London: Arnold, 1998.

Giroux, Henry. *The Mouse That Roared.* New York: Rowman and Littlefield, 1999.

———. *Channel Surfing: Racism, The Media, and the Deconstruction of Today's Youth.* New York: St. Martin's Press, 1998.

———. "Teenage Sexuality, Body Politics, and the Pedagogy of Display." In *Youth Culture: Identity in a Postmodern World,* edited by Jonathon S. Epstein. Malden, MA: Blackwell Publishers, 1998.

Gitlin, Todd. *Media Unlimited: How the Torrent of Images and Sounds Overwhelms Our Lives.* New York: Metropolitan Books, 2001.

———. "Media Sociology: The Dominant Paradigm." *Theory and Society* 6 (1978): 205–253.

Gittins, Diana. *The Child in Question.* New York: St. Martin's Press, 1998.

Glassner, Barry. *The Culture of Fear: Why Americans Are Afraid of the Wrong Things.* New York: Basic Books, 1999.

Goldman, Robert, and Stephen Papson. *Sign Wars: The Cluttered Landscape of Advertising.* New York: The Guilford Press, 1996.

Gorman, Lyn, and David McLean. *Media and Society in the Twentieth Century: A Historical Introduction.* New York: Blackwell, 2003.

Griffiths, Mark. "Violent Video Games and Aggression: A Review of the Literature." *Aggression and Violent Behavior* 4 (1999): 203–212.

Gunter, Barrie, and Jill L. McAleer. *Children and Television: The One Eyed Monster?* New York: Routledge, 1990.

Hartley, John. *The Politics of Pictures: The Creation of the Public in the Age of Popular Media.* London: Routledge, 1992.

Heins, Marjorie. *Not In Front of the Children: "Indecency," Censorship, and the Innocence of Youth.* New York: Hill and Wang, 2001.

Heintz, James, Nancy Folbre, and the Center for Popular Economics. *The Ultimate Field Guide to the U.S. Economy.* New York: The New Press, 2000.

Henke, Lucy. "Young Children's Perceptions of Cigarette Brand Advertising Symbols: Awareness, Affect, and Target Market Identification." *Journal of Advertising* 24 (1995): 13–28.

Hine, Thomas. *The Rise and Fall of the American Teenager: A New History of the American Adolescent Experience.* New York: Perennial, 1999.

Hodge, Robert, and David Tripp. *Children and Television: A Semiotic Approach.* Stanford: Stanford University Press, 1986.

Hoffner, Cynthia, et al. "The Third-Person Effect in Perceptions of the Influence of Television Violence." *Journal of Communication* 51 (2001): 283–298.

Ingraham, Chrys. *White Weddings: Romancing Heterosexuality in Popular Culture,* 2nd ed. New York: Routledge, 2008.

James, Allison, Chris Jenks, and Alan Prout. *Theorizing Childhood.* New York: Teacher's College Press, 1998.

James, Allison, and Alan Prout. *Constructing and Reconstructing Childhood: Contemporary Issues in the Sociological Study of Childhood.* London: Falmer Press, 1997.

Jenkins, Henry, ed. *The Children's Culture Reader.* New York: New York University Press, 1998.

John, Deborah Roedder. "Consumer Socialization of Children: A Retrospective Look at Twenty-Five Years of Research." *Journal of Consumer Research* 26 (1999): 204.

Johnson, Steven. *Everything Bad is Good for You: How Today's Popular Culture is Actually Making Us Smarter.* New York: Riverhead Books, 2005.

Jones, Gerard. *Killing Monsters: Why Children Need Fantasy, Super Heroes, and Make-Believe Violence.* New York: Basic Books, 2002.

Kelley, Peter, David Buckingham, and Hannah Davies. "Talking Dirty: Children, Sexual Knowledge and Television." *Childhood* 6, no. 22 (1999): 221–242.

Kincaid, James R. *Child-Loving: The Erotic Child in Victorian Literature.* New York: Routledge, 1992.

Kincheloe, Joe L. "The New Childhood: Home Alone as a Way of Life." In *The Children's Culture Reader,* edited by Henry Jenkins. New York: New York University Press, 1998.

King, Cynthia M. "Effects of Humorous Heroes and Villains in Violent Action Films." *Journal of Communication* 1 (2000): 5–24.

Kitsuse, John, and Malcolm Spector. *Constructing Social Problems.* Edison, NJ: Transaction Publishers, 2000.

Kitzinger, Jenny. "Who Are You Kidding? Children, Power, and the Struggle Against Sexual Abuse." In *Constructing and Reconstructing Childhood: Contemporary Issues in the Sociological Study of Childhood,* edited by Allison James and Alan Prout. London: Falmer Press, 1997.

Krcmar, Marina, and Kathryn Greene. "Predicting Exposure to and Uses of Television Violence." *Journal of Communication* 3 (1999): 24–45.

Linn, Susan. *Consuming Kids: The Hostile Takeover of Childhood.* New York: The New Press, 2004.

Louv, Richard. *Childhood's Future.* New York: Anchor Books, 1990.

Majors, Richard, and Janet Mancini Billson, *Cool Pose: The Dilemmas of Black Manhood in America.* New York: Touchstone, 1992.

Males, Mike A. *The Scapegoat Generation: America's War on Adolescents.* Monroe, ME: Common Courage Press, 1996.

———. *Framing Youth: Ten Myths about the Next Generation.* Monroe, ME: Common Courage Press, 1999.

Mander, Jerry. *Four Arguments for the Elimination of Television.* New York: Morrow Quill Paperbacks, 1978.

Mangleberg, Tamara F., and Terry Bristol. "Socialization and Adolescents' Skepticism Toward Advertising." *Journal of Advertising* 27 (1998): 11–20.

Medved, Michael. *Hollywood vs. America: Popular Culture and the War on Traditional Values.* New York: HarperCollins, 1992.

Morley, David. *Television, Audiences and Cultural Studies.* New York: Routledge, 1992.

Nasaw, David. *Children of the City: At Work and at Play.* New York: Oxford University Press, 1986.

Olney, Martha. *Buy Now, Pay Later: Advertising, Credit, and Consumer Durables in the 1920s.* Chapel Hill: University of North Carolina Press, 1991.

Palladino, Grace. *Teenagers: An American History.* New York: Basic Books, 1996.

Postman, Neil. *Amusing Ourselves to Death: Public Discourse in the Age of Show Business.* New York: Penguin Books, 1985.

Potter, W. James, and Ron Warren. "Considering Policies to Protect Children From TV Violence." *Journal of Communication* 4 (1996): 116–138.

Quart, Alissa. *Branded: The Buying and Selling of Teenagers.* New York: Basic Books, 2003.

Robinson, Thomas N., Helen L. Chen, and Joel D. Killen. "Television and Music Video Exposure and Risk of Adolescent Alcohol Use." *Pediatrics* (1998): 102–107.

Rose, Tricia. "'Fear of a Black Planet': Rap Music and Black Cultural Politics in the 1990s." *Journal of Negro Education* 60 (1991): 279.

Sargent, James D., et al. "Effect of Parental R-Rated Movie Restriction on Adolescent Smoking Initiation: A Prospective Study." *Pediatrics* 114 (2004): 149–156.

———. "Exposure to Smoking Depictions in Movies." *Archives of Pediatric and Adolescent Medicine* 161 (2007): 849–856.

Schudson, Michael. *Advertising, the Uneasy Persuasion: Its Dubious Impact on American Society.* New York: Basic Books, 1984.

Schwartz, Hillel. *Never Satisfied: A Cultural History of Diets, Fantasies and Fat.* New York: The Free Press, 1986.

Scott, Derek. "The Effect of Video Games on Feelings of Aggression." *The Journal of Psychology* 129 (1995): 121–133.

Seidel, Ruth. *Keeping Women and Children Last: America's War on the Poor.* New York: Penguin, 1998.

Seiter, Ellen. "Children's Desires/Mother's Dilemmas: The Social Contexts of Consumption." In *The Children's Culture Reader,* edited by Henry Jenkins. New York: New York University Press, 1998.

———. *Television and New Media Audiences.* Oxford: Oxford University Press, 1999.

Snyder, Leslie B., et al. "Effects of Alcohol Advertising Exposure on Drinking Among Youth." *Archives of Pediatric and Adolescent Medicine* 160 (2006): 18–24.

Spigel, Lynn. "Seducing the Innocent: Childhood and Television in Postwar America." In *The Children's Culture Reader,* edited by Henry Jenkins. New York: New York University Press, 1998.

Springhall, John. *Youth, Popular Culture and Moral Panics: Penny Gaffs to Gangsta-Rap, 1830–1996.* New York: St. Martin's Press, 1998.

Steinberg, Shirley R., and Joe L. Kincheloe, eds. *Kinderculture: The Corporate Construction of Childhood.* Boulder: Westview Press, 1998.

Sternheimer, Karen. "A Media Literate Generation? Adolescents as Active, Critical Viewers: A Cultural Studies Approach." Ph.D. dissertation, University of Southern California, 1998.

———. "Blaming Television and Movies Is Easy and Wrong." *Los Angeles Times,* February 4, 2001, p. M5.

———. *Kids These Days: Facts and Fictions About Today's Youth.* Lanham, MD: Rowman and Littlefield, 2006.

———. "Do Video Games Kill?" *Contexts* 6, no 1. (2007): 13–17.

———. "Hollywood Doesn't Threaten Family Values." *Contexts 8,* no. 4 (2008): 44–48.

Thorne, Barrie. *Gender Play: Girls and Boys in School.* New Brunswick, NJ: Rutgers University Press, 1993.

———. "Re-Visioning Women and Social Change: Where are the Children?" *Gender and Society* 1 (1987): 85–109.

Tobin, Joseph. *Good Guys Don't Wear Hats: Children's Talk about the Media.* New York: Teacher's College Press, 2000.

Vandewater, Elizabeth A., Mi-suk Shim, and Allison G. Caplovitz. "Linking Obesity and Activity Level with Children's Television and Video Game Use." *Journal of Adolescence* 27, no. 1 (2004): 71–85.

Wertham, Frederic. "Such Trivia as Comic Books." In *The Children's Culture Reader,* edited by Henry Jenkins. New York: New York University Press, 1998.

Winn, Marie. *The Plug-In Drug: Television, Computers and Family Life.* New York: Penguin, 2002.

Wooden, Wayne S., and Randy Blazak. *Renegade Kids, Suburban Outlaws: From Youth Culture to Delinquency.* 2nd ed. Belmont, CA: Wadsworth, 2001.

Woodhead, Martin. "Psychology and the Cultural Construction of Children's Needs." In *Constructing and Reconstructing Childhood: Contemporary Issues in the Sociological Study of Childhood,* edited by Allison James and Alan Prout. London: Falmer Press, 1997.

Zelizer, Viviana A. "Kids and Commerce," *Childhood* 9 (2002): 375–396.

———. *Pricing the Priceless Child: The Changing Social Value of Children.* Princeton, NJ: Princeton University Press, 1994.

Index